This Guide is designed to assist Commander's with legal situations by helping them to recognize and avoid issues, or to take immediate actions necessary to preserve the situation when legal issues arise.

THIS PUBLICATION IS NOT MEANT TO REPLACE OR SUPERCEDE THE INDEPENDENT LEGAL ADVICE OF YOUR SERVICING JUDGE ADVOCATE.

COMMENTS OR SUGGESTIONS
Should be sent to:

Office of the Dean
The Judge Advocate General's Legal Center and School
600 Massie Road
Charlottesville, VA 22903-1781

PHONE: 434-971-3300

E-MAIL: moe.lescault@us.army.mil

Published

June 2012

The Judge Advocate General's Legal Center and School

All Photos by:

www.defenseimagery.com

Visual Information Department, TJAGLCS

Commander's Legal Handbook

TABLE OF CONTENTS

Preface – Part I

THE COMMANDER'S RESPONSIBILITY TO PRACTICE PREVENTIVE LAW

"An ounce of prevention is worth a pound of cure."

-- Benjamin Franklin

1. BE PROACTIVE, NOT JUST REACTIVE

This Handbook is designed to assist you in taking proper immediate action when faced with a variety of legal issues that might arise during your command. The purpose of your actions should be to preserve the legal situation until you can consult with your servicing Judge Advocate. However, like most aspects of your command responsibilities, you can fail if you just wait for things to come to you. You need to be proactive in preventing problems before they occur.

In the legal arena, this means establishing and enforcing high standards, ensuring your Soldiers are fully aware of those standards and properly trained to comply with them. You must also properly train your Soldiers on all Army policies and higher level command standards so that they also understand and comply with them. Soldiers must also be well-versed in the Army Values and be able to apply those values to real-world situations, which will usually keep them well within legal bounds.

All Soldiers have seen issues in the news that can occur when we are not proactive about discipline and standards: Abuse of prisoners, desecration of corpses, hazing, and sexual assault to name recent examples. All of these circumstances present serious legal issues. But, fundamentally, they also represent a breakdown in unit standards, training, and discipline. Your objective as a Commander should be to develop solid systems and a command climate that prevents legal issues, rather than just reacting to them. In sum, it is every bit as important to train your Soldiers to maintain a high level of discipline and compliance with law, policy, and military standards, as it is to train them to perform your Mission Essential Task List (METL). In legal circles, we call this effort to prevent legal problems before they arise by properly training Soldiers, "preventive law." The responsibility to practice preventive law belongs to the Commander.

2. PREVENTIVE LAW

While responsibility for practicing preventive law remains with the Commander, your servicing Judge Advocate stands ready to assist you in meeting this responsibility. One of the most valuable services a Judge Advocate can provide to a Commander is eliminating problems before they ever occur through a robust preventive law program.

While preventive law is often contemplated in the context of the legal assistance program, e.g. a class on avoiding unscrupulous payday lenders or auto dealers using bait and switch schemes, the concept of preventive law is central to good order and discipline as well. For example, proper training and emphasis on the standards contained in a General Order #1 prior to entering a Theater of Operations can go a long way toward avoiding the types problems mentioned above. Your Judge Advocate can help you to properly emphasize these standards in a number of ways. For example, they can help you to cover how previous Soldiers have violated this directive and the administrative and punitive action that followed the offenses without violating due process, privacy, or practicing undue command influence. They can also help you to analyze systems and look at weak points and behaviors in your organization that, while not violating the law now, might lead to legal issues. For example, they can help you to craft policies for barracks living arrangements, curbing abuse of alcohol, and providing security while respecting privacy – all of which can help to prevent sexual assaults.

So, as you read and use this guide, please do not use it as an excuse to avoid your servicing Judge Advocate. We hope that you will reach out to your lawyer, and that they will reach out to you, so that through your relationship with this important member of your personal staff, you can receive the advice and assistance you need to have an exceptional and rewarding command experience.

Preface – Part II

TOP TEN SITUATIONS WHEN YOU SHOULD IMMEDIATELY CONSULT WITH YOUR SERVICING JUDGE ADVOCATE

1. AFTER RECEIVING A REPORT OF ANY CRIMINAL OFFENSE

Many offenses have reporting or other policy requirements, such as sexual assault, sexual harassment, hazing, etc. Your servicing JA will ensure that all of these requirements are met and then can advise you on your options to handle the report and/or the offense.

2. BEFORE APPOINTING AN INVESTIGATING OFFICER

If you need to initiate a commander's inquiry, an AR 15-6 informal or formal investigation (including EO investigations), or a line of duty or financial liability investigation of property loss, ask your servicing JA for assistance. Your servicing JA can offer advice on the appropriate type of investigation as well as assist in drafting the appointment memorandum that governs the scope of the investigation.

3. BEFORE CONDUCTING ANY SEARCH (FOR EXAMPLE: DRUG TEST, BREATH TEST, BARRACKS ROOM)

Your servicing JA will be able to confirm whether you have sufficient information (or probable cause) to conduct the search, thus enabling you to use the search results in follow-up administrative, non-judicial or courts-martial proceedings.

4. WHENEVER YOU ARE CONSIDERING ANY ADVERSE PERSONNEL ACTION AGAINST A SOLDIER.

Your Servicing JA will help you to ensure that your action complies with all law and regulation and is feasible before you announce your intention to pursue the action. Adverse actions include, but are not limited to, flagging a soldier, administrative separation, removing the Soldier from certain status positions (such as drill sergeant), relief for cause, and issuing a memorandum of reprimand.

5. BEFORE ADMINISTERING NONJUDICIAL PUNISHMENT UNDER UCMJ ARTICLE 15.

Your Servicing JA will help you to ensure that your action complies with the UCMJ and can be supported at Court-martial if the Article 15 is declined.

6. AFTER RECEIVING A FAMILY SUPPORT OR DEBT COLLECTION COMPLAINT

Your servicing JA can identify what type of support is required, identify if an exception exists, identify if "payment in kind" is appropriate, and assist in doing "the math" when formulas must be used in the event of multiple dependent children located in various households. Additionally, they can confirm that the letter you must draft within fourteen days meets the requirements of AR 608-99. Similarly, Soldiers are expected to pay their debts to creditors, but only creditors are entitled to assistance from the Command, debt collectors are not. Your servicing JA can help you to determine the status of the entity requesting your assistance and what your proper options are as a commander.

7. BEFORE APPROVING ANY FUNDRAISING ACTIVITY

Fundraising approval authority is subject to state law and current installation policy. Regardless of whether it is for your FRG or some other entity, you need to discuss this fully with your JA before taking any action.

8. BEFORE PROVIDING (OR AGREEING TO PROVIDE) SUPPORT TO ANY PRIVATE ORGANIZATION (PO)

Support to POs is limited by the Joint Ethics Regulation (JER) and subject to the proper approving authority. All POs must be supported equally with no preferential treatment (that is, if you provide support to one PO, you must be prepared to provide similar support to all similarly situated POs).

9. BEFORE COLLECTING MONIES FOR DEPARTURE GIFTS

Your servicing JA can define a "donating group" and inform you of the limitations for soliciting in the government workplace. Furthermore, he can make suggestions to ensure there is no improper pressure on subordinates or an appearance of impropriety.

10. BEFORE PURCHASING CERTAIN ITEMS WITH OFFICIAL FUNDS

Certain items that have become traditional in military culture are not allowed to be purchased with official funds, or have very specific rules governing their purchase. These types of items include, but are not limited to, commander's coins, T-shirts, food items, and bottled water. Your servicing JA can help you to ensure your purchase is proper.

MILITARY JUSTICE

Section 1

THIS PAGE IS INTENTIONALLY BLANK

Chapter 1

INTRODUCTION TO MILITARY JUSTICE

1. SOURCES OF AUTHORITY

The military justice system derives its authority from three major sources:

A. The Uniformed Code of Military Justice (UCMJ)

The UCMJ is a federal law and the basis of our military justice system. It determines what conduct is criminal, establishes the various types of courts, and sets forth the procedures to be followed in the administration of military justice. You can find the UCMJ in Appendix 2 of the MCM, United States, 1984 or in 10 United States Code (USC) §§801-940.

B. The Manual for Courts- Martial (MCM)

The MCM is an executive order that details the rules for administering military justice. For example, it sets forth the rules of evidence for courts-martial and contains a list of maximum punishments for each offense. Each company-size unit should have a copy of the MCM.

C. Army Regulation 27-10

AR 27-10 supplements the MCM and is the basic Army regulation for administering military justice.

2. ROLE OF COMMANDERS

Commanders are responsible for both enforcing the law and protecting Soldiers' rights. Unit discipline and morale may depend on how wisely its commander exercises his or her authority. Commanders are also responsible for providing administrative support to judicial proceedings. In addition to ensuring that accused Soldiers appear at all proceedings, in uniform, commanders may also be required to provide witnesses, vehicles, drivers, escorts, and bailiffs for those proceedings.

3. RIGHTS OF SOLDIERS

The military justice system provides for certain fundamental rights and safeguards that must be considered in any case involving criminal conduct.

A. Presumption of Innocence

Under our legal system, everyone is presumed innocent until a court or commander finds them guilty beyond a reasonable doubt. A court or commander may make a fair and just decision only after hearing all the evidence relating to the guilt or innocence of an accused.

B. Legal Counsel

Laws prohibit compulsory self-incrimination and provide that anyone suspected of committing a crime has the right to consult with a lawyer. Congress realized that soldiers may not understand their rights and may be intimidated by the mere presence of a superior. Therefore, under military law no one may question a suspect without first determining that the suspect understands the nature of the offense, the right to remain silent, and the right to counsel. If interrogators violate these rights, the evidence obtained may not be used against the accused. You must protect your unit members' rights and preserve the government's case by ensuring that your subordinate commanders understand and comply with UCMJ, Article 31, and right-to-counsel requirements.

C. Search and Seizure

The United States Constitution protects every citizen from unreasonable searches and seizures; however, the right to privacy is not absolute. Courts have balanced individuals' rights against society's needs and have established rules for determining when a search is reasonable. The evidence obtained from unreasonable searches may not be used in a trial. This discourages indiscriminate invasion of privacy by government officials. **Under military law, you may authorize searches if you determine such searches will not violate Soldiers' rights. However, a court-martial may well review your decisions. You should consult your judge advocate before ordering a search or a seizure.**

D. Prompt Action

The Sixth Amendment to the Constitution and UCMJ, Article 10, guarantee the right to a speedy trial. The accused soldier has the right to be advised of the charges against him as early as possible. Normally, the accused must come to trial within 120 days of either arrest or preferral of charges, whichever is earlier. Actions that you take may trigger the speedy trial clock without you knowing it. If you place any restrictions on an accused, talk to your judge advocate immediately. A speedy trial assists both the government and the accused. Testimony given soon after an incident is more reliable than that given after a long period. Also, witnesses are likely to leave the area during a delay.

4. THE COURT-MARTIAL SYSTEM

A. Justice is the goal of the court-martial system

As in all American criminal courts, courts-martial are adversarial proceedings. That is, lawyers representing the government and the accused present the facts, legal aspects, and arguments most favorable to each side. In doing so, they follow the rules of procedure and evidence. Based upon these presentations, the judge decides questions of law. The court-martial members apply the law and decide questions of fact.

B. Duties of Counsel

At a court-martial, a trial counsel represents the government, and a defense counsel represents the accused. Each counsel is duty-bound to do everything possible within the law to represent the interests of his or her client.

C. Determination of Criminal Conduct

A crime is an act for which the law provides a penalty. Violations of Army regulations, state and federal laws, and the orders of superiors may constitute criminal conduct punishable under the UCMJ. You can resolve any question of what constitutes criminal conduct under the UCMJ by calling your staff judge advocate or trial counsel. A soldier's conduct may be substandard or personally offensive without being criminal.

D. Types of Courts-Martial

The court-martial system consists of three types of courts-martial: a summary court-martial, a special court-martial, and a general court-martial.

1) Summary Court-Martial

A summary court-martial (SCM) is a court composed of one officer who may or may not be a lawyer. The SCM handles minor crimes of enlisted soldiers and has simple procedures. The maximum punishment, which depends upon the rank of the accused, is limited to confinement for one month (for E4s and below), forfeiture of two-thirds pay for one month, and reduction in grade. An SCM may not try an accused against his will. If he objects, you may consider trial by a higher court-martial. The accused does not have the right to military counsel at an SCM, although he or she will see a trial defense attorney before the court-martial.

2) Special Court-Martial

A special court-martial (SPCM) can try enlisted soldiers and consists of a military judge, at least three court members (unless the accused chooses to be tried by a military judge alone), a trial counsel, and a defense counsel. The maximum sentence is a bad conduct discharge (BCD), confinement for twelve months, forfeiture of two-thirds pay per month for twelve months, and reduction to the lowest enlisted grade. (See MCM, R.C.M. 201(f)(2)(B).) If a BCD is adjudged, a verbatim record of trial is required, and the accused has a right to an automatic appeal to the Army Court of Military Review.

3) General Court-Martial

A general court-martial (GCM) tries the most serious offenses. It consists of a military judge, at least five members (unless the accused elects to be tried by a military judge alone), a trial counsel, and a defense counsel. Unless waived by the accused, a formal investigation (an “Article 32” investigation) must occur before a general court-martial may try the case. The GCM may adjudge the most severe sentences authorized by law, including the death penalty.

E. Typical Army Court-Martial Process

The following is a diagram of a *typical* court-martial process. The process for some courts-martial may differ in some respects from the diagram, but ordinarily a court-martial follows the process below. Note that while all three types of courts-martial are depicted on the diagram, an accused Soldier will only be tried by the one type of court convened in his case.

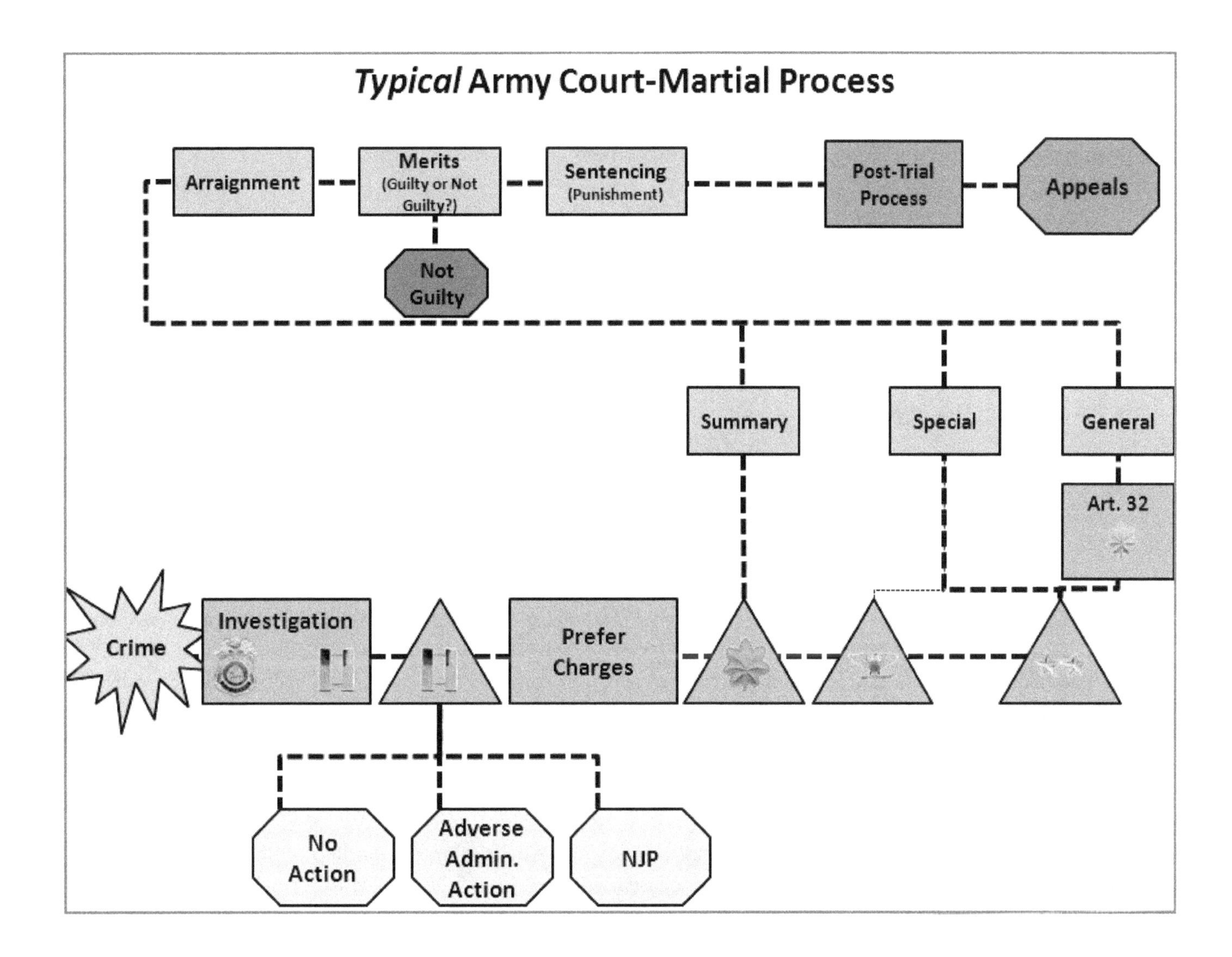

Chapter 2

MISCONDUCT: OPTIONS AND DUTIES OF THE COMMANDER

This chapter provides an OVERVIEW of the considerations and decisions that need to be made by the Commander from the time she learns of misconduct through a decision on how the situation will be resolved. Many of the areas are discussed in more detail in later chapters of the Guide. Cross-references are provided in that instance. Your servicing Judge Advocate is always available to talk through these options with you. You should consult with them early and often as you think through these options.

1. OVERALL RESPONSIBILITIES

A. A Commander's System

The disciplinary system in the military is a Commander owned and operated system. Commanders must act responsibly and in support of the goals of the system in order to protect their prerogatives.

B. Goals of the System

There are dual goals in our system that often must be balanced in the commander's judgment. First is the discipline of the unit, that is, maintaining good order and discipline. The second – preserving the fact and appearance of justice – is equally important and is intertwined with the first.

C. The Commander's Role

The commander plays a quasi-judicial role in the system, making decisions that in the civilian sector would be made by professional prosecutors or judges. Commanders must remain neutral and detached from the circumstances and make the best decision for the unit, the Soldier, and the interest of Justice. Each case must be individually considered in the context of a consistent disciplinary philosophy.

2. INVESTIGATE

The Commander's primary obligation at this stage is to expeditiously, fairly, and impartially gather all of the facts surrounding the situation. There are several options for investigating depending on the circumstances. Your servicing Judge Advocate can discuss these options with you and help you to determine the best course of action. For serious crimes, like drug offenses, sexual assaults, etc., you need to report the offense to CID immediately. For less serious crimes that involve property or people, you need to report the offense to the military police. Contact your Judge Advocate to ensure you are complying with your reporting requirements. These law enforcement organizations generally will conduct the investigation. For crimes that affect discipline without also affecting property or people, you may be the owner of the investigation.

A. Preliminary (informal) investigation. (aka "Commander's Inquiry")

"Upon receipt of information that a member of the command is accused or suspected of committing an offense . . . triable by court-martial, the immediate commander shall make or cause to be made a preliminary inquiry into the charges or suspected offenses." Rule for Courts-martial (R.C.M.) 303. This can be a very informal investigation. No appointment letter is required.

B. AR-15-6 Investigation (See Chapter 14)

You may do a 15-6, especially if you are not sure whether a criminal offense has been committed. Often, these investigations involve formal appointments. If you want to do a 15-6, contact your trial counsel or administrative law attorney.

C. Article 32, UCMJ Investigation

"[N]o charge or specification may be referred to a general court-martial for trial until a thorough and impartial investigation of all the matters set forth therein has been made in substantial compliance with this rule." R.C.M. 405(a). For cases that are being considered for a general court-martial, your battalion commander (the summary court-martial convening authority) or brigade commander (the special court-martial convening authority) may appoint an Article 32 investigation. No case can go to a general court-martial without having first been investigated at an Article 32. At the Article 32, the accused and his or her counsel will be present.

3. CONSIDER ALTERNATIVES TO DISPOSE OF THE MATTER

A. No action/dismissal. Sometimes the appropriate action is no action or dismissal.

B. Nonpunitive/Adverse administrative action

- Flag. (**See Chapter 26**)
- Letter of reprimand (Local or OMPF Filing).
- Bar to Reenlistment (Impose/appeal/lift). (**See Chapter 29**)
- Relief for cause.
- Administrative separation (which chapter, type of discharge, notification or board) (**See Chapters 27 & 28**).

C. Nonjudicial punishment (Article 15) (See Chapters 5 & 6)

- Summarized
- Company-grade
- Field-grade
- Other Decisions: Suspend punishment, Filing determination, Appellate action).

D. Judicial action. (See Chapter 1)

Consult with your Servicing Judge Advocate immediately if you believe the situation will warrant judicial action. Chapter 1 contains a description of the types of course available, which are: Summary, Special, Special Empowered to Adjudge a Bad Conduct Discharge (BCD), General Court-Martial.

E. RCM 306(b) Factors

When determining the disposition of a matter, the Commander must consider the factors listed in Rule for Courts-martial 306(b), which are:

- Character and service of accused
- Nature of offense,

- Effect on unit good order and discipline,
- Appropriateness of punishment allowed,
- Motive of accuser/victim,
- Reluctance of victim to testify
- Cooperation of accused
- Treatment of similar offenses
- Admissibility of evidence
- Other issues

Your servicing Judge Advocate can assist you in discussing and considering these factors as they relate to a particular set of facts.

4. PRETRIAL RESTRAINT (R.C.M. 304)

Absent emergency or exigent circumstances, you should ALWAYS discuss the case with your servicing Judge Advocate before imposing pretrial restraint of any type.

A. Types of pretrial restraint. R.C.M. 304(a)

- Conditions on liberty. Conditions on liberty include pulling pass privileges and ordering an accused not to contact someone else. These types of conditions do not trigger the speedy trial clock.
- Restriction in lieu of arrest. Restriction in lieu of arrest includes restricting an accused to an area on post, requiring him or her to sign in a various intervals, etc. These types of restrictions trigger the speedy trial clock.
- Arrest. The line between restriction in lieu of arrest and arrest is not clear. Generally, if the accused is still going to work, then he or she is not in arrest. However, if the restrictions you put on the accused are too strict, a court might conclude that the accused was under arrest. Arrest triggers both the speedy trial clock and another protection that is found in Article 10 of the UCMJ. Under Article 10, someone that is being held in arrest or pretrial confinement gets the highest priority for having his or her case processed. If the government is not moving the case at a reasonable pace, the case can be dismissed with prejudice. In addition, if the conditions are so strict that the accused is essentially in jail, then the accused may be entitled to other relief. *The best thing to do is to consult your Judge Advocate about any conditions you put on an accused.*
- Pretrial confinement. There is no bail system in the military. If you order an accused into confinement, he will stay there unless your decision is overruled. The presumption is that Soldiers will not go into pretrial confinement. ***Only grounds for pretrial confinement: accused likely to flee or to commit additional serious criminal misconduct.***

B. Procedures for pretrial confinement? R.C.M. 305.

- To order someone into pretrial confinement, you must have reasonable grounds that the person committed an offense that is triable by court-martial; and confinement is necessary because the accused is a flight risk OR will commit serious future misconduct, AND lesser forms of restraint are inadequate. It is not enough that the accused is a pain in the neck or a hassle. He must either be a flight risk OR have the potential to commit SERIOUS future misconduct, which could include SERIOUS threats to your unit's discipline and readiness. You don't have to try lesser forms of restraint first – sometimes lesser forms will be obviously inadequate. Keep in mind that once the accused goes into pretrial confinement, you are responsible for his well-being while he is in confinement (you or someone from your command will likely have to visit him or her on a regular basis) and you will be responsible for bringing the accused to his attorney for case work and to all of the proceedings.

- Within 48-hours of ordering the accused into confinement, your decision must be reviewed by a neutral and detached officer. Within 72-hours, you must memorialize your decision into a memorandum. Within 7-days, a magistrate will review your decision and decide whether continued pretrial confinement is necessary.

5. TRIAL DECISIONS

A. Request for Discharge in Lieu of Court-Martial. Chapter 10, AR 635-200.

1) Requirements.

- Offense must carry a punitive discharge as a possible punishment or,
- Combination of charges would permit a BCD under R.C.M. 1003(d) <u>and</u>
- Case is referred to a court authorized to adjudge a punitive discharge.

2) Only a General Court-Martial convening authority may approve or disapprove.

3) Type of discharge: Usually Under Other than Honorable Conditions.

4) When to recommend/accept?

Some examples: Unlikely court will give much of a sentence; saves child victims from testifying; precludes massive outlay of resources; unit preparing to deploy, if no negative effect on command disciplinary climate.

B. Pretrial Agreements. R.C.M. 705.

- Many courts-martial are resolved by pretrial agreements. Made between accused and convening authority. You may be asked for your recommendation on whether the convening authority should accept a pretrial agreement.
- Either side, government or defense, may initiate.
- When to recommend that the convening authority accept a pretrial agreement? Some examples: good sentence; saves resources; speeds process, reluctant witnesses.
- Increasing flexibility regarding possible terms of agreement: e.g. reduction, confinement or forfeitures, rehabilitation, restitution, deferral of forfeitures, and some forms of unlawful command influence.
- Counter-offers are permitted; you may be asked for your recommendation if there is a counter-offer.

Chapter 3

UNLAWFUL COMMAND INFLUENCE (UCI)

1. SHIFT IN ROLE

In your legal role as a commander, you must have a slightly different mindset than as an operational commander. You play a quasi-judicial role within the military justice system that precludes you from directing subordinate commanders in the way that you might in an operation. Even if you think that you are "mentoring" and "coaching," you can commit UCI. See the readings in the Appendix to this Chapter for a good explanation of why commanders should not coach and mentor subordinates when it comes to the military justice system.

2. FRAMEWORK

A. Accusatory (the process of bringing charges) v. adjudicative (the actual trial)

Accusatory UCI happens when someone that is responsible for bringing charges or processing charges takes a certain action because someone else pressured him or her to take that action. Adjudicative UCI is UCI that taints the trial process itself – the military judge, the defense counsel, the members, or a witness is pressured to do or not do something.

B. Apparent v. actual

UCI does not have to actually occur for there to be a problem. If the situation just looks bad – as in, members of the public would think that the system is unfair – then that can be enough for the military judge to grant the accused some relief.

C. Inadvertent v. intentional

A commander or superior does not have to intend to commit UCI or have some sinister purpose. A commander or superior can have perfectly good intentions and still commit UCI. This often happens when commanders coach or mentor subordinates about military justice or issue policy letters.

D. The MCM v. administrative matters

The principles of UCI fully apply to Article 15s and all courts-martial. Because this concept arises in the UCMJ, it is generally limited to procedures that are found in the UCMJ. Therefore, accusatory UCI concepts generally do not apply to administrative proceedings like administrative separation boards. In fact, there are several regulations that include requirements for subordinates to initiate separation boards, GOMORs, or grade reduction boards. The Secretary of the Army can direct a subordinate to initiate a GOMOR or a separation board. A superior officer cannot do the same for a court-martial or Article 15. However, the concept of adjudicative UCI does apply to administrative proceedings because it is a violation of the UCMJ to tamper with an administrative proceeding.

E. What Are Things you can do that are NOT UCI?

- Withhold authority over types of offenses or types of offenders. Often, battalion commanders withhold drug offense and certain types of assaults to their level, and often, commanding generals withhold the authority to punish officers and senior NCOs.
- Reach down and take specific cases.
- Send cases back down with guidance to resolve at their level, with their tools (including taking no action).

3. PROBLEM AREAS

A. Deployed commander communicating to rear detachment commander

Rear detachment commanders usually brief the forward commander on what is going on in detachment. That can be a problem when the rear commander briefs legal actions to the forward commander. The forward commander may give explicit instructions on what to do in cases, or there might be implicit approval of certain actions but not others. If you are a rear detachment commander and you have UCMJ authority, you must exercise it independent from that forward commander. If your forward commander wants information on the legal actions in the rear unit, have your Judge Advocate communicate that information. Your Judge Advocate will be vigilant toward the UCI concerns.

B. Policy memos, OPDs, and mentoring

Commanders are used to coaching and mentoring across the full spectrum of leadership and often want to share their philosophy on military justice as they try to develop junior leaders. When this coaching and mentorship covers military justice, however, problems arise. Subordinate commanders may start to change their actions based not on what they think the appropriate action is, but based on what they think their superior wants to see. Congress was aware of this tension and wrote in Article 37 that it is okay to give general instruction on military justice on things like procedure and what constitutes offenses. Once you start to talk about specifics approaches to specific types of problems, you start to approach the line that is UCI. In Appendix B, you will see some readings on this problem. Note that this tension has been around for a long time. You will not be the first commander that will want to coach and mentor on military justice, and you won't be the last. The best thing to do is to talk to your Judge Advocate about what you want to say and have your Judge Advocate scrub your language for UCI issues.

C. Subordinates committing UCI without your knowledge

As you gain experience and responsibility in the court-martial process, you tend to commit fewer mistakes and instead, have to deal with the mistakes of your subordinates.

4. EXAMPLES OF UCI

- "I am absolutely uncompromising about discipline in the leader ranks."
- "I am going to CRUSH leaders who fail to lead by example."
- "There is no place in the Army for drug users."
- "Reduction in grade and $500 is a starting point."
- "TDS is the enemy."
- "The accused is a scumbag. Stay away from him."

- "You testified for the accused? You have embarrassed the unit."
- PAO comments: "They will likely be discharged from the Army."

5. PREVENTING A PROBLEM

- Have your Judge Advocate give a class to your unit on unlawful command influence and the ways that people in at your level of command sometimes commit unlawful command influence.
- Have your Judge Advocate review signature or release of statements.
- Lash up the SJA and PAO.
- Focus on the process, not the result; focus on the offense, not the offender. If you need to make a public statement about a case, use language like this:

"[This type of misconduct] has no place in the Army. [This type of misconduct] erodes unit cohesion and mission effectiveness. Allegations of [this type of misconduct] will be thoroughly investigated and appropriate action will be taken based on that investigation."

6. FIXING A PROBLEM

While each problem is unique, there are some common steps you might consider. You wall want to consult with your servicing Staff Judge Advocate as the first step in any case. If you take proactive actions to cure UCI before the case goes to trial, then the military judge may find that your actions were sufficient to solve the problem.

A. Consult with your SJA.

B. Issue a revised policy statement.

C. Conduct an investigation.

D. Take corrective action against someone who commits UCI.

E. Transfer offenders.

F. Apologize.

G. Provide a briefing on duty to testify.

APPENDIX A
THE 10 COMMANDMENTS OF UNLAWFUL COMMAND INFLUENCE

COMMANDMENT 1:	Do not stack the panel, nor select nor remove court-members in order to obtain particular result in a particular trial.
COMMANDMENT 2:	Do not disparage the defense counsel or the military judge.
COMMANDMENT 3:	Do not communicate an inflexible policy on disposition or punishment.
COMMANDMENT 4:	Do not place outside pressure on the judge or court-members to obtain a particular decision.
COMMANDMENT 5:	Do not intimidate witnesses or discouraged them from testifying.
COMMANDMENT 6:	Do not order a subordinate to dispose of a case in a certain way.
COMMANDMENT 7:	Do not coach or mentor subordinate commanders on military justice without talking to your legal advisor first.
COMMANDMENT 8:	Do not disparage the accused or tell others not to associate with him, and do not allow subordinates to do so, either.
COMMANDMENT 9	Ensure that subordinates and staff do not commit unlawful command influence, inadvertently or not.
COMMANDMENT 10	If a mistake is made, raise the issue immediately and cure with an appropriate remedy.

APPENDIX B
RECURRING PROBLEM: THE POLICY STATEMENT

When commanders make policy statements about the military justice system, particularly about what types of offenses warrant what kinds of courts or sentences, commanders run the risk that they will commit both adjudicative UCI (some witnesses may not now come forward on the accused's behalf, and some panel members may now punish in accordance with what they believe the convening authority believes) and accusatory UCI (some commanders may transmit a case because that is what they think their commander wants them to do, not because that is their independent decision).

Commanders are used to coaching and mentoring their subordinates in all areas of command responsibility and leadership, but here, the law has carved out an exception. Commanders should consult with their staff judge advocates before entering this area.

Note that Art. 37(a) exempts general instructional or informational courses on military justice if such courses are designed solely for the purpose of instructing members of the command in the substantive and procedural aspects of courts-martial. Commanders should consider asking their staff judge advocate to provide general instruction, and should allow judge advocates to give advice on particular cases.

The readings below help illuminate the line between mentorship and unlawful command influence.

United States v. Treakle, 18 M.J. 646 (A.C.M.R. 1984)

The duties of a division commander as a court-martial convening authority and as the primary leader responsible for discipline within the division are among the most challenging a commander can perform. On the one hand, effective leadership requires a commander to supervise the activities of his subordinates diligently and ensure that state of good order and discipline which is vital to combat effectiveness. On the other hand, he must exercise restraint when overseeing military justice matters to avoid unlawful interference with the discretionary functions his subordinates must perform. The process of maintaining discipline yet ensuring fairness in military justice requires what the United States Court of Military Appeals has called "a delicate balance" in an area filled with perils for the unwary. Many experienced line officers have expressed similar conclusions. Excerpts from two particularly useful and authoritative examples are reproduced [below].

Correction of procedural deficiencies in the military justice system is within the scope of a convening authority's supervisory responsibility. Yet in this area, the band of permissible activity by the commander is narrow, and the risks of overstepping its boundaries are great. Interference with the discretionary functions of subordinates is particularly hazardous. While a commander is not absolutely prohibited from publishing general policies and guidance which may relate to the discretionary military justice functions of his subordinates, several decades of practical experience under the Uniform Code of Military Justice have demonstrated that the risks often outweigh the benefits. The balance between the command problem to be resolved and the risks of transgressing the limits set by the Uniform Code of Military Justice is to be drawn by the commander with the professional assistance of his staff judge advocate. Although the commander is ultimately responsible, both he and his staff judge advocate have a duty to ensure that directives in the area of military justice are accurately stated, clearly understood and properly executed.

Excerpts from a letter which the Powell Committee recommended The Judge Advocate General of the Army send to officers newly appointed as general court-martial convening authorities. (Committee on the Uniform Code of Military Justice, Good Order and Discipline in the Army: Report to Honorable Wilber M. Bruckner, Secretary to the Army, 17–21 (18 Jan 1960)).

Dear :

Because it is of the utmost importance that commanders maintain the confidence of the military and the public alike in the Army military justice system, the following suggestions are offered you as a commander who has recently become a general court-martial convening authority, in the hope that they will aid you in the successful accomplishment of your military functions and your over-all command mission.

A serious danger in the administration of military justice is illegal command influence. Congress, in enacting the Uniform Code of Military Justice, sought to comply with what it regarded as a public mandate, growing out of World War II, to prevent undue command influence, and that idea pervades the entire legislation. It is an easy matter for a convening authority to exceed the bounds of his legitimate command functions and to fall into the practice of exercising undue command influence. In the event that you should consider it necessary to issue a directive designed to control the disposition of cases at lower echelons, it should be directed to officers of the command generally and should provide for exceptions and individual consideration of every case on the basis of its own circumstances or merits. For example, directives which could be interpreted as requiring that all cases of a certain type, such as larceny or prolonged absence without leave, or all cases involving a certain category of offenders, such as repeated offenders or offenses involving officers, be recommended or referred for trial by general court-martial, must be avoided. This type of directive has been condemned as illegal by the United States Court of Military Appeals because it is calculated to interfere with the exercise of the independent personal discretion of commanders subordinate to you in recommending such disposition of each individual case as they conclude is appropriate, based upon all the circumstances of the particular case. The accused's right to the exercise of that unbiased discretion is a valuable pretrial right which must be protected. All pretrial directives, orientations, and instructions should be in writing and, if not initiated or conducted by the staff judge advocate, should be approved and monitored by him.

The results of court-martial trials may not always be pleasing, particularly when it may appear that an acquittal is unjustified or a sentence inadequate. Results like these, however, are to be expected on occasion. Courts-martial, like other human institutions, are not infallible and they make mistakes. In any event, the Uniform Code prohibits censuring or admonishing court members, counsel, or the law officer with respect to the exercise of their judicial functions. My suggestion is that, like the balls and strikes of an umpire, a court's findings or sentence which may not be to your liking be taken as 'one of those things.' Courts have the legal right and duty to make their findings and sentences unfettered by prior improper instruction or later coercion or censure.

Excerpts from an article by General William C. Westmoreland discussing the relationship of military justice to good order and discipline in the Army. (Westmoreland, Military Justice—A Commander's Viewpoint, 10 Am.Crim.L.Rev. 5, 5–8 (1971)).

As a soldier and former commander, and now as Chief of Staff of the Army, I appreciate the need for a workable system of military justice. Military commanders continue to rely on this system to guarantee justice to the individual and preserve law and order within the military.

An effective system of military justice must provide the commander with the authority and means needed to discharge efficiently his responsibilities for developing and maintaining good order and discipline within his organization. Learning and developing military discipline is little different from learning any discipline, behavioral pattern, skill, or precept. In all, correction of individuals is indispensable.... The military commander should have the widest possible authority to use measures to correct individuals, but some types of corrective action are so severe that they should not be entrusted solely to the discretion of the commander. At some point he must bring into play judicial processes. At this point the sole concern should be to accomplish justice under the law, justice not only to the individual but to the Army and society as well.

I do not mean to imply that justice should be meted out by the commander who refers a case to trial or by anyone not duly constituted to fulfill a judicial role. A military trial should not have a dual function as an instrument of discipline and as an instrument of justice. It should be an instrument of justice and in fulfilling this function, it will promote discipline.

The protection of individual human rights is more than ever a central issue within our society today. An effective system of military justice, therefore, must provide of necessity practical checks and balances to assure protection of the rights of individuals. It must prevent abuses of punitive powers, and it should promote the confidence of military personnel and the general public in its overall fairness. It should set an example of efficient and enlightened disposition of criminal charges within the framework of American legal principles. Military justice should be efficient, speedy, and fair.

THIS PAGE IS INTENTIONALLY BLANK

Chapter 4

COMMANDER'S PRELIMINARY INQUIRY (R.C.M. 303)

If a commander receives information that a member of his or her command is accused or suspected of committing an offense or offenses triable by court-martial, the immediate commander is required to make *or cause to be made* a preliminary inquiry into the charges or suspected offenses. This preliminary inquiry is usually informal. In the case of simple, minor offenses the inquiry may simply be a matter of the commander obtaining information from the suspected offender's chain of command. In complex or serious cases the commander should seek the assistance of law enforcement investigators when conducting the preliminary inquiry. **If there is any doubt as to whether to seek the assistance of law enforcement, the commander should contact the command's judge advocate.**

The inquiry should gather all reasonably available evidence on:

- Guilt or innocence;
- Aggravation; and
- Extenuation and Mitigation.

A commander who is a **special or general courts-martial convening authority** should not personally conduct the preliminary inquiry, but instead should appoint another officer to do so. This will avoid the problem of the convening authority becoming an "accuser" under Article 1(9), UCMJ (and thus losing the ability to convene a court-martial against the accused Soldier).

THIS PAGE IS INTENTIONALLY BLANK

Chapter 5

NONJUDICIAL PUNISHMENT – ARTICLE 15, UCMJ

1. REFERENCES

- UCMJ art. 15.
- MANUAL FOR COURTS-MARTIAL, UNITED STATES pt. V (2008) [hereinafter MCM].
- U.S. DEP'T OF ARMY, REG. 27-10, LEGAL SERVICES: MILITARY JUSTICE chs. 3, 4, 21 (3 October 2011) [hereinafter AR 27-10].

2. INTRODUCTION

Proceedings under Article 15 are not criminal prosecutions. Nonjudicial punishment (NJP) provides commanders with an essential and prompt means of maintaining good order and discipline, and promotes positive behavior changes in service members without the stigma of a court-martial.

3. AUTHORITY TO IMPOSE NONJUDICIAL PUNISHMENT

A. Who may impose?

1) Commanders

"Commanders" are commissioned or warrant officers who exercise primary command authority over an organization; is the person looked to by superior authorities as the individual chiefly responsible for maintaining discipline in the organization. AR 27-10, para. 3-7a.

This can include detachment commanders and commanders of provisional units. Whether an officer is a commander is determined by the duties he or she performs, not necessarily by the title of the position occupied. AR 27-10, para. 3-7a.

2) Joint Commanders (See AR 27-10, para. 3-7b.)

A multi-Service commander or officer in charge, to whose command soldiers are assigned or attached, may impose nonjudicial punishment upon such Soldiers. A multi-Service commander or officer in charge, alternatively, may designate one or more Army units and will for each such Army unit designate an Army commissioned officer as commanding officer for the administration of nonjudicial punishment.

B. Can Article 15 authority be delegated? (AR 27-10, para. 3-7c.)

Article 15 authority ***may not*** be delegated. However, the **exception** is that General court-martial convening authorities and commanding generals can delegate Article 15 authority to one deputy or assistant commander or *instead* to the chief of staff (if the chief of staff is general officer or frocked to general officer rank). The delegation must be in writing.

C. Can Article 15 Authority of Subordinate Commanders Be Limited?

The short answer is, "Yes." However, only certain types of limitations are permissible and there are some limits that are expressly not permitted.

1) Permissible limitations (AR 27-10, para. 3-4c.)

The superior commander may *totally* withhold all Article 15 Authority from the subordinate. Alternatively, the superior commander may *partially* withhold authority, for example over certain categories of personnel (i.e., all officer cases), particular offenses (i.e., all cases involving drugs), or individual cases (i.e., the disposition of SPC Smith's case). There is no requirement that limitations be written but is a good idea to do so (e.g., write a memorandum or publish in post regulation).

2) Impermissible limitations (MCM pt. V, para. 1d(2); AR 27-10, para. 3-4b.)

The superior commander cannot direct a subordinate commander to impose an Article 15. If the authority to issue nonjudicial punishment remains with the subordinate, it is up to the subordinate to decide, independently, how to dispose of the case, by either issuing nonjudicial punishment or not. Similarly, the superior commander cannot issue regulations, orders, or "guides" that either directly or indirectly suggest to subordinate commanders that:

- Certain categories of offenders or offenses are to be disposed of under Article 15.
- Predetermined kinds or amounts of punishment are to be imposed for certain categories of offenders or offenses.

4. WHO CAN RECEIVE NONJUDICIAL PUNISHMENT

A. Military Personnel of a Commander's Command (AR 27-10, para. 3-8.)

- Assigned.
- Affiliated, attached, or detailed.
- The "Beans and Bullets" Rule. AR 27-10, para. 3-8a(3)(b). Look to the facts to determine where the Soldier slept, ate, was paid, performed duty, the duration of the status, and other similar factors. If the facts show the Commander is providing the Soldier these services, then the Soldier can be considered 'of the command' of the Commander for purposes of imposing nonjudicial punishment.

B. Personnel of Other Armed Forces (services) (AR 27-10, para. 3-8c.)

An Army commander is not prohibited from imposing NJP on members of his or her command that are from other services. However, if an Army commander imposes NJP on members of another service, he or she may only do so under the circumstances and procedures outlined for imposing NJP prescribed by that member's parent service.

5. HOW TO DECIDE WHAT OFFENSES ARE APPROPRIATE FOR NJP

A. Relationship to administrative corrective measures

NJP should be used when administrative corrective measures (for example, denial of pass privileges, counseling, extra training, administrative reductions in grade, administrative reprimands) are inadequate due to the nature of the minor offense or because of the servicemember's service record. NJP is generally used to address intentional disregard of or failure to comply with standards of military conduct, while administrative corrective measures generally are used to address misconduct resulting from simple neglect, forgetfulness, laziness, inattention to instructions, sloppy habits, and similar deficiencies. AR 27-10, para. 3-3a.

Commanders and supervisors need to ensure that extra training does not become extra duty (punishment) that was given without following NJP procedures. Extra training must relate directly to the deficiency observed and must be oriented to correct that particular deficiency, although extra training can occur after duty hours. AR 27-10, para. 3-3c.

B. NJP may be imposed for minor offenses (MCM pt. V, para. 1e; AR 27-10, para. 3-9.)

Whether an offense is minor depends on several factors:

- The nature of the offense and the circumstances surrounding its commission;
- The offender's age, rank, duty assignment, record and experience;
- The maximum sentence imposable for the offense if tried by a general court-martial.

As a rule of thumb, a minor offense is one that does not authorize the imposition of a dishonorable discharge or confinement in excess of one year if tried at a general court-martial. MCM pt. V, para. 1e. However, the maximum punishment authorized for an offense is not controlling. Determining what is a minor offense versus a major offense is within the discretion of the imposing commander.

C. Limitations

1) Double punishment prohibited

Once Article 15 imposed, cannot impose another Article 15 for same offense or substantially same misconduct. Commanders need to bring all known offenses that are determined to be appropriate for disposition by NJP and that are ready to be considered at that time. This includes all offenses arising from a single incident or course of conduct. MCM pt. V, para. 1f(3); AR 27-10, para. 3-10.

2) Statute of limitations

Except in very limited and rare circumstances, NJP may not be used for offenses which were committed more than 2 years before the date of imposition.

3) Civilian courts

NJP may not be imposed for an offense that has been tried by a federal court. NJP may not be imposed for an offense that has been tried by a state court unless the Commander complies with Chapter 4 of AR 27-10. If you think you have such a case, discuss it with your servicing Judge Advocate before taking any action.

4) Courts-Martial

NJP should not be used when it is clear that only a court-martial will meet the needs of justice and discipline.

D. Preliminary inquiry. (See Chapter 4)

Prior to deciding on how to handle the disciplinary issue at hand, Commanders need to conduct a preliminary inquiry under R.C.M. 303. The inquiry can be informal and can be conducted personally or by someone else in the command. The person conducting the inquiry should gather all reasonably available evidence related to guilt or innocence, aggravation, and extenuation and mitigation. The inquiry should cover whether an offense was committed; whether the Soldier was involved; and the character and military record of the accused. Having conducted an investigation and considering the factors in the prior sentence, the commander should decide whether to impose NJP based upon:

- The nature of the offense;
- The record of the servicemember;
- The need for good order and discipline;
- The effect of NJP on the servicemember and the servicemember's record. MCM pt. V, para. 1d(1).

The commander should initiate the NJP procedure only after determining that the Soldier *probably* committed the offense and that the NJP procedure is appropriate. NJP should be conducted at the lowest level of command commensurate with the needs of discipline. If the commander believes that his or her authority is insufficient to impose proper NJP, then he or she should send the case to a superior using DA Form 5109. A superior commander may also return a case to a subordinate commander for appropriate disposition.

6. TYPES OF ARTICLE 15S AND PUNISHMENTS

A. Summarized Article 15 (AR 27-10, para. 3-16.)

Summarized Article 15's may only be used with enlisted Soldiers. In summarized proceedings, the punishment cannot exceed:

- 14 days extra duty
- 14 days restriction
- An oral admonition or reprimand, **or**
- Any combination thereof.

Summarized Article 15's may be imposed by company or field grade officers and are recorded on DA Form 2627-1.

B. Formal Article 15 (AR 27-10, para. 3-17.)

Formal Article 15's are appropriate whenever:

- Soldier is an officer, or
- Punishment (for any soldier) might exceed 14 days extra duty, 14 days restriction, oral admonition or reprimand, or any combination thereof.

Formal Article 15's are classified as company grade Article 15s, field grade Article 15s, and general officer Article 15s. Technically, "general officer Article 15s" are only imposed on officers (general officers can impose greater punishments on officers that other commanders can). General officers can impose Article 15s on enlisted personnel, too, but the available punishments are the same as those available to field grade officers. All formal Article 15's are recorded on DA Form 2627.

The maximum available punishment is based on rank of imposing commander (company grade, field grade, or for officer offenders, general officer) and the rank of the soldier receiving the punishment. AR 27-10, para. 3-19, tbl. 3-1. This table of punishments is reproduced in Tables 5-1 and 5-2 below. Usually, commanding generals withhold authority over officer misconduct using the local AR 27-10. Company grade or field grade NJP over another officer is very rare.

TABLE 5-1: ENLISTED PUNISHMENTS

	Summarized	Company Grade	Field Grade
Extra Duty	14 days	14 days	45 days
Restriction	14 days	14 days	60 days (45 days if combined with extra duty)
Correctional Custody		7 days (E1-E3)	30 days (E1-E3)
Reduction		1 grade (E1-E4)	1 or more grade (E1-E4) 1 grade (E5-E6)
Forfeitures		7 days	½ of 1 month's pay for 2 months
Reprimand / Admonition	Oral	Oral /written	Oral/written

TABLE 5-2: OFFICER PUNISHMENTS

	Company Grade	Field Grade	General Officer
Restriction	30 Days	30 Days	60 Days or 30 Days Arrest in Quarters
Forfeitures			½ of 1 month's pay for 2 months
Reprimand / Admonition	Written	Written	Written

C. Reduction in grade

In general, a commander who can promote to a certain grade can also reduce from that grade. Officers and enlisted soldiers above the grade of E-6 cannot be reduced at an Article 15.

D. Forfeiture of pay

Forfeitures are based on grade to which reduced, whether or not reduction is suspended. Forfeitures may be applied against a soldier's retired pay. AR 27-10, para. 3-19*b*(7)(b).

E. Admonition and reprimand

Officer admonitions and reprimands must be in writing. Enlisted admonitions and reprimands can be oral or in writing. Admonitions and reprimands imposed under NJP should state clearly that they were imposed as punishment under Art. 15. This is to contrast them with admonitions and reprimands given as an administrative matter, which have different procedures. *See* AR 600-37. Written admonitions and reprimands are prepared in memorandum format and attached to the DA Form 2627.

F. Combination of punishments (AR 27-10, para. 3-19b(8))

Commanders can combine punishments. No two or more punishments involving the deprivation of liberty may be combined to run either consecutively or concurrently, except that restriction and extra duty may be combined but not to run for a period in excess of the maximum duration allowed for extra duty. For officers, arrest in quarters may not be imposed in combination with restriction.

G. When Does Punishment Begin?

Punishment generally begins on the day imposed. Unsuspended punishments of reduction and forfeiture take effect on the day imposed. Commanders can delay other punishments for up to 30 days for legitimate reasons (quarters, TDY, brief field problem). However, once commenced, deprivation of liberty punishments will run continuously unless the Soldier is at fault or is incapacitated (cannot pause deprivation of liberty once it has commenced because of a field exercise).

7. NOTICE REQUIREMENTS (THE "FIRST READING")

A. Soldier must be notified of the following

- Commander's intention to dispose of the matter under Article 15.
- Offense(s) of which the Soldier is suspected.
- Maximum punishment that the commander could impose under Article 15.
- Soldier's rights under Article 15.

B. Delegating the notice responsibility

The commander may delegate the notice responsibility to any subordinate who is a SFC or above (if senior to soldier being notified). The commander still needs to personally sign the DA Form 2627 or 2627-1. This is a good way to involve the first sergeant or command sergeant major.

For a script that can be used during the first reading, *see* AR 27-10, app. B.

8. SOLDIER'S RIGHTS

A. Formal Article 15's

During a formal Article 15, the Soldier is entitled to the following rights.

1) A copy of DA Form 2627

Items 1 and 2 must be completed on the copy the Soldier receives that the defense counsel may review and properly advise the Soldier.

2) Reasonable decision period and to consult with counsel

This period is usually 48 hours. However, the actual period is determined by the complexity of the case and the availability of counsel. So the period can be longer than 48 hours. Additionally, the Soldier can request a delay, which the imposing commander can grant for good cause.

3) Right to remain silent

4) Right to Demand trial by court-martial (unless attached to or embarked on a vessel)

5) Right to Request an open or closed hearing (AR 27-10, para. 3-18(g)(2))

Ordinarily, hearings are open. An open hearing usually takes place in the commander's office with the public allowed to attend. In practical terms, an open hearing means the office door would be open; a closed hearing, the office door would be closed. The commander should consider all facts and circumstances when deciding whether the hearing will be open or closed.

6) Right to Request a spokesperson

The spokesperson need not be a lawyer. Trial Defense Service does not usually provide counsel for Article 15 hearings. The TDS counsel will advise the Soldier, and then the Soldier will attend the hearing on their own. However, the Soldier may retain a lawyer at his or her own expense.

7) Right to Examine available evidence

8) Right to Present evidence and call witnesses (AR 27-10, para. 3-18i.)

The commander determines if the witness is reasonably available, considering that witness and transportation fees are not available. Reasonably available witnesses will ordinarily only be those at the installation concerned.

9) Right to Appeal

The Soldier has five calendar days to file an appeal to the next superior authority in the chain of command. The superior authority should act on the appeal within five calendar days (three calendar days for summarized proceedings). While the punishment generally runs during the appeals period, if the command takes longer than the designated period, and the Soldier requests, the punishments involving deprivation of liberty will be interrupted until the appeal is completed.

B. Summarized

The rights in a summarized proceeding are similar to the formal proceeding, but are limited to the following:

- Reasonable decision period (normally 24 hours).
- Demand trial by court-martial.
- Remain silent.
- Hearing.
- Present matters in defense, extenuation, and mitigation.
- Confront witnesses.
- Appeal.

9. HEARING

A. The hearing is non-adversarial

This means that the hearing is not like a courtroom hearing (ie, a court-martial). Neither the Soldier nor their spokesperson (or retained lawyer) may examine or cross-examine witnesses unless allowed by the commander. However, the Soldier or spokesperson or lawyer can indicate to the imposing commander the relevant issues or questions that they would like the commander to explore or ask witnesses about.

B. In the commander's presence unless extraordinary circumstances

The Soldier will be allowed to personally present matters in defense, extenuation, or mitigation to the Commander, except when appearance is prevented by the unavailability of the Commander or by extraordinary circumstances (ie – the Soldier is stationed at a remote geographic location separate from the Commander).

C. Rules of evidence

Commander is not bound by the formal rules of evidence, except for the rules pertaining to privileges. Privileges include spouses not being required to testify against their spouse and clergy not being required to testify against their parishioner.

The Commander may consider any matter the he or she believes is relevant (including, e.g. unsworn statements and hearsay). But beware that if the Soldier turns down the Art. 15, the Military Rules of Evidence will apply at a court-martial. So, evidence that the commander considers at Article 15 may not be admissible at the court-martial.

D. Degree of Proof

As a criminal law matter, the commander must be convinced beyond a reasonable doubt that the Soldier is guilty of the offense in order to find the Soldier guilty and punish him or her.

10. CLEMENCY

The imposing commander, a successor in command, or the next superior authority may grant clemency. Clemency can include the following processes.

A. Suspension of the Punishment

The execution of a punishment of reduction or forfeiture may be suspended for no more than four months. Other punishments may be suspended for no more than six months. For summary Art. 15s, suspensions are for no more than three months. The suspended punishment is automatically remitted if no misconduct during the suspension period.

1) Vacation of Suspension

If the Solder violates a punitive article of the UCMJ (or other stated condition) during the suspension period, the commander may vacate the suspension. If the vacation involves a condition on liberty, reduction in rank, or forfeiture of pay, the commander should hold a hearing as outlined in AR 27-10, para. 3-25. For the vacation of other punishments, the Soldier should be given notice and an opportunity to respond. If the Soldier is absent without leave when the commander proposes vacation, special rules apply. In this instance, ensure that you consult with your servicing Judge Advocate. The conduct that led to the vacation can serve as a separate basis for a new NJP action.

No appeal is authorized from the vacation of a suspended sentence.

B. Mitigation

The commander can reduce the quantity or quality of the punishment.

C. Remission

The commander can cancel any portion of the unexecuted punishment.

D. Setting aside and restoration

Commanders can set aside any part or amount of a punishment, whether executed or unexecuted, and restore whatever rights, privileges or property that was affected are restored. This should only be done when there was "clear injustice," or an unwaived legal or factual error that clearly and affirmatively injured the substantial rights of the Soldier. Generally, this type of clemency should occur within four months from the date that punishment was imposed.

11. FILING

A. Summarized Article 15

DA Form 2627-1 is filed locally. The form is destroyed two years after imposition of the Article 15 or upon the transfer of the Soldier from the unit.

B. Formal Article 15

1) Specialist/Corporal (E-4) and below

The original DA Form 2627 is filed locally in the unit nonjudicial punishment or unit personnel files. The form is destroyed two years after imposition of the Article 15 or upon transfer of the Soldier to another general court-martial convening authority.

2) All other soldiers

- *Performance fiche or restricted fiche of OMPF*

In addition to the local filing discussed above, the Commander may file the Article 15 in the Soldier's Official Military Personnel File (OMPF). If filing in the OMPF, the Commander must decide whether to file the Article 15 in the performance portion of the file or the restricted portion. The performance section is routinely used by career managers and selection boards for the purpose of assignment, promotion, and schooling selection. The restricted section contains information not normally viewed by career managers or selection boards, so filing in the restricted portion benefits the Soldier.

NOTE: If an E5 or above already has an Art. 15 in restricted fiche, AR 27-10 requires that it will be redirected to performance fiche.

- *Factors Informing the Commander's Filing Decision*

A commander's decision where to file is as important as the decision relating to the imposition of NJP itself. Commanders should consider:

- Interests of the Soldier's career.
- Soldier's age, grade, total service, whether Soldier has prior NJP, and recent performance.
- Army's interest in advancing only the most qualified personnel for positions of leadership, trust, and responsibility.
- Whether the conduct reflects unmitigated moral turpitude or lack of integrity, patterns of misconduct, evidence of serious character deficiency, or substantial breach of military discipline.

C. Review of the Filing Decision by Superior Authority

The imposing commander's filing decision is subject to review by superior authority. However, the Superior commander cannot withhold the subordinate commander's filing determination authority.

12. APPEALS

The Soldier only has the right to one appeal under Article 15. This appeal operates as follows.

A. Time limits to appeal

The Soldier has a "reasonable" time to appeal. However, after five calendar days, the appeal is presumed to be untimely and may be rejected.

B. Who acts on an appeal?

The next superior commander generally handles the appeal. The superior authority should act on appeal within five calendar days (three calendar days for summarized proceedings). While the punishment generally runs during the appeals period, if the command takes longer than the designated period, and the Soldier requests, the punishments involving deprivation of liberty will be interrupted until the appeal is completed.

C. Procedure for submitting appeal

The Soldier submits their appeal through the imposing commander using the appropriate space on DA Form 2627. The submission of additional matters is optional. However, if additional materials are submitted, they must be forwarded to the appellate authority.

D. Action by appellate authority

The appellate authority may conduct an independent inquiry into the matter. They may also take appellate action, even if Soldier does not appeal.

1) Legal Review

In certain circumstances, the Article 15 must be referred to the OSJA for a **legal review** prior to action on the appeal. This is discussed in note 9 on the reverse side of DA Form 2627. Circumstances requiring a legal review include:

- Reduction in one or more pay grades from E4 or higher, or

- More than 7 days arrest in quarters, 7 days correctional custody, 7 days forfeiture of pay, or 14 days of either extra duty or restriction

You may *always* refer an Article 15 for legal review in any case, regardless of punishment imposed. Review is typically done by the trial counsel.

2) Matters considered

The appellate authority must review the appropriateness of the punishment and whether the proceedings were conducted under law and regulations. Their consideration is not limited to the written matters in the record; the appellate authority may make additional inquiries. The appellate authority may consider the record of the proceedings, any matters submitted by the service member, any matters considered during the legal review, and any other appropriate matters. The rules do not require that the service member be given notice and an opportunity to respond to any additional matters considered.

3) Appellate Authority's Options

In acting on the Appeal, the Appellate authority may:

- Approve the punishment.
- Suspend all or any part of the punishment.
- Mitigate the punishment.
- Remit all or any part of the punishment.
- Set Aside the Article 15. This includes setting aside the earlier NJP in order to refer the case to court-martial.

E. Petition to the Department of the Army Suitability Evaluation Board (DASEB)

Sergeants (E-5) and above may petition to have DA Form 2627 transferred from the performance to the restricted fiche. The Soldier must present evidence that the Article 15 has served its purpose and transfer would be in the best interest of the Army.

Soldiers can also petition for complete removal of the Article 15. Normally, petitions are not considered until at least one year after imposition of punishment. Soldiers may seek assistance with these types of petition from the Trial Defense Service or Legal Assistance Office at their installation.

13. PUBLICIZING ARTICLE 15'S

It is permissible for commanders to publish the results of Article 15's, but they must delete the Soldier's social security number and relevant privacy information.

A. Timing

Commanders may announce the result at next unit formation after punishment is imposed, or, if the Article 15 is appealed, after the decision on appeal. Additionally Commanders can post the results on the unit bulletin board.

B. Commander Considerations

When considering whether to publicize Article 15's or not, the Command must avoid inconsistent or arbitrary policies. So, the commander should decide whether they will publish the Article 15's or not, and then be consistent in publishing them throughout the command tour. Additionally, before publishing the punishments of sergeants and above, consider:

- The nature of the offense.
- The individual's military record and duty position.
- The deterrent effect.
- The impact on unit morale or mission.
- The impact on the victim.
- The impact on the leadership effectiveness of the individual concerned.

14. SUPPLEMENTAL ACTIONS

Supplemental Action is any action taken by an appropriate authority to suspend, vacate, mitigate, remit, or set aside a punishment under formal Art. 15 proceedings after action has been taken on an appeal, or the DA Form 2627 has been distributed to agencies outside the unit (personnel, finance). Supplemental actions must be recorded on a DA Form 2627-2.

Chapter 6

COMPANY GRADE ARTICLE 15 SCRIPT

In the following script, BOLD language are instructions and notes, NORMAL PRINT is what you would read/say to the Soldier.

Appendix B of AR 27-10 is the source document for this script. It has been modified for clarity and to make it easier to follow the recommended procedures.

Note: As commander, you may delegate performance of the Notification, Election of Rights, and Appellate Rights sections to an appropriate subordinate. Your First Sergeant is especially well suited for this role.

1. NOTIFICATION

Note: The commander may delegate the Notification portion.

Note: It is important the commander sign following Item 2 on the DA Form 2627 before Notification takes place. Leave the Date and Time blocks blank. The person performing the notification should fill in these blanks with the current time and date at the actual Notification.

CDR/1SG: As your commanding officer, (I have)(the company commander has) disciplinary powers under Article 15 of the UCMJ. (I have)(The commander has) received a report that you violated the Uniform Code, and (I am)(the commander is) considering imposing nonjudicial punishment. This is not a formal trial like a court-martial. As a record of these proceedings (I)(he) will use DA Form 2627. I now hand you this form. Read items 1 and 2. Item 1 states the offense(s) you are reported to have committed and item 2 lists the rights you have in these proceedings. Under the provisions of Article 31 of the UCMJ, you are not required to make any statement or provide any information concerning the alleged offense(s). If you do, it may be used against you in these proceedings or in a trial by court-martial. You have the right to consult with a lawyer as stated in item 2.

Note: Wait for the soldier to read items 1 and 2 of DA Form 2627. Allow him or her to retain a copy of the form until the proceedings are finished and the commander has either imposed punishment or decided not to impose it.

CDR/1SG: Do you understand item 1? Do you understand the offense(s) you are reported to have committed?

Soldier: Yes/No.

Note: If the soldier does not understand the offense(s), explain the offense(s) to him/her.

CDR/1SG: Do you understand item 2? Do you have any questions about your rights in these proceedings?

Soldier: Yes/No.

Note: If the soldier does not understand his or her rights, explain them in greater detail. If the soldier asks a question you cannot answer, recess the proceedings. You may find the answer in one of the following sources: Article 15, UCMJ; Part V of the Manual for Courts-Martial (MCM); AR 27-10, Chapter 3; or contact your JA office.

CDR/1SG: There are some decisions you have to make.

CDR/1SG: Number One. You have to decide whether you want to demand trial by court-martial. If you demand a court-martial, these proceedings will stop. (I)(the commander) then will have to decide whether to initiate court-martial proceedings against you. If you were to be tried by court-martial for the offense(s) alleged against you, you could be tried by summary court-martial, special court-martial, or general court-martial. If you were to be tried by special or general court-martial you would be able to be represented by a military lawyer appointed at no expense to you or by a civilian lawyer of your choosing at no expense to the government.

CDR/1SG: Number Two. If you do not demand trial by court-martial, you must then decide whether you want to present witnesses or submit other evidence in defense, extenuation, and/or mitigation. Your decision not to demand trial by court-martial will not be considered as an admission that you committed the offense(s); you can still submit evidence in your behalf.

CDR/1SG: Evidence in defense is facts showing that you did not commit the offense(s) stated in item 1. Even if you cannot present any evidence in defense, you can still present evidence in extenuation or mitigation.

CDR/1SG: Evidence in extenuation is circumstances surrounding the offense, showing that the offense was not very serious.

CDR/1SG: Evidence in mitigation is facts about you, showing that you are a good soldier and that you deserve light punishment.

CDR/1SG: Number Three. You can make a statement and request to have a spokesperson appear with you and speak on your behalf. (I)(The commander) will interview any available witnesses and consider any evidence you think (I)(he/she) should examine.

CDR/1SG: Number Four. Finally, you must decide whether you wish to request that the proceedings be open to the public. Do you understand the decisions you have to make?

Soldier: Yes/No.

Note: If the soldier does not understand, explain each of the decisions to the soldier.

CDR/1SG: If you do not demand trial by court-martial and after you have presented your evidence, (I am)(the commander is) convinced that you committed the offense, (I)(he/she) could then punish you. The maximum punishment (I)(he/she) could impose on you would be:

> E1-E4: Admonition/reprimand; 14 days extra duty; 14 days restriction; forfeiture of 7 days pay; and reduction in rank of one grade.
>
> E5-E6: Admonition/reprimand; 14 days extra duty; 14 days restriction; and forfeiture of 7 days pay.

CDR/1SG: You should compare this punishment with the punishment you could receive in a court-martial.

Note: If the soldier requests to be informed of the maximum court-martial sentence you may state the following: The maximum sentence you could receive in a court-martial is _______________ (sentence) for the offense(s).

Note: Part IV, MCM lists for each punitive article the punishments a court-martial may impose for violations of the various Articles of the UCMJ. You may inform the soldier that referring the charges to a summary or special court-martial would reduce the maximum sentence. For example, a summary court may not impose more than 1 month of confinement at hard labor. A special court may not impose more than 6 months of confinement.

Note: You should not inform the soldier of the particular punishment you/the commander may consider imposing until all evidence has been considered.

CDR/1SG: As Item 2 points out, you have a right to talk to an attorney before you make your decisions. A military lawyer whom you can talk to free of charge is located at ________________. Would you like to talk to an attorney before you make your decisions?

Soldier: Yes/No.

Note: If the answer is yes, go to (1) below. If the answer is no, continue at (2) below.

(1) CDR/1SG: I will provide you whatever assistance I can to help you consult an attorney. I encourage you to consult the attorney promptly. You may consult with an attorney by telephone. You are to notify me if you encounter any difficulty in consulting an attorney.

Note: Skip the following statement and go to the next one.

(2) CDR/1SG: I understand you do not wish to consult an attorney. You should understand you are provided an opportunity to do so.

CDR/1SG: You now have 48 hours to think about what you should do in this case. You may advise (me) (the commander) of your decision at any time within the 48-hour period. If you do not make a timely demand for trial or if you refuse to sign that part of DA Form 2627 indicating your decision on these matters, (I)(the commander) can continue with these Article 15 proceedings even without your consent.

CDR/1SG: You are dismissed unless you have made all your decisions and are fully prepared to proceed immediately. Do you want to wish to proceed immediately?

Soldier: Yes/No.

Note: If the answer is no, go to (1) below. If the answer is yes, continue at (2) below.

(1) CDR/1SG: You are dismissed.

Note. At this point, you should recess the proceedings.

(2) CDR/1SG: I understand you do not wish consult with an attorney, have made your decisions, and are prepared to proceed immediately.

2. ELECTION OF RIGHTS

Note: The commander may delegate the performance of the Election of Rights portion.

Note: If conducted during the same session as the Notification, skip the next statement.

CDR/1SG: As your commander, (I have)(the commander has) disciplinary powers under Article 15 of the UCMJ. (I have)(The commander has) received a report that you violated the Uniform Code, and (I am)(the commander is) considering imposing nonjudicial punishment. This is not a formal trial like a court-martial. As a record of these proceedings, I will use DA Form 2627. I am handing you this form. (I)(The First Sergeant) initially notified you of this charge on ____________.

CDR/1SG: Turn your attention to Item 3 of the DA Form 2627. Do you demand trial by court-martial?

Soldier: Yes/No.

Note: If the answer is yes, go to (1) below. If the answer is no, continue at (2) below.

(1) CDR/1SG: Initial Block a, sign and date Item 3. Because you have demanded trial by court-martial, these proceedings will stop. (I)(The commander) now must decide whether to initiate court-martial proceedings against you. I will notify you when (I have)(the commander has) reached a decision. You are dismissed.

Note: This concludes the proceeding.

(2) CDR/1SG: Initial Block b of Item 3 indicating your choice to not demand trial by court-martial.

CDR/1SG: An open hearing means that the proceeding is open to the public. If the hearing is closed, only you, I, designated soldiers of the chain of command, available witnesses and a spokesperson, if designated, will be present. Do you request an open hearing?

Soldier: Yes/No.

CDR/1SG: Initial Block b(1) of Item 3 indicating your choice.

CDR/1SG: Do you wish to be accompanied by a spokesperson?

Soldier: Yes/No.

CDR/1SG: Initial Block b(2) of Item 3 indicating your choice.

CDR/1SG: Do you want to submit any evidence showing that you did not commit the offense(s), or explaining why you committed the offense(s), or any other information about yourself that you would like me to know? And/or do you wish to have any witnesses testify, including witnesses who would testify about your good past military record or character?

Soldier: Yes/No.

CDR/1SG: Initial Block b(3) of Item 3 indicating your decision, and sign and date the form in the space provided under that item.

Note: Wait until the soldier initials the blocks and signs and dates the form.

Note: In the event the soldier does not make a decision within the specified time or refuses to complete or sign item 3 of DA Form 2627, see paragraph 3-18f of AR 27-10.

3. PRESENTATION OF EVIDENCE AND MATTERS

***Note:* The *commander cannot delegate* the Presentation of Evidence and Matters portion.**

Note: If the soldier has no witnesses or matters to present, the commander may skip to Imposition of Punishment.

Note: ***If the commander delegated both the Notification and Election of Rights for this Article 15, making this is the first time the soldier is appearing before the commander, read the following statement. If not, the commander may skip to the next statement.***

CDR: As your commander, I have disciplinary powers under Article 15 of the UCMJ. I have received a report that you violated the Uniform Code, and I am considering imposing nonjudicial punishment. This is not a formal trial like a court-martial. As a record of these proceedings, I will use DA Form 2627. I am handing you this form. You were initially notified of this charge on _____________.

CDR: Do you need additional time to gather your evidence?

Soldier: Yes/No.

Note: If the soldier needs additional time to gather his or her evidence, give the soldier a reasonable period to gather the evidence. Tell the soldier when the proceedings will resume and recess the proceedings.

Note: If the soldier has witnesses and/or evidence, and the soldier is prepared to present them, proceed as follows:

CDR: I will now examine whatever matters you wish to present.

Note: Insure that the soldier has the opportunity he or she deserves to present any evidence.

CDR: Do you have any further evidence to present?

Soldier: Yes/No.

Note: Consider the evidence presented. If the evidence persuades you that you should not punish the soldier, terminate the proceedings, inform the soldier, and destroy all copies of DA Form 2627. If you are convinced that the soldier committed the offense(s) beyond a reasonable doubt and deserves to be punished, proceed to Imposition of Punishment.

4. IMPOSITION OF PUNISHMENT

***Note:* The *commander cannot delegate* the Imposition of Punishment portion.**

Note: ***If the soldier presented evidence and matters to the commander, skip the following statement and go one to the next one.***

CDR: As your commander, I have disciplinary powers under Article 15 of the UCMJ. I have received a report that you violated the Uniform Code, and I am considering imposing nonjudicial punishment. This is not a formal trial like a court-martial. As a record of these proceedings, I will use DA Form 2627. I am handing you this form. (I)(The First Sergeant) initially notified you of this charge on _____________.

CDR: I have considered all the evidence. I am convinced that you committed the offense(s). I impose the following punishments:

Note: Announce punishment. Many Legal Offices prefer you do not annotate the punishment on the DA Form 2627. They may provide you a punishment worksheet to use. Consult with your Legal Office to determine the preferred method.

Note: After you have imposed punishment, complete Items 4, 5 and 6 of DA Form 2627, and sign and date in the blanks below Item 6.

5. APPELLATE ADVICE

Note: The commander may delegate the Appellate Advice portion.

Note: Hand the DA Form 2627 and the punishment worksheet (if used) to the soldier.

CDR/1SG: Read the (DA Form 2627)(punishment worksheet) which lists the punishment (I have)(the commander has) just imposed on you. Now read Item 6 which points out that you have a right to appeal this punishment to ___________. You can appeal if you believe that you should not have been punished at all, or that the punishment is too severe. Any appeal should be submitted within 5 calendar days. An appeal submitted after that time may be rejected. Even if you appeal, the punishment is effective today (unless the imposing commander sets another date). Once you submit your appeal, it must be acted upon by _________ within 5 calendar days, excluding the day of submission. Otherwise, any punishment involving deprivation of liberty (correctional custody, restriction or extra duty), at your request, will be interrupted pending the decision on the appeal.

CDR/1SG: Do you understand your right to appeal?

Soldier: Yes/No.

CDR/1SG: Do you desire to appeal?

Soldier: Yes/No.

Note: If the answer is yes, go to (2) below. If the answer is no, continue at (1) below.

(1) CDR/1SG: If you do not want to appeal, initial Block a in Item 7 and sign and date in the blanks below Item 7.

Note: Now give the soldier detailed orders as to how the commander wants him or her to carry out the punishments.

CDR/1SG: You are dismissed.

Note: This concludes the proceeding.

(2) CDR/1SG: Do you want to submit any additional matters to be considered in an appeal?

Soldier: Yes/No.

Note: If the answer is yes, go to (2) below. If the answer is no, continue at (1) below.

(1) CDR/1SG: Initial Block b in Item 7 and sign and date the blanks below Item 7. I will notify you when I learn what action has been taken on your appeal. You are dismissed.

Note: This concludes the proceeding.

(2) CDR/1SG: If you intend to appeal and do not have the additional matters with you, Item 7 will not be completed until after you have obtained all the additional material you wish to have considered on appeal.

CDR/1SG: Do you have your additional material with you?

Soldier: Yes/No.

Note: If the answer is yes, go to (2) below. If the answer is no, continue at (1) below.

(1) CDR/1SG: When you have obtained this material, return with it by __________(Five calendar days from imposition of punishment). At that time, you will complete Item 7 by initialing Block c and signing and dating in the blanks below. After you complete Item 7, I will send the DA Form 2627 and the additional matters you submit to ______________ (Appeal authority). Remember that the punishment will not be delayed (unless the imposing commander sets another date).

CDR/1SG: You are dismissed.

Note: This concludes the proceeding.

(2) CDR/1SG: Give me the material. Complete Item 7 by initialing Block c and signing and dating in the blanks below. After you complete Item 7, I will send the DA Form 2627 and the additional matters you submit to __________ (Appeal authority). Remember that the punishment will not be delayed (unless the imposing commander sets another date).

CDR/1SG: You are dismissed.

Note: This concludes the proceeding.

THIS PAGE IS INTENTIONALLY BLANK

Chapter 7

SEARCH & SEIZURE

1. INTRODUCTION

The Fourth Amendment protects individuals from "unreasonable" searches and seizures, and requires that searches and seizures be based upon probable cause and a warrant. The Fourth Amendment applies to Soldiers - they do not waive their Fourth Amendment rights when they join the Army. However, the Fourth Amendment applies to Soldiers differently than it does to civilians. This is because a Soldier's privacy rights are balanced against not only law enforcement needs but also against military necessity and national security. Consequently, a search may be considered reasonable in a military setting, but would not be so in the civilian world.

An example of how the Fourth Amendment applies to Soldiers differently than it does to civilians is search authorizations. A civilian search "warrant" must be in writing, under oath, and issued by a civilian magistrate. A military search "authorization," on the other hand, need not be in writing, need not be under oath, and may be issued by a commander. Despite these technical distinctions, the terms "search warrant" and "search authorization" basically mean the same thing and are often used interchangeably.

Another example of how the Fourth Amendment applies to Soldiers differently than to civilians is urinalysis testing. Most civilians presently are not subject to random urinalysis testing for illegal drug use. Soldiers, however, must give urine samples during routine health and welfare inspections. This greater intrusion into a Soldier's privacy is justified because of the detrimental impact that illegal drug use has on military operations and national security.

Searches and seizures need not always be based on probable cause and a search warrant or authorization. There are several situations where the Fourth Amendment does not apply, such as searches of government property or seizures of items in plain view. There are also situations where the Fourth Amendment applies but no probable cause or warrant is required. For example, administrative inspections such as health and welfare inspections, urinalysis inspections, gate inspections, and inventories need not be based on probable cause or a warrant.

The search and seizure rules are complex and constantly changing because of court interpretations. Therefore, the best advice is to contact your legal adviser whenever a search and seizure issue comes up. Your legal adviser can assist you with proposed courses of action, and recommend alternatives which will decrease the likelihood that evidence may be found inadmissible at a court-martial.

2. PROBABLE CAUSE AND WARRANTS

A. Probable Cause

1) Defined

There is probable cause to search when there are reasonable grounds to believe that items connected with criminal activity are located in the place or on the person to be searched.

2) Evaluating Probable Cause

A commander may determine that probable cause exists based on his or her personal observations, or information from others. The commander's task is to determine from the totality of the circumstances whether it is reasonable to conclude that evidence of a crime is in the place to be searched. Probable cause determinations should be based on factual and reliable information.

a. FACTUAL BASIS

If the commander did not personally observe the information, but is relying on an informant, the following can use the following criteria to evaluate the factual basis of the information:

- **Personal observation.** The trustworthiness of information can be established if the informant personally observed the criminal activities. In drug cases, you should also inquire why the informant believes that what he or she saw was drugs. You should determine whether the informant had a class on drug identification, furnished reliable information in the past, or had substantial experience with drugs.
- **Admission of the suspect.** An informant's information is considered reliable if based on statements he or she heard the suspect or an accomplice make.
- **Self-verifying detail.** The factual basis of an anonymous tip may be established if the tip is so detailed that the information must have been obtained as a result of a personal observation.

b. RELIABILITY

The commander should also be satisfied as to the credibility of the person furnishing the information. This may be established by one or more of the following:

- **Demeanor.** When the information is personally given to the commander, the commander can judge the informant's believability at that time. In many cases the individual may be a member of the commander's unit and the commander is in the best position to judge the credibility of the person. Even when the person is not a member of the commander's unit, the commander can personally question the individual and determine the consistency of statements made by the individual.
- **Past reliability.** This is one of the easiest methods for establishing believability: knowledge that the informant has proven reliable in the past. A commander should examine the underlying circumstances of past reliability, such as a record that the informant has furnished correct information in the past.
- **Corroboration.** Corroboration means that other facts back up the information provided. Corroboration and the demeanor of the person are particularly important when questioning first-time informants with no established record of past reliability.
- **Declaration against interest.** The person furnishing the information may provide information that is against that person's penal interest. For example, when a person knowingly admits to an offense and has not been promised any benefit, he or she may be prosecuted for that offense. This lends a great degree of reliability to the information furnished.
- **Good citizen informants.** Often, the informant's background renders him or her credible. For instance, a victim or a bystander with no reason to lie may be considered reliable. In

addition, law enforcement officers and good Soldiers are generally considered reliable sources of information.

B. Search Warrants and Authorizations

1) Commander's Authorization

A commander may authorize searches of his or her Soldiers and equipment, or areas he or she controls, when there is probable cause to believe that items connected with criminal activity are located in the place or on the person to be searched. When time permits, the commander should consult a legal adviser first. A commander may not delegate the authority to authorize searches to others in the unit. The power to authorize a search, however, may devolve to an acting commander if the commander is absent. The authority of an acting commander to authorize searches should be documented in writing by the absent commander.

2) Magistrate's and Judge's Authorization

A magistrate (designated JAG officer) or a military judge on your installation can also authorize searches. Using a magistrate to authorize a search may be preferable to requesting authorization from a commander for several reasons. First, commanders may be involved in an investigation related to a search and their neutrality could become an issue. Second, the magistrate may authorize searches anywhere on an installation; therefore, issues of scope of authority are avoided. Third, if a search authorization is contested at trial, the commander will not have to testify.

3) Procedures for Obtaining an Authorization to Search

AR 27-10, Military Justice (3 October 2011), sets out the procedures for obtaining an authorization to search. Written or oral statements (including those obtained by telephone or radio), sworn or unsworn, should be presented to the commander, magistrate, or military judge. The authorizing official will then decide whether probable cause to search exists, based upon the statements and will issue either a written or an oral authorization to search. Written statements and authorizations are preferred to avoid problems later if the search is challenged at trial. When granting authority to search, the authorizing official must specify the place to be searched and the things to be seized. A sample affidavit in support of a request for search authorization (DA Form 3744) is contained in AR 27-10; DA Form 3745 is a search authorization form.

4) Scope of an Authorized Search

Once authorization to search has been obtained, the person conducting the search must carefully comply with the limitations imposed by the authorization. Only those locations which are described in the authorization may be searched and the search may be conducted only in areas where it is likely that the object of the search will be found. For example, if an investigator has authority to search the quarters of a suspect, the investigator may not search a car parked on the road outside. Likewise, if an authorization states that an investigator is looking for a 25-inch television, the investigator may not look into areas unlikely to contain a TV, such as a medicine cabinet or file cabinet.

5) Detention

Pending Execution of Search Authorizations. An authorization to search for contraband implicitly carries the limited authority to detain occupants of a home, apartment, or barracks room while the search is conducted. Police may also detain occupants leaving the premises at the time police arrive to execute the search authorization.

C. Commander Must Be Neutral and Detached

A commander, much like a judge, must remain objective when deciding whether there is sufficient information to justify a search authorization. When a commander is actively involved in a criminal investigation, he or she is disqualified from acting as the authorizing official.

A commander is not neutral and detached if he or she initiated or orchestrated the investigation or conducted the search personally. On the other hand, knowledge of an on-going investigation within the unit, disdain for certain kinds of crime, and personal information or knowledge about a suspect's character does not disqualify a commander from granting a search authorization.

If a commander is unsure whether a court will view his or her involvement in a particular case as disqualifying, the commander should play it safe by sending the person seeking the authorization to the military magistrate or to the next higher commander who has no involvement with the case.

3. WHEN THE FOURTH AMENDMENT DOES NOT APPLY

A. Nongovernmental Searches

The Fourth Amendment only protects Soldiers against searches by U.S. government officials. It does not cover searches by private persons or foreign officials.

1) Private Searches

The Fourth Amendment does not prohibit searches by private persons (roommates or family members), unless the private search was directed by a commander or police investigator. Be careful when working with unit informants. Telling them to "keep your eyes open" is permissible; telling them to bring you evidence may violate the Fourth Amendment and render the evidence inadmissible.

2) Foreign Searches

The Fourth Amendment applies only to the U.S. Government. Searches by German or Korean police need not comply with the Fourth Amendment unless the foreign search is directed, conducted, or participated in by U.S. agents. Foreign police may freely exchange criminal information with the military police.

B. No Reasonable Expectation of Privacy

The Fourth Amendment does not apply unless the suspect has a reasonable expectation of privacy in the area searched.

1) Government Property

A Soldier has no reasonable expectation of privacy in most government property, including military vehicles, tents, common tool kits, and office desks. No authorization is required to search these places. But the Fourth Amendment does cover items issued for personal use, such as wall lockers, foot lockers, and field gear. These items may be examined only during inspections and authorized searches.

2) Government E-Mail and Computer Systems

Although government e-mail, computers, and cell phones should follow the rules stated above for government property, appellate case law has found a reasonable expectation of privacy in these areas in certain circumstances. Changes in technology and how we use it often occur faster than case law can adapt to them, so consult your trial counsel or legal advisor if you want to search for digital evidence on a government information system. Depending on the circumstances, an authorization may not be required, especially if there was a proper DOD log-on banner on the device to be searched, and a properly filled out user agreement signed by the individual to be searched.

3) Abandoned Property

There is generally no expectation of privacy in abandoned property, such as a car abandoned on a public road, on-post quarters after a person has checked out, items thrown from a window or to the ground, garbage containers placed on a street curb, or a building destroyed by fire. Therefore, no authorization or probable cause is required to search or seize these items.

4) Open View (Plain View)

What a person knowingly exposes to the public is not subject to Fourth Amendment protection. For example, the exterior of a car parked on a public street is not protected by the Fourth Amendment. An item is in plain view if law enforcement (or military personnel) can see it from a place they have a lawful right to be in. For example, a platoon sergeant conducting room inspections has a right to be in each barracks room. If he sees a bong on a desk in the room, that bong is in plain view and there is no reasonable expectation of privacy in the item.

5) Sensory Aids

So long as a person is lawfully present in an area, he or she may properly use low-technology devices that enhance the senses. For example, flashlights may be used to look inside cars and dogs may sniff autos, luggage, or field gear. On the other hand, a thermal imaging device may not be used to observe activity inside a private home. In addition, special rules exist for the use of wiretaps and electronic "bugs." See your trial counsel if you feel electronic surveillance is necessary.

4. EXCEPTIONS TO THE FOURTH AMENDMENT

A. Exigent Circumstances

In emergencies, where the delay necessary to get a warrant would result in the removal, destruction, or concealment of evidence, a warrant is not required. However, probable cause is still required in these situations. For example, a staff duty officer walking through a barracks who smells marijuana coming from a Soldier's room may enter the room and "freeze" the situation. If he apprehends the Soldier for using marijuana, he may conduct a search of the Soldier incident to apprehension and may also seize any items in plain view. He should then seek authorization before he searches the rest of the room.

B. Automobile Exception

If there is probable cause to search an automobile, a warrant or authorization is generally not required. For example, if a staff duty officer has probable cause to believe that drugs are located in a Soldier's car, he may search the car without obtaining a warrant or search authorization. This exception exists because such evidence may be easily lost if the automobile is driven away before a warrant or authorization is obtained. The entire automobile may be searched, to include the trunk.

C. Consent Searches

A Soldier may consent to a search. However, the consent must be voluntary and not coerced by the influence of rank or position. When requesting consent you should advise the Soldier that he or she has the right not to consent. If the Soldier does consent, he or she can withdraw the consent at any time. In this case, the search must stop immediately. A Soldier may consent to a partial search (for example, everything in the room, but not the wall locker). Article 31 rights and written consent are recommended but not required. Do not "threaten" a Soldier that the search will be conducted even if he or she refuses to give consent.

D. Search Incident to Apprehension

Any person who has been properly apprehended may be searched in order to ensure the safety of the apprehending person and others, and to prevent destruction of evidence. Only the person's clothing and body and any areas within the person's reach may be searched. When a person is apprehended in an automobile, the entire passenger compartment may be searched, but only if the individual is within reaching distance of the passenger compartment at the time of the search, or if it is reasonable to believe the vehicle contains evidence of the crime the individual was just arrested for. The scope of this vehicle search incident to apprehension includes the glove box, console, back seat and under the seats, but does not include the trunk.

E. Inspections

1) General

Inspections are a function of command. The commander has the inherent right to inspect the barracks to ensure the command is properly equipped, maintained, and ready, and that personnel are present and fit for duty. A commander conducting an inspection may find items that could aid in a criminal prosecution. These items may be seized and used as evidence for an Article 15 or court-martial.

a. PRIMARY PURPOSE TEST

An inspection must have a primary administrative purpose. For example, inspections to ensure security, readiness, cleanliness, order, and discipline are permissible. Inspections may include an examination to locate and confiscate unlawful weapons and other contraband, since confiscation of contraband is a means of ensuring security, readiness, and order. An inspection whose primary purpose is to obtain evidence for an Article 15 or court-martial is not permissible, and any evidence discovered will be inadmissible. An inspection may have a dual purpose (both administrative and criminal) so long as the primary purpose is administrative.

b. SCOPE

The scope of an inspection must reflect its purpose. If the purpose is broad (general security, readiness, fitness for duty) then the intrusion may be broad (unroll sleeping bags, check inside pockets, unlock containers). If the purpose of the inspection is narrow (for example, only to check helmet accountability), then one cannot inspect beyond that purpose.

c. SUBTERFUGE RULE

An inspection may not be used as a subterfuge for a search. This normally takes place when a commander "feels" an individual has contraband in his possession or living area but lacks sufficient information to amount to probable cause, and uses an "inspection" to search that person for the contraband. Evidence discovered during an improper inspection usually is not admissible for court-martial (although technically admissible at an Article 15, commanders should be aware that if a Soldier refuses Article 15, there may not be enough evidence to prove a crime at a court-martial). If (1) an inspection immediately follows a report of a specific offense and was not previously scheduled, or (2) specific persons are targeted, or (3) specific persons are subjected to substantially different intrusions, then the government must show by clear and convincing evidence that the primary purpose of the examination was administrative, and that the inspection was not a ruse for an illegal criminal search. The commander's testimony is crucial to this issue.

2) Health and Welfare Inspections

The most common type of inspection is a commander's inspection of the unit to protect the health and welfare of the unit's Soldiers. The primary purpose of such an inspection must be administrative. Commanders should ensure that the scope of the inspection is consistent with the purpose and that everyone is treated alike. For example, if one Soldier's wall locker is inspected with "extra care" during a health and welfare inspection, the inspection will likely be found to be an unlawful subterfuge for a criminal search.

3) Drug Dogs

A commander conducting a health and welfare inspection may use a drug detector dog to enhance the senses of individuals conducting the inspection. Drug detector dogs may be used to inspect barracks, automobiles, and other areas, but as a matter of DA policy, will not be used to inspect persons. Drug dogs may not sniff individual Soldiers or formations. When a request is made for a handler and dog to go to a particular unit, the commander requesting the team should ask the provost marshal about the reliability of the dog and handler. Before the dog is used, the handler should demonstrate the reliability of the dog. The test for reliability consists of certification from an approved training course, the training and utilization alert record, and performance demonstrated to the commander.

4) Lost Weapons Lock-downs

The commander has the right to conduct an inspection for weapons or ammunition after a unit has been firing or has found a weapon missing. The commander or designated representatives may inspect all persons who were on the range and others who were in a position to steal the weapon, and their barracks and private automobiles. Commanders should exercise caution and ensure the inspection is conducted consistent with the primary purpose test and all Soldiers are treated alike.

5) Gate Inspections

A gate inspection is another form of an administrative inspection. An installation commander may authorize gate inspections to check drivers' licenses and vehicle registrations, deter drug traffic, reduce DWI incidents, prevent terrorist attacks, deter larcenies, or any other legitimate administrative purposes. Inspections may include all vehicles, or only those designated by the commander, such as every tenth vehicle.

a. WRITTEN GUIDANCE

The installation commander must issue written instructions defining the purpose (e.g. security, drugs, or and DWIs), times, locations, and methods for gate inspections. It is important to limit the discretion of the gate guards conducting the inspection. Some discretion to consider traffic patterns is permissible so long as it is provided by the written guidance.

b. NOTICE

All persons must receive notice in advance that they are subject to inspection upon entry, while within the confines, and upon departure from the installation. A warning sign or visitor's pass are common ways to give notice.

c. DRUG DOGS / TECHNOLOGICAL AIDS

Metal detectors, drug dogs, and other technological aids may be used during gate inspections.

d. CIVILIAN EMPLOYEES

Civilian employees may be entitled to overtime pay when their working conditions are affected by gate inspection delays. Check the local collective bargaining agreement to gauge this impact.

e. ENTRY INSPECTIONS

Civilians entering the installation may only be inspected with their consent. If they refuse to consent, they should be denied access to the installation. Soldiers may be ordered to comply with an inspection, and may be inspected over their objection, using reasonable force, if necessary.

f. EXIT INSPECTIONS

Civilians exiting the installation may be inspected over their objection, using reasonable force if necessary. Civilians who refuse to comply with an exit inspection should be informed of possible administrative sanctions (loss of post driving privileges, bar letter). Immediately notify the installation commander if this happens. If contraband is found, detain the civilians and notify the local civilian police. The standard for exit inspections for Soldiers is the same as for entry inspections; they may be ordered to submit to an inspection and reasonable force may be used if necessary.

6) Inventories

a. GENERAL

A commander is required to conduct an inventory of a Soldier's property when the Soldier is AWOL, admitted to the hospital, or on emergency leave. See para. 12-14, AR 700-84, Issue and Sale of Personal Clothing (18 Nov 2004). The commander or a designated representative should also inventory the property of an individual who has been placed in military or civilian confinement. See para. 10-8, AR 190-47, The U.S. Army Correctional System (15 Jun 2006). If the person conducting the inventory discovers items that would aid in a criminal prosecution, those items may be seized and used as evidence.

b. AUTOMOBILES

Under some circumstances, automobiles may also be inventoried. When a person is arrested for DWI or for some other offense which requires transportation to the MP station, the person's vehicle may be secured. If the vehicle is impounded, it may be inventoried. If a person is arrested for DWI just as he pulls into his quarters' parking lot, there is no reason to impound the vehicle. But if the person is arrested on an outer road of the post where there is a possibility of vandalism, the vehicle may be impounded and inventoried.

5. APPREHENSIONS

A. Contacts and Stops and Apprehensions

1) Contacts

Officers, NCOs, and MPs may initiate "contact" with persons in any place they are lawfully situated. Generally, such contacts are not "apprehensions" subject to the Fourth Amendment. Most contacts do not result from suspicion of criminal activity. Examples of lawful contacts include questioning witnesses to crimes and warning pedestrians that they are entering a dangerous neighborhood. These types of contacts are entirely reasonable, permissible, and within the normal activities of law enforcement personnel and commanders. They are not detentions in any sense.

2) Stops

An officer, NCO, or MP who reasonably suspects that a person has committed, is committing, or is about to commit a crime has the obligation and authority to stop that person. Both pedestrians and occupants of vehicles may be stopped. If the person is a suspect and is to be questioned, Article 31 warnings should be read. The stop must be based on more than a hunch. The official making the stop should be able to state specific facts to support the decision to stop an individual. If the individual making the stop reasonably suspects the stopped person is armed and dangerous, they may frisk or pat down the person for weapons.

3) Apprehensions

Arrests in the military are called apprehensions. Any officer, noncommissioned officer, or military policeman may apprehend individuals when there is probable cause to apprehend. Generally, a person is apprehended when he or she is not free to leave. The person making the apprehension should identify himself or herself and tell the suspect he or she is under apprehension. The suspect should also be told the reason for the apprehension and read his or her Article 31 rights, preferably from a rights warning card, as soon as practicable. If the suspect resists apprehension he or she may be prosecuted for resisting apprehension or disobeying an order. Civilians may be detained until military or civilian police arrive.

B. Probable Cause to Apprehend

A person may be apprehended only if there is probable cause that the person has committed a crime. Probable cause to apprehend is a common sense appraisal based on all of the facts and circumstances present. An example of probable cause to apprehend is when you or some other reliable person has seen an individual commit a violation of the UCMJ, such as using marijuana, assaulting someone, breaking another's property, or being drunk and disorderly.

C. Arrest Warrants

Generally, if there is probable cause, no authorization to apprehend (arrest warrant) is required in the military. There is one important exception, however; that is when you apprehend someone in a "private dwelling," such as on-post family quarters, or any off-post quarters. If the person to be apprehended is in a "private dwelling," the apprehending officer must obtain authorization to make the apprehension from a military magistrate or the commander with authority over the private dwelling (usually the installation commander). Barracks and field encampments are not considered private dwellings; therefore, no special authorization is needed to apprehend someone there. Also, to apprehend a person at off-post quarters requires coordination with civilian authorities and may require an arrest warrant from a civilian judge.

6. URINALYSIS TESTS

A. Use of Test Results

There are four kinds of urine tests: inspections, probable cause tests, consent tests, and fitness-for-duty tests. Results from inspection, probable cause, and consent urine tests may be used for Article 15, court-martial and administrative separation purposes. The results of a fitness-for-duty test may not be used as a basis for an Article 15 or court-martial. In addition, a positive fitness-for-duty test result may not be used in an administrative separation action unless the Soldier receives an honorable discharge. See AR 635-200, Personnel Separations, Enlisted Personnel (6 June 2005).

Command-directed. Be wary of the term "command-directed" urinalysis. Any urine test ordered by the commander (inspection, probable cause, fitness-for-duty) is "command-directed." The ability to use the test results for UCMJ or separation purposes depends on the type of test (inspection, probable cause, consent), not on whether or not it is labeled "command-directed." A fitness-for duty test is normally "command-directed," but a positive result may not be used for UCMJ purposes.

B. Urinalysis inspections

1) Unit integrity

A unit urinalysis test is merely another form of inspection. All of the Soldiers in a unit may be tested or Soldiers may be "randomly" selected, usually based on the final digit of their social security number, for testing. Alternatively, a portion of the unit (platoon, section, squad) may be tested.

2) Battalion Prevention Leader

When the government loses a urinalysis case it is rarely due to laboratory errors. Army urine testing laboratories are now widely regarded as the models for comparison and employ the most stringent scientific testing equipment and techniques. When the government loses a urinalysis case or decides not to prosecute one, it is primarily due to problems at the unit level, usually with the chain of custody. Many of these problems stem from the Battalion Prevention Leader. If a commander takes a Soldier who cannot perform adequately as a squad leader and makes that Soldier the Battalion Prevention Leader, it is likely that there will be problems.

C. Probable cause urine tests

Probable cause urine tests follow the same rules as other probable cause searches. If, under the totality of the facts and circumstances, a commander has a reasonable belief that a Soldier has used drugs, then he may order the Soldier to provide a urine sample. The results of that test are admissible. Common examples of probable cause urine tests are (1) when drugs are discovered on a Soldier's person, car, wall locker or field gear; and (2) when a Soldier has been observed using drugs.

D. Consent urine tests

1) Consent must be voluntary

A consent urine test is a form of consent search. No probable cause or authorization is required, but the commander must be able to show that the Soldier voluntarily consented to provide a urine sample and was not coerced by the rank or position of the person requesting the sample. Article 31 rights are not required to prove voluntary consent, but if the Soldier is asked questions about his suspected drug use, then Article 31 rights would be required.

2) What to do if the Soldier asks questions

If a Soldier asks the commander, "What are my options?" a new problem arises. In response to the "what are my options" question, the commander should explain the differences between a consent urine test and one ordered by the commander. The results of a consent urine test may be the basis for an Article 15, court-martial or administrative elimination. The results of a fitness-for-duty urine test may not. If the Soldier understands these differences and nevertheless consents, the consent will probably be viewed as voluntary.

3) Consent as a back-up

If a commander has probable cause to order a urine test, he may still request a consent sample as a precautionary alternative. If the Soldier asks "what are my options" the commander should explain that the results of a consent urine test are admissible and, if the Soldier refuses to consent, the commander may order a urine test. However, the commander should also tell the Soldier that if the commander orders the test, the results may not be admissible if it is later determined that the commander did not have probable cause. In this case, the test results may not be used for Article 15 or court-martial purposes and may only be used in an administrative separation if the Soldier receives an honorable discharge.

E. Fitness-for-duty urine tests

1) Results inadmissible

AR 600-85, Army Substance Abuse Program (1 2 February 2009, RAR 001 2 Dec 2009) provides that a commander may order a urine test to determine the "fitness-for-duty" of any Soldier when the commander observes, suspects, or otherwise becomes aware that the Soldier may be affected by illegal drug use. The results of such a fitness-for-duty test are inadmissible for court-martial purposes. They are inadmissible because AR 600-85 balances the needs of the military with the individual privacy rights of the Soldier and will not allow test results based on mere suspicion to be used for punishment. A commander can order a Soldier to provide a urine sample based solely on mere suspicion; but because this is not based upon probable cause, an inspection, or consent, the results may only be used to refer the Soldier for rehabilitative treatment or separate him from the service with an honorable discharge. Before a commander orders a Soldier to provide a urine sample, the commander should understand the admissibility of the urinalysis results to prevent later confusion when the results come back.

2) Suspicion is less than probable cause

Reasonable suspicion sufficient to order a fitness for duty test must be based upon facts which a commander can articulate. However, it need not amount to probable cause.

F. Confirmatory testing

One of the most difficult cases that a commander must handle is when a senior NCO, particularly one who is a "good Soldier," tests positive for drug use. The Soldier may deny drug use and challenge the validity of the testing procedures at the unit and the lab, often focusing on minor irregularities that do not invalidate the results. A commander has a few options to resolve these dilemmas.

1) Polygraphs

Offer the Soldier the opportunity to take a polygraph. A Soldier may not be required to take a polygraph, but if he consents to take one, the local CID polygrapher can be invaluable in distinguishing those who did not use drugs from those who only swear that the urine test was wrong. Few of these "wronged" Soldiers will be willing to take a polygraph, and many of those who do will admit to the drug use after failing the polygraph test. The polygraph results are inadmissible at a court-martial, but they can be used to help a commander decide the proper disposition of a case.

2) Blood and DNA testing

When a Soldier alleges that his or her urine sample was switched with someone else's, the sample can be tested to ensure that the blood type of the positive sample is the same as the Soldier's blood type. This method does not eliminate any possibility of error, but it may help determine whether the positive urine sample was, in fact, the Soldier's sample. DNA found in the urine can also be compared with the Soldier's DNA to confirm that the positive sample was submitted by the Soldier. Unless there is evidence that the Soldier's urine sample was switched, the government is not required to perform blood or DNA testing.

3) Hair testing

If a Soldier denies ever using drugs, his or her hair may be tested to confirm this allegation. Since traces of drugs are deposited in a drug user's hair as the hair grows, a hair sample will provide a history of an individual's drug use. Although hair analysis may be unable to detect a single use of drugs, it will be able to detect chronic use. The government is generally not required to pay for hair testing.

APPENDIX A
COMMANDER'S GUIDE TO ARTICULATE PROBABLE CAUSE TO SEARCH

1. Probable cause to authorize a search exists if there is a reasonable belief, based on facts, that the person or evidence sought is at the place to be searched. Reasonable belief is more than mere suspicion. Witness or source should be asked three questions:

a. **What is where and when?** Get the facts!

(1) Be specific: how much, size, color, etc.

(2) Is it still there (or is information stale)?

(a) If the witness saw a joint in barracks room two weeks ago, it is probably gone; the information is stale.

(b) If the witness saw large quantity of marijuana in barracks room one day ago, it is probably still there; the information is not stale.

b. **How do you know?** Which of these apply:

(1) "I saw it there." Such personal observation is extremely reliable.

(2) "He [the suspect] told me." Such an admission is reliable.

(3) "His [the suspect's] roommate/wife/friend told me." This is hearsay. Get details and call in source if possible.

(4) "I heard it in the barracks." Such rumor is unreliable unless there are specific corroborating and verifying details.

c. **Why should I believe you?** Which of these apply:

(1) Witness is a good, honest Soldier; you know him from personal knowledge or by reputation or opinion of chain of command.

(2) Witness has given reliable information before; he has a good track record (CID may have records).

(3) Witness has no reason to lie.

(4) Witness has truthful demeanor.

(5) Witness made statement under oath. ("Do you swear or affirm that any information you give is true to the best of your knowledge, so help you God?")

(6) Other information corroborates or verifies details.

(7) Witness made admission against own interests.

2. The determination that probable cause exists must be based on facts, not only on the conclusion of others.

3. The determination should be a common sense appraisal of the totality of all the facts and circumstances presented.

4. Make a written note of the reasons why you authorized the search in case authorization becomes an issue later.

5. Talk to your legal advisor!

APPENDIX B
DRUG DETECTION TIMES

Time periods which drugs and drug metabolites remain in the body at levels sufficient to detect are listed below. **Source: FTDTL, Ft Meade, (301) 677-7086/7085.**

Drug	Approximate Retention Time
THC (marijuana)	1-5 days*
Cocaine	2-4 days
Amphetamines /methamphetamines	3 days (ecstasy)
Barbiturates	1-2 days
Opiates	1-3 days
PCP	3 days
LSD	12 hours – 3 days**
Steroids	3 days or longer***

* Longer than 5 days indicates chronic or heavy use.

** LSD is only tested if command makes a specific request through AFIP.

*** Length of detection determined by type and duration of use. Testing is only done at UCLA; you must make a specific request to that lab to test for steroids.

Note – Only 10-50% of submitted samples are tested for PCP, Oxycodone/Oxymorphone, and Codeine/Morphine.

Chapter 8

SELF-INCRIMINATION, CONFESSIONS, AND RIGHTS WARNING

1. Sources of the Rights

A Soldier's privilege against self-incrimination and right to counsel come from four sources:

A. The Fifth Amendment

"No person . . . shall be compelled in any criminal case to be a witness against himself, nor be deprived of life, liberty, or property, without due process of law. . . ."

B. Uniform Code of Military Justice

1) Article 31(a), UCMJ

"No person subject to this chapter may compel any person to incriminate himself or to answer any question the answer to which may tend to incriminate him."

2) Article 31(b), UCMJ

"No person subject to this chapter may interrogate, or request any statement from an accused or a person suspected of an offense without first informing him . . ."

C. The Sixth Amendment

"In all criminal prosecutions, the accused shall . . . enjoy the right to have the Assistance of Counsel for his defense."

D. Army Regulations

1) AR 15-6 – Investigations

No military witness or respondent will be compelled to incriminate himself (*see* Article 31, UCMJ).

No witness or respondent not subject to the UCMJ will be deprived of his rights under the Fifth Amendment.

2) AR 27-10 - Nonjudicial Punishment

The imposing commander will ensure that the Soldier is notified of his right to remain silent and his right to consult with counsel.

3) AR 635-200 - Enlisted Personnel Separations

Article 31, UCMJ, applies to board procedures.

This list of regulations is not exhaustive; other regulations also impose a rights warning requirement. Always review regulations governing a specific type of investigation or proceeding to decide if rights warnings are required.

2. THE RIGHTS WARNING DECISION

How do you decide if you must actually read the rights warnings? The answer is: whenever you intend to conduct official questioning of a suspect or accused, you must read a rights warning. Each element of this standard is discussed below:

A. Official

The first part of the rule requires rights warnings when the questioner acts in an official capacity. Law enforcement personnel and commanders almost always act in an official capacity. In contrast, when a Soldier brags about criminal conduct in response to a friend's question, those statements may be used against the Soldier because the friend is not acting in an "official" capacity and is not required to read rights warnings to the Soldier. The Soldier's act of bragging indicates that he or she did not feel pressured or coerced into talking about the crime, so the rationale underlying the rights warning requirement does not apply.

B. Questioning

Questioning is a broad term and includes any formal or informal words or actions that are designed to elicit (or reasonably likely to result in) an incriminating response. *See* Mil. R. Evid. 305. In your official capacity, if you are trying to get the Soldier to tell you something that you can use against him or her, you are questioning the Soldier. For example, it is questioning if you bring a Soldier suspected of stealing a rifle into your office and attempt to get a response by showing the Soldier the recently recovered stolen weapon.

It is not questioning when a Soldier volunteers information or spontaneously gives information without any "words or actions reasonably likely to elicit an incriminating response" from the commander. If you simply listen to the Soldier, there is no requirement to stop the Soldier and advise him or her of their rights. If you want to question the Soldier after any volunteered information, then you must give rights warnings.

C. Suspect or accused

You do not have to advise all Soldiers of their rights before questioning them. Witnesses, who are not suspected or accused of offenses, need not be advised of any privilege against self-incrimination, even though you are conducting official questioning. A Soldier becomes a suspect when you believe, or have enough information such that you reasonably should believe that the Soldier committed an offense. Because of this "reasonableness" standard, you cannot avoid rights warnings by simply saying that you did not suspect the Soldier being questioned. A Soldier becomes an "accused" after court-martial charges have been preferred against him.

D. Summary

When you **officially question** a **suspect** or **accused**, you must read the rights warnings prior to the questioning. If you must re-interview the suspect, you should complete another rights advisement before questioning, and ensure defense counsel is present if necessary.

3. RIGHTS WARNINGS

Rights warnings should be read verbatim from DA Form 3881, Rights Warning Procedure/Waiver Certificate (attached below) or GTA 19-6-6, How to Inform Suspect/Accused Persons of Their Rights (Rights Warning Card) (attached below).

4. Voluntary Waiver of Rights

After reading the rights warnings to the suspect, ask these questions:

- Do you understand your rights? (Yes)
- Do you want a lawyer? (No)
- Are you willing to make a statement? (Yes)

If the answers in the parentheses are given, the suspect has waived his or her rights and you may proceed with your interview. If the suspect does not understand his or her rights, you should explain the rights further; if he or she wants to remain silent or see an attorney, you should stop the interview, make a note of the request, and call your trial counsel. Be sure to specifically note whether the suspect wants to remain silent, have an attorney, or both. Different rules apply to each request.

5. Presence of Counsel

In certain circumstances, defense counsel must be present before questioning a Soldier about misconduct. For example, if charges have been preferred against a Soldier, then defense counsel must be present before questioning the Soldier about the charged offenses. However, if the questioning focuses on uncharged misconduct, defense counsel may not have to be present. Even if no charges are preferred, if the Soldier in a previous custodial interrogation requests to consult with a lawyer, then normally a defense counsel must be present before conducting a subsequent interrogation. This area can be very complicated; therefore, contact your trial counsel before questioning a Soldier who has had charges preferred against him, or has previously asked for a lawyer.

6. REMEDY: EXCLUSION

If the questioning official violates the voluntariness doctrine; the requirement to give rights warnings; the rules on obtaining a waiver; or, the rules about the presence of counsel, then any statement obtained from a suspect that might have been used against the suspect at trial will be excluded from evidence. Any evidence derived from the statement must also be excluded. For example, if the statement told investigators where a stolen weapon was hidden, and the weapon was recovered based upon that statement, then the weapon itself would also have to be excluded if the statement was improperly obtained. This can be catastrophic, but may not always be the end of the government's case. If the trial counsel can prove the case with evidence that was obtained independently of the inadmissible statement, then the prosecution may go forward.

RIGHTS WARNING PROCEDURE/WAIVER CERTIFICATE

For use of this form, see AR 190-30; the proponent agency is ODCSOPS

DATA REQUIRED BY THE PRIVACY ACT

AUTHORITY: Title 10, United States Code, Section 3012(g)

PRINCIPAL PURPOSE: To provide commanders and law enforcement officials with means by which information may be accurately identified.

ROUTINE USES: Your Social Security Number is used as an additional/alternate means of identification to facilitate filing and retrieval.

DISCLOSURE: Disclosure of your Social Security Number is voluntary.

1. LOCATION		2. DATE	3. TIME	4. FILE NO.
5. NAME *(Last, First, MI)*		8. ORGANIZATION OR ADDRESS		
6. SSN	7. GRADE/STATUS			

PART I - RIGHTS WAIVER/NON-WAIVER CERTIFICATE

Section A. Rights

The investigator whose name appears below told me that he/she is with the United States Army ______________________________ ______________________________ and wanted to question me about the following offense(s) of which I am suspected/accused: ______________________________

Before he/she asked me any questions about the offense(s), however, he/she made it clear to me that I have the following rights:

1. I do not have to answer any question or say anything.
2. Anything I say or do can be used as evidence against me in a criminal trial.
3. *(For personnel subject othe UCMJ* I have the right to talk privately to a lawyer before, during, and after questioning and to have a lawyer present with me during questioning. This lawyer can be a civilian lawyer I arrange for at no expense to the Government or a military lawyer detailed for me at no expense to me, or both.

   \- or -

   (For civilians not subject to the UCMJ) I have the right to talk privately to a lawyer before, during, and after questioning and to have a lawyer present with me during questioning. I understand that this lawyer can be one that I arrange for at my own expense, or if I cannot afford a lawyer and want one, a lawyer will be appointed for me before any questioning begins.
4. If I am now willing to discuss the offense(s) under investigation, with or without a lawyer present, I have a right to stop answering questions at any time, or speak privately with a lawyer before answering further, even if I sign the waiver below.

5. COMMENTS *(Continue on reverse side)*

Section B. Waiver

I understand my rights as stated above. I am now willing to discuss the offense(s) under investigation and make a statement without talking to a lawyer first and without having a lawyer present with me.

WITNESSES *(If available)*	3. SIGNATURE OF INTERVIEWEE
1a. NAME *(Type or Print)*	
b. ORGANIZATION OR ADDRESS AND PHONE	4. SIGNATURE OF INVESTIGATOR
2a. NAME *(Type or Print)*	5. TYPED NAME OF INVESTIGATOR
b. ORGANIZATION OR ADDRESS AND PHONE	6. ORGANIZATION OF INVESTIGATOR

Section C. Non-waiver

1. I do not want to give up my rights

   ☐ I want a lawyer ☐ I do not want to be questioned or say anything

2. SIGNATURE OF INTERVIEWEE

ATTACH THIS WAIVER CERTIFICATE TO ANY SWORN STATEMENT *(DA FORM 2823)* SUBSEQUENTLY EXECUTED BY THE SUSPECT/ACCUSED

DA FORM 3881, NOV 89 EDITION OF NOV 84 IS OBSOLETE USAPA 2.01

PART II - RIGHTS WARNING PROCEDURE

THE WARNING

1. WARNING - Inform the suspect/accused of:
   a. Your official position.
   b. Nature of offense(s).
   c. The fact that he/she is a suspect/accused.
2. RIGHTS - Advise the suspect/accused of his/her rights as follows:
   "Before I ask you any questions, you must understand your rights."
   a. "You do not have to answer my questions or say anything."
   b. "Anything you say or do can be used as evidence against you in a criminal trial."
   c. (For personnel subject to the UCMJ) "You have the right to talk privately to a lawyer before, during, and after questioning and to have a lawyer present with you during questioning. This lawyer can be a civilian you arrange for at no expense to the Government or a military lawyer detailed for you at no expense to you, or both."

   - or -

   (For civilians not subject to the UCMJ) You have the right to talk privately to a lawyer before, during, and after questioning and to have a lawyer present with you during questioning. This lawyer can be one you arrange for at your own expense, or if you cannot afford a lawyer and want one, a lawyer will be appointed for you before any questioning begins."
   d. "If you are now willing to discuss the offense(s) under investigation, with or without a lawyer present, you have a right to stop answering questions at any time, or speak privately with a lawyer before answering further, even if you sign a waiver certificate."

Make certain the suspect/accused fully understands his/her rights.

THE WAIVER

"Do you understand your rights?"
(If the suspect/accused says "no," determine what is not understood, and if necessary repeat the appropriate rights advisement. If the suspect/accused says "yes," ask the following question.)

"Have you ever requested a lawyer after being read your rights?"
(If the suspect/accused says "yes," find out when and where. If the request was recent *(i.e., fewer than 30 days ago)*, obtain legal advice whether to continue the interrogation. If the suspect/accused says "no," or if the prior request was not recent, ask him/her the following question.)

"Do you want a lawyer at this time?"
(If the suspect/accused says "yes," stop the questioning until he/she has a lawyer. If the suspect/accused says "no," ask him/her the following question.)

"At this time, are you willing to discuss the offense(s) under investigation and make a statement without talking to a lawyer and without having a lawyer present with you?" *(If the suspect/accused says "no," stop the interview and have him/her read and sign the non-waiver section of the waiver certificate on the other side of this form. If the suspect/accused says "yes," have him/her read and sign the waiver section of the waiver certificate on the other side of this form.)*

SPECIAL INSTRUCTIONS

WHEN SUSPECT/ACCUSED REFUSES TO SIGN WAIVER CERTIFICATE: If the suspect/accused orally waives his/her rights but refuses to sign the waiver certificate, you may proceed with the questioning. Make notations on the waiver certificate to the effect that he/she has stated that he/she understands his/her rights, does not want a lawyer, wants to discuss the offense(s) under investigation, and refuses to sign the waiver certificate.

IF WAIVER CERTIFICATE CANNOT BE COMPLETED IMMEDIATELY: In all cases the waiver certificate must be completed as soon as possible. Every effort should be made to complete the waiver certificate before any questioning begins. If the waiver certificate cannot be completed at once, as in the case of street interrogation, completion may be temporarily postponed. Notes should be kept on the circumstances.

PRIOR INCRIMINATING STATEMENTS:

1. If the supsect/accused has made spontaneous incriminating statements before being properly advised of his/her rights he/she should be told that such statements do not obligate him/her to answer further questions.
2. If the suspect/accused was questioned as such either without being advised of his/her rights or some question exists as to the propriety of the first statement, the accused must be so advised. The office of the serving Staff Judge Advocate should be contacted for assistance in drafting the proper rights advisal.

NOTE: If 1 or 2 applies, the fact that the suspect/accused was advised accordingly should be noted in the comment section on the waiver certificate and initialed by the suspect/accused.

WHEN SUSPECT/ACCUSED DISPLAYS INDECISION ON EXERCISING HIS OR HER RIGHTS DURING THE INTERROGATION PROCESS: If during the interrogation, the suspect displays indecision about requesting counsel (for example, "Maybe I should get a lawyer."), further questioning must cease immediately. At that point, you may question the suspect/accused only concerning whether he or she desires to waive counsel. The questioning may not be utilized to discourage a suspect/accused from exercising his/her rights. (For example, do not make such comments as "If you didn't do anything wrong, you shouldn't need an attorney.")

COMMENTS *(Continued)*

REVERSE OF DA FORM 3881

USAPA V2.01

HOW TO INFORM SUSPECT/ACCUSED PERSONS OF THEIR RIGHTS

Use this card only when DA Form 3881, Rights Warning Procedure/Waiver Certificate, cannot be used. Complete DA Form 3881 as soon as possible.

VERBAL RIGHTS WARNING

Inform the person of your official position, the nature of the offense(s), and the fact that he/she is a suspect/accused. Then read him/her the following--do not paraphrase; read verbatim:

"BEFORE I ASK YOU ANY QUESTIONS, YOU MUST UNDERSTAND YOUR RIGHTS."

1. "YOU DO NOT HAVE TO ANSWER MY QUESTIONS OR SAY ANYTHING."

2. "ANYTHING YOU SAY OR DO CAN BE USED AS EVIDENCE AGAINST YOU IN A CRIMINAL TRIAL."

3. (For personnel subject to the UCMJ) "YOU HAVE THE RIGHT TO TALK PRIVATELY TO A LAWYER BEFORE, DURING, AND AFTER QUESTIONING AND TO HAVE A LAWYER PRESENT WITH YOU DURING QUESTIONING. THIS LAWYER CAN BE A CIVILIAN YOU ARRANGE FOR AT NO EXPENSE TO THE GOVERNMENT OR A MILITARY LAWYER DETAILED FOR YOU AT NO EXPENSE TO YOU, OR BOTH."

   (For civilians not subject to the UCMJ) "YOU HAVE THE RIGHT TO TALK PRIVATELY TO A LAWYER BEFORE, DURING, AND AFTER QUESTIONING AND TO HAVE A LAWYER PRESENT WITH YOU DURING QUESTIONING. THIS LAWYER CAN BE ONE YOU ARRANGE FOR AT YOUR OWN EXPENSE, OR IF YOU CANNOT AFFORD A LAWYER AND WANT ONE, A LAWYER WILL BE APPOINTED FOR YOU BEFORE ANY QUESTIONING BEGINS."

4. "IF YOU ARE NOW WILLING TO DISCUSS THE OFFENSE(S) UNDER INVESTIGATION, WITH OR WITHOUT A LAWYER PRESENT, YOU HAVE A RIGHT TO STOP ANSWERING QUESTIONS AT ANY TIME, OR SPEAK PRIVATELY WITH A LAWYER BEFORE ANSWERING FURTHER, EVEN IF YOU SIGN A WAIVER CERTIFICATE."

Make certain the suspect/accused fully understands his/her rights, then say:

"DO YOU WANT A LAWYER AT THIS TIME?"

"AT THIS TIME, ARE YOU WILLING TO DISCUSS THE OFFENSE(S) UNDER INVESTIGATION AND MAKE A STATEMENT WITHOUT TALKING TO A LAWYER AND WITHOUT HAVING A LAWYER PRESENT WITH YOU?"

(See DA Form 3881 for more detailed instructions.)
Department of the Army Graphic Training Aid
Supersedes GTA 19-6-5, July 1985 GTA 19-6-6, June 1991

Chapter 9

PUNITIVE ARTICLES OF THE UNIFORM CODE OF MILITARY JUSTICE (UCMJ) (AS OF JUNE 2012)

77 - Principals
78 - Accessory after the fact
79 - Conviction of lesser included offenses
80 - Attempts
81 - Conspiracy
82 - Solicitation
83 - Fraudulent enlistment, appointment, or separation
84 - Effecting unlawful enlistment, appointment, or separation
85 - Desertion
86 - Absence without leave (AWOL)
87 - Missing movement
88 - Contempt toward officials
89 - Disrespect toward a superior commissioned officer
90 - Assaulting or willfully disobeying superior commissioned officer
91 - Insubordinate conduct toward warrant officer, noncommissioned, or petty officer
92 - Failure to obey order or regulation
93 - Cruelty and maltreatment
94 - Mutiny and sedition
95 - Resistance, flight, breach of arrest, and escape
96 - Releasing prisoner without proper authority
97 - Unlawful detention
98 - Noncompliance with procedural rules
99 - Misbehavior before the enemy
100 - Subordinate compelling surrender
101 - Improper use of countersign
102 - Forcing a safeguard
103 - Captured or abandoned property
104 - Aiding the enemy
105 - Misconduct as a prisoner
106 - Spies
106a - Espionage
107 - False official statements
108 - Military property: sale, loss, damage, destruction, or wrongful disposition
109 - Property other than military property: waste, spoilage, or destruction
110 - Improper hazarding of vessel
111 - Drunken or reckless operation of vehicle, aircraft, or vessel
112 - Drunk on duty
112a - Wrongful use, possession, etc., of controlled substances
113 - Misbehavior of sentinel or lookout
114 - Dueling
115 - Malingering
116 - Riot or breach of peace
117 - Provoking speeches or gestures
118 - Murder
119 - Manslaughter
119a - Death or injury of an unborn child
120 - Rape and sexual assault
120a - Stalking
120b - Rape and sexual assault of a child
120c - Other sexual misconduct
121 - Larceny and wrongful appropriation
122 - Robbery
123 - Forgery
123a - Making, drawing, or uttering check, draft, or order without sufficient funds
124 - Maiming
125 - Sodomy
126 - Arson
127 - Extortion
128 - Assault
129 - Burglary
130 - Housebreaking
131 - Perjury
132 - Frauds against the United States

133 - Conduct unbecoming an officer and gentleman

134 - General article

Clause 1 – Disorders and neglects to the prejudice of good order and discipline in the armed forces

Clause 2 - Conduct of a nature to bring discredit upon the armed forces

Clause 3 - Crimes and offenses not capital

134 - Listed offenses:

- Abusing public animal
- Adultery
- Assault, with intent to murder, voluntary manslaughter, rape, robbery, sodomy, arson, burglary, or housebreaking
- Bigamy
- Bribery and graft
- Burning with intent to defraud
- Check, worthless, making and uttering – by dishonorably failing to maintain funds
- Child endangerment
- Child pornography
- Cohabitation, wrongful
- Correctional custody – offenses against
- Debt, dishonorably failing to pay
- Disloyal statements
- Disorderly conduct, drunkenness
- Drinking liquor with prisoner
- Drunk prisoner
- Drunkenness – incapacitation for performance of duties through prior wrongful indulgence in intoxicating liquor or any drug
- False or unauthorized pass offenses
- False pretenses, obtaining services under
- False swearing
- Firearm, discharging through negligence
- Firearm, discharging – willfully, under such circumstances as to endanger human life
- Fleeing scene of accident
- Fraternization
- Gambling with subordinate
- Homicide, negligent
- Impersonating a commissioned officer, warrant, noncommissioned, or petty officer, or an agent or official
- Indecent language
- Jumping from vessel into the water
- Kidnapping
- Mail: taking, opening, secreting, destroying, or stealing
- Mail: depositing or causing to be deposited obscene matters in
- Misprision of serious offense
- Obstructing justice
- Wrongful interference with adverse administrative proceeding
- Pandering and prostitution
- Parole, Violation of
- Perjury: subornation of
- Public record: altering, concealing, removing, mutilating, obliterating, or destroying
- Quarantine: medical, breaking
- Reckless Endangerment
- Restriction, breaking
- Seizure: destruction, removal, or disposal of property to prevent
- Self-injury without intent to avoid service
- Sentinel or lookout: offenses against or by
- Soliciting another to commit an offense
- Stolen property: knowingly receiving, buying, concealing
- Straggling
- Testify: wrongful refusal
- Threat or hoax designed or intended to caused panic or public fear
- Threat, communicating
- Unlawful entry
- Weapon: concealed carrying
- Wearing unauthorized insignia, decoration, badge, ribbon, device, or lapel pin

Chapter 10

URINALYSIS

1. SCIENTIFIC ASPECTS OF URINALYSIS PROGRAM

A. What Urinalysis Test Proves

Urine test proves only past use; it proves that drug or drug metabolites (waste products) are in the urine. Urine test does not prove: Impairment; Single or multiple usages; Method of ingestion; or, Knowing ingestion.

B. Drugs Tested

- Marijuana (THC metabolite) and Cocaine (BZE metabolite).
- Other drugs tested (some only upon request):
- LSD – removed from testing in 2006. Still screened periodically under the "prevalence program."
- Opiates (morphine, codeine, 6-MAM metabolite of heroin)
- PCP
- Amphetamines; including designer amphetamines MDMA, MDA, MDEA
- Oxymorphone/Oxycodone
- Anabolic steroids – testing only done by UCLA.

C. Cut-off Levels

DOD and urine testing laboratories have established "cut-off" levels. Samples which give test results below these cut-off levels are reported as negative. A sample is reported as positive only if it gives test results above the cut-off level during both the screening (every positive screened twice) and the confirming test. Source: DoD Standard Drug Testing Panel, *available at* http://tricare.mil/tma/ddrp/Program-Policy-Archives.aspx. Cut-off levels for different tests are in the tables below.

Cut-off levels for screening tests (EMIT and IA)	
Drug	ng/ml
Marijuana (THC)	50
Cocaine (BZE)	150
Amphetamine/Methamphetamine	500
Designer Amphetamines (MDMA, MDA, MDEA)	500
Opiates	
Morphine/Codeine	2000
Oxycodone/Oxymorphone	100
6-monoacetylmorphine (heroin)	10
Phencyclidine (PCP)	25

Cut-off levels for GC/MS test	
Drug	*ng/ml*
Marijuana (THC)	15
Cocaine (BZE)	100
Amphetamine/Methamphetamine	100
Designer Amphetamines (MDMA, MDA, MDEA)	500
Opiates	
Morphine	4000
Codeine	2000
Oxycodone/Oxymorphone	100
6-monoacetylmorphine (heroin)	10
Phencyclidine (PCP)	25

D. Drug Detection Times

1) Time periods which drugs and drug metabolites remain in the body at levels sufficient to detect are listed below

Drug	*Approx. Retention Time*
Marijuana (THC) (Half-life 36 hours)	
Acute dosage (1-2 joints)	2-3 days
Marijuana (eaten)	1-5 days
Moderate smoker (4 times per week)	5 days
Heavy smoker (daily)	10 days
Chronic smoker	14-18 days (may exceed 20 days)
Cocaine (BZE) (Half-life 4 hours)	2-4 days
Amphetamines	1-2 days (2-4 days if heavy use)
Barbiturates	
Short-acting (e.g. Secobarbital)	1 day
Long-acting (e.g. Phenobarbital)	2-3 weeks
Opiates	2 days
Phencyclidine (PCP)	14 days

2) Factors which affect retention times

- Drug metabolism and half-life.
- Donor's physical condition.
- Donor's fluid intake prior to test.
- Donor's method and frequency of ingestion of drug.

3) Detection times may affect

- Probable cause. Information concerning past drug use may not provide probable cause to believe the Soldier's urine contains traces of drug metabolites, unless the alleged drug use was recent.
- Jurisdiction over reservists. Reservists may not be convicted at a court-martial for drug use unless use occurred while on federal duty.

2. COMMANDERS' OPTIONS

A. Courts-Martial

Court-martial procedures are complex and the Military Rules of Evidence apply. USAR Soldiers must have committed the offense while in a UCMJ Article 2 status for commanders to court-martial.

B. Non-judicial Punishment

Nonjudicial punishment procedures are relatively simple. Military Rules of Evidence do not apply. The burden of proof is beyond a reasonable doubt.

USAR Soldiers must have committed the offense while in a UCMJ Article 2 status for commanders to impose non-judicial punishment.

C. Administrative Separations

All Soldiers identified as drug abusers **will** be processed for administrative separation. AR 600-85, paras. 10-6 and 16-8a(3); *See also*, AR 635-200, para. 14-12c(2) and AR 135-178, para. 12-1d. "Processed for separation or discharge" means that separation action will be initiated and processed through the chain of command to the separation authority for appropriate action. Commanders may recommend retention or suspension of discharge, if warranted.

D. Other Discretionary Actions

1) Denial of Pass or Leave Privileges

2) Prohibitions on the Consumption of Alcohol

This may be appropriate in cases of alcohol offenses.

3) Confiscation of Drug-Related Contraband

3. LAWFUL TYPES OF URINALYSIS

A. Probable Cause Urinalysis

- A urinalysis test is constitutional if based upon probable cause. Mil. R. Evid. 312(d) and 315.
- A warrant or proper authorization may be required.

B. Inspections

- A urinalysis is constitutional if it is part of a valid random inspection.

- Beware of subterfuge under Mil. R. Evid. 313(b). Targeting specific Soldiers for inspections following the report of an offense is unlawful.

C. Consent Urinalysis

- A urinalysis is constitutional if obtained with consent. Mil. R. Evid 314(e).
- Consent must be voluntary under totality of the circumstances. However, consent is involuntary if commander announces his intent to order the urine test should the accused refuse to consent. Mil. R. Evid. 314(e)(4).
- It's OK to Trick. Permissible to use trickery to obtain consent as long as it does not amount to coercion. For example, asking a Soldier to consent to a urinalysis for medical reasons, and then testing for drug purposes would be lawful trickery.

D. Medical Urinalysis

A urinalysis is constitutional if conducted for a valid medical purpose. Mil. R. Evid. 312(f). However, in the Army, most medical tests may only be used for limited purposes. AR 600-85, para. 10-12, and Table 10-1.

E. Fitness for Duty Urinalysis

A commander may order a urinalysis based upon reasonable suspicion to ensure a Soldier's fitness for duty even if the urinalysis is not a valid inspection and no probable cause exists. Results of such tests may only be used for limited purposes. *See* AR 600-85, para. 10-12(a)(1).

Chapter 11

FRATERNIZATION AND IMPROPER SENIOR-SUBORDINATE RELATIONSHIPS

1. REFERENCES

- Manual for Courts-Martial, 2008 Edition
- AR 600-20, Army Command Policy, dtd RAR 4 August 2011

A. Overview

The Army's policy regarding senior-subordinate relationships imposes prohibitions on many personal and business relationships between officers and enlisted service members. The policy does, however, permit many relationships in settings such as community-based organizations, church activities, sports events, and family and unit social functions. Violations of the policy may be punishable under the UCMJ, as violations of a lawful general regulation.

B. Officer-Enlisted Personal Relationships

Officer-enlisted dating, sharing of living quarters (other than due to operational necessity), and engagement in intimate or sexual relationships is prohibited. This policy applies to relationships both between Army officers and enlisted members, and between Soldiers and members of other branches of the services, one of whom is enlisted and the other of whom is an officer. There is an exception for Guard and Reserve Soldiers when the relationship exists primarily due to civilian acquaintanceship as long as they are not in an activated status. The regulation also prohibits relationships between trainees and permanent party Soldiers, even when the same rank, as well as recruits and recruiters.

C. Personal Relationships Between Soldiers of Different Ranks

The policy strictly prohibits relationships between Soldiers of different rank (whether the relationships are officer-officer, officer-enlisted, or enlisted-enlisted, but does not preclude relationships based on position, e.g. CO and XO where both are O-3s) that have any of the following effects:

- Actually or appear to compromise the integrity of supervisory authority or the chain of command.
- Cause actual or perceived partiality or unfairness.
- Involve or appear to involve the improper use of rank or position for personal gain.
- Are, or are perceived to be, exploitative in nature.
- Cause an actual or clearly predictable adverse impact on discipline, authority, morale or the command's ability to accomplish its mission.

D. Business Relationships and Gambling

All business relationships between officers and enlisted service members, except for landlord-tenant relationships and one-time business transactions (such as the sale of a car) are prohibited. Furthermore, the policy prohibits the borrowing and lending of money (no de minimis exception), and commercial solicitations, between officers and enlisted personnel. There is an exception for Guard and Reserve Soldiers when the relationship exists primarily due to civilian employment. Gambling between officers and enlisted personnel is strictly prohibited, e.g. an NCAA pool with a monetary buy-in.

E. Team-Building Relationships

Social contacts between officers and enlisted members, or between Soldiers of different ranks, in forums such as community organizations, church activities, sports events, family gatherings, and unit social functions are permitted.

F. Enforcement of Policy

The policy recognizes that commanders are responsible for enforcing the terms and conditions of the policy. It also recognizes, however, that all military personnel share the responsibility for maintaining professional relationships.

1) Responsibility of All Soldiers

While the senior member in a relationship generally is in the best position to terminate or limit the relationship; the policy holds accountable all Soldiers concerned who violate the policy.

2) Commanders' Options

Commanders have a wide variety of options at their disposal in addressing violations of the policy. These options include, but are not necessarily limited to, the following:

- Counseling.
- Orders to Cease the Conduct Violative of the Policy.
- Verbal or Written Reprimands.
- Reassignment.
- Adverse Evaluation Reports.
- Nonjudicial Punishment.
- Separation from the Army.
- Bar to Reenlistment.
- Denial of Promotion.
- Court-Martial.

3) UCMJ Violations

Violations of the policy may be punished as violations of one or more of the following punitive articles under the UCMJ:

- Articles 90 & 92: Disobedience of a Lawful Order or Regulation.
- Article 133: Conduct Unbecoming an Officer.
- Article 134: Fraternization.
- Article 134: Adultery.

Chapter 12

PROPER RESPONSES TO REPORTS OF SEXUAL ASSAULT

One of the most sensitive issues that you will have to deal with as a company commander is an allegation of sexual assault where the victim, the alleged offender, or both are in your company. Army policy on sexual assault is found in Army Regulation 600-20, Chapter 8. Here is the policy statement from your senior leaders, found in paragraph 8-2:

> "Sexual assault is a criminal offense that has no place in the Army. It degrades mission readiness by devastating the Army's ability to work effectively as a team . . . Sexual assault is incompatible with Army values and is punishable under the UCMJ and other Federal and local civilian laws . . . The Army will treat all victims of sexual assault with dignity, fairness, and respect . . . The Army will treat every reported sexual assault incident seriously by following proper guidelines."

1. IDENTIFY AND MEET THE SEXUAL ASSAULT RESPONSE TEAM

Early in your command, you should identify and meet the key professionals that will assist you in this area. In addition to your servicing judge advocate, you will have a:

- **Special Victim Prosecutor (SVP)** identified for your organization. SVPs are specially-trained judge advocates that assist with domestic violence and sexual crimes cases.
- The SHARP/SARC (**Sexual Assault Response Coordinator**) is the principal POC for sexual assault and sexual harassment. Every Battalion has at least one SARC. DoDD 6495.01 (Jan. 23, 2012) states: "The SARC shall serve as the SINGLE POINT OF CONTACT for coordinating appropriate and responsive care for sexual assault victims."
- You will also have **Unit Victim Advocates** (UVA) assigned to your organization. Know who these people are and how to contact them. They can also help you to establish a meaningful training program that can help you to get ahead of this problem.

2. PREVENTING SEXUAL ASSAULT

Get involved early so that you can set the conditions that will prevent sexual assaults from happening in the first place. We know that ***most*** sexual assaults:

- Happen to women;
- To Soldiers that are within the first four months of their assignment to the unit;
- Within 18 months of entry onto active-duty;
- Involve alcohol;
- Occur late on Friday and Saturday nights; and
- Occur in high-density housing.

Understand these conditions and work to control them.

3. REPORTS OF SEXUAL ASSAULT

There are two kinds of reports: restricted and unrestricted. Victims can only make restricted reports to a select group of people (Sexual Assault Response Coordinators (SARC), Victim Advocates, chaplains, and health care professionals). If you hear about a report, then it is an unrestricted report.

The point of this chapter is to highlight two immediate action drills that you need to know cold. The guidelines you are required to follow are found in paragraph 8-4 and in Appendix G of AR 600-20. You need to go to these references to ensure that you completely comply with them, and you need to seek help from those who have special training in this issue.

A. IMMEDIATE ATION DRILL 1: RELAY THE REPORT TO LAW ENFORCEMENT

At your level, you have very little discretion in the moments after you learn about an allegation of a sexual assault. **If you learn about an allegation of sexual assault, you must report that allegation to CID. Period.**

Sexual assault is a crime defined as intentional sexual contact, characterized by use of force, physical threat or abuse of authority or when the victim does not or cannot consent. Sexual assault includes rape, nonconsensual sodomy (oral or anal sex), indecent assault (unwanted, inappropriate sexual contact or fondling), or attempts to commit these acts.

If the allegation is of a sexual crime that does not meet that definition, you must report it to the military police. In general, you should just report those to CID also and if they feel the issue should be investigated by the military police instead, they can refer the file to them.

You also need to inform your chain of command, servicing judge advocate, and the SARC.

You are not supposed to make a credibility judgment about the victim. In fact, the Department of Defense defines a victim of sexual assault as anyone who makes an allegation of sexual assault. You do not get to choose whether the person who made the complaint is a victim – the Department of Defense has said that she is. You must treat the victim with dignity and respect at all times.

Law enforcement agents, prosecutors, and defense counsel will develop the evidence in the case and will eventually present what they have learned to commanders for the decision on what to do with the case, and if the case goes to court-martial, to the judge or panel to decide the case. Later in the process, you will be asked to recommend what should happen in the case. At that point, you will make an independent, individual decision on what you believe should be the action taken in the case, based on all of the information you now know.

Current Department of Defense policy is that the authority to dispose of allegations of rape, sexual assault, or forcible sodomy is WITHHELD TO BRIGADE COMMANDERS. You cannot dispose of a sexual assault case, meaning that you cannot make a case go away, if you are in command below that level. You can make a recommendation to superiors that no action be taken (or whatever you think is the appropriate action in the case), but you must transmit the case to your superiors.

B. IMMEDIATE ACTION DRILL 2: SAFEGUARD THE VICTIM

Dealing with a victim is complex business. You have to be careful not to re-traumatize them with the actions that you take. One of the most important first steps is to make sure the victim has a victim advocate and then work with that victim advocate. Victim advocates are specially trained and will help you to interact with and safeguard the victim.

You need to take immediate actions to ensure that the victim is safe. In the military, many of our victims and alleged offenders work in the same unit. They may have daily interaction. You should consider issuing a military protective order (DD Form 2873) to the alleged offender to minimize contact and safeguard the victim. You may also consider other forms of pretrial restraint against the alleged offender, to included pretrial confinement.

Recognize also that victims can be subject to harassment from others, to include the alleged offender's spouse or significant other, and friends of the alleged offender.

Under current law, the victim can request a transfer from the unit, and you (or the first commander authorized to transfer the victim) must make a decision within 72-hours. The presumption is that you will transfer the victim. If you deny the transfer, then the victim can appeal your decision to the first general officer in the chain of command, and that general officer must act within another 72-hours.

In some cases, the victim may not want to transfer from the unit. In those cases, consider transferring the alleged offender.

4. REGISTERED SEX OFFENDERS

If one of your Soldiers is convicted of an offense for which he or she needs to register as a sex offender and the Soldier is still in your formation, then the chain of command needs to take certain actions. Generally, this scenario occurs if the Soldier is tried at a court-martial and convicted, but receives a sentence of less than four months confinement with no punitive discharge, or the Soldier is convicted by a civilian court after he or she enlists. For a list of qualifying convictions, see AR 27-10, ch. 24. In those situations, consider the following administrative courses of action. It is very important, however, that you consult your servicing Judge Advocate before proceeding.

A. Separation UPAR 600-20 and 635-200

You **MUST** initiate a separation action in accordance with AR 600-20, para. 8-5o(34) and under AR 635-200, ch. 14. This does not mean that you must separate, however you must initiate the action and consider the Soldier for separation.

Note that if the Soldier was tried at a court-martial that could have given him a punitive discharge and the court-martial did not punish him or her with a punitive discharge, then the Soldier cannot be given an other than honorable discharge at this separation proceeding if the only cause of the separation is the same misconduct.

B. Bar to Reenlistment

If the Soldier is retained under that separation procedure, you may issue a bar to reenlistment under AR 601-280, para. 8-3a.

C. Security Clearance

You may choose to revoke the Soldier's security clearance under AR 380-67, para. I-13b(1)(c).

D. Administrative Reduction

If the Soldier was convicted at a civilian trial, you may initiate administrative reduction procedures under AR 600-8-19, para. 10-3.

E. Administrative Reprimand

You may issue an administrative reprimand under AR 600-37, para. 3-4.

THIS PAGE IS INTENTIONALLY BLANK

Chapter 13

VICTIM-WITNESS ISSUES

1. REFERENCES

- www.sexualassault.army.mil
- Army Reg. 600-20, Army Command Policy, Sexual Assault, Ch. 7 & 8 (RAR, 27 April 2010)
- Army Reg. 27-10, Chapter 18 (Victim Witness Assistance)
- DoDD 6495.01, Sexual Assault Prevention and Response Program (January 23, 2012)
- DoDI 6495.02, Sexual Assault Prevention and Response Program Procedures (13 Nov 2008)

2. SEXUAL HARASSMENT/ASSAULT RESPONSE AND PREVENTION (SHARP) PROGRAM (AR 600-20, CH. 8)

SHARP reflects the Army's commitment to eliminate incidents of sexual assault and sexual harassment. The goals of SHARP are to: create a climate that minimizes sexual assault incidents; create a climate that encourages victims to report incidents of sexual assault without fear; establish sexual assault training & awareness programs to educate Soldiers, focus on the "bystanders" to the incident, encouraging them to protect and support their fellow Soldiers; ensure sensitive and comprehensive treatment to restore victim's health and well-being

A. Sexual Assault is a crime

Sexual Assault means "intentional sexual contact, characterized by use of force, physical threat or abuse of authority or when the victim does not or cannot consent." Sexual acts which are unauthorized by either person involved ordinarily constitute a crime. 2. Consent: A sexual assault victim is not required to offer physical resistance. Consent is not demonstrated by how a Soldier dresses, or by whether there is some past relationship with the alleged offender. It is defined by the actions of the offender. Consent is not given when a person uses force, threat of force, or coercion or when the victim is asleep, incapacitated, or unconscious.

B. Command responsibilities regarding sexual assault allegations / cases

1. Installation commanders

- Ensure 24/7 sexual assault response capability and Victim Advocate availability.
- Provide and train SARC (Sexual Assault Response Coordinators) and Victim Advocates (VA).
- Educate all Soldiers and staff of restricted/unrestricted reporting policies.
- Establish written procedures for reporting of sexual assault throughout the chain of command and to law enforcement.

2. Unit commanders

- Ensure victim safety. Consider a Military Protective Order (MPO). Inform both military and civilian authorities if a MPO is issued.
- Advise the victim of the need to preserve evidence (e.g.: by not bathing, washing garments or bed linen.

- Encourage the victim to report the incident to law enforcement, and to get a medical examination immediately (even beyond 72 hours). Coordinate victim transport & movement, engaging the minimum number of personnel.
- Notify the SARC of the incident.
- Notify CID & other law enforcement of the incident as soon as victim safety & treatment is arranged, but no later than 24 hours after the report.
- Inform the victim of resources available on the internet from Military One Source, http://www.militaryonesource.mil, 1.800.342.9647.
- Determine whether the victim or the suspect need or desire to be transferred or reassigned. See, Directive-Type Memorandum (DTM) 11-063 – Expedited Transfer of Military Service Members Who File Unrestricted Reports of Sexual Assault (11 December 2011), http://www.sapr.mil/media/pdf/policy/DTM-11-063.pdf
- Keep victims informed of proceedings, at a minimum within 15 days of the beginning of disciplinary proceedings and every 30 days thereafter.
- Update battalion or higher level commander within 14 days, & monthly thereafter
- Appoint two Unit VAs per battalion level.
- Appoint deployable SARCs and VAs.
- Disposition of collateral misconduct, and reassignment or separation decisions must be made within policy guidelines.
- Flag alleged offenders.

NOTE: Authority to dispose of cases that result from an allegation of sexual assault is withheld to the Brigade commander level and above.

C. Sexual Harassment (AR 600-20, ch. 7)

Sexual Harassment is a form of gender discrimination that involves unwelcomed sexual advances, requests for sexual favors and other verbal and physical conduct of a sexual nature, where submission to or rejection of the conduct may affect a person's career, or where the behavior "creates an intimidating, hostile or offensive working environment." The Army has zero tolerance for sexual harassment. Sexual harassment complaints are handled by EO. AR 600-20, Appendix D.

D. Victim Witness Assistance Program (AR 27-10, ch. 18)

This program is supervised by the SJA office, is established to support all victims of crime and witnesses to crime. The program supports military justice prosecution efforts.

E. Victim Rights (DODI 1030.1, para. 4.4) include

- Fair treatment and respect for dignity and privacy;
- Reasonable protection from accused;
- Notification of court proceedings;
- Presence at all public court proceedings related to the offense, unless court determines victim's testimony would be materially affected by other testimony;
- Confer with Government attorney;
- Receive available restitution; and
- Receive information about conviction, sentencing, imprisonment and release of accused.

INVESTIGATIONS

Section 2

Chapter 14

INTRODUCTION TO ADMINISTRATIVE INVESTIGATIONS

This chapter provides an OVERVIEW of the considerations when conducting various administrative investigations. Many of the areas are discussed in more detail in later chapters of the Guide. Cross-references are provided in that instance.

1. REFERENCES.

- DODI 6055.07, Mishap Notification, Investigation, Reporting, and Record Keeping, 6 June 2011.
- AR 15-6, Procedure for Investigating Officers and Boards of Officers, 2 October 2006.
- AR 385-10, The Army Safety Program, 23 August 2007 (w/RAR, 14 June 2010).
- AR 600-8-1, Army Casualty Program, 30 April 2007 (as amended by Army Directive 2009-02, The Army Casualty Program (Dover Media Access and Family Travel), 3 April 2009).
- AR 600-8-4, Line of Duty Policy, Procedures, and Investigations, 4 September 2008.
- AR 600-34, Fatal Training/Operational Accident Presentations to the Next of Kin, 2 January 2003.
- AR 735-5, Policies and Procedures for Property Accountability, 28 February 2005.
- Army Directive 2010-01, Conduct of AR 15-6 Investigations Into Suspected Suicides and Requirements for Suicide Incident Family Briefs, 26 March 2010.
- Army Directive 2010-02, Guidance for Reporting Requirements and Redacting Investigations Reports of Deaths and Fatalities, 26 March 2010.
- DA Pam 735-5, Financial Liability Officer's Guide, 9 April 2007.
- www.apd.army.mil (Official Army regulation and pamphlet website).

2. INTRODUCTION.

All the Services have specific procedures for various types of administrative investigations. In the absence of more specific regulatory guidance, the Army uses AR 15-6, Procedure for Investigating Officers and Boards of Officers. AR 15-6 contains the basic rules for Army regulatory boards. If an investigation is appointed under a specific regulation, that regulation will control the proceedings.

Commanders have inherent authority to investigate any matter under their responsibility, unless otherwise prohibited or limited, if undertaken for the purpose of furthering the good order and discipline of their command. Administrative investigations are different from criminal investigations and are usually conducted by non-law enforcement personnel. However, administrative investigations may form the basis for criminal charges, or may lead to criminal investigation. (See Appendix B, AR 195-2, Criminal Investigation Activities, to determine which UCMJ offenses are investigated by CID, MPI, or unit commander.)

3. WHAT DO WE INVESTIGATE?

- Training accidents
- Operational accidents
- Combat operations (e.g. friendly fire, hostile deaths)

- Garrison operations
- Minor misconduct
- Serious misconduct
- Complaints and inquiries
- Property damage
- Off-duty and on-duty incidents

4. WHY DO WE INVESTIGATE?

- To gather, analyze, and record relevant information
- To collect, assemble, analyze, and record available evidence about a particular matter
- To discover information upon which to make decisions
- To ascertain facts and to report them to the appointing authority
- To learn lessons and correct mistakes
- To find the truth

****Treat every investigation as if it will be scrutinized by Congress and released to the family/public****

Chapter 15

AR 15-6 INVESTIGATIONS

This chapter provides an OVERVIEW of procedures for conducting investigations in accordance with Army Regulation 15-6.

1. AR 15-6, PROCEDURES FOR INVESTIGATING OFFICERS AND BOARDS OF OFFICERS

A. Applicability

Applies to the Active Army, the Army National Guard, and the U.S. Army Reserve, unless otherwise stated within the regulation.

1) Purpose

AR 15-6 establishes procedures for investigations and boards of officers not specifically authorized by any other directive. AR 15-6 or any part of it may be made applicable to investigations or boards that are authorized by another directive, but only by specific provision in that directive or in the memorandum of appointment (i.e., AR 635-200, Active Duty Enlisted Administrative Separations, authorizing formal separation boards IAW AR 15-6 for enlisted Soldiers.) In case of a conflict between the provisions of AR 15-6, when made applicable, and the provisions of a specific directive authorizing the investigation or board, the specific regulation would govern.

Even when not specifically made applicable, AR 15-6 may be used as a general guide for investigations or boards authorized by another directive, but in that case, its provisions are not mandatory (i.e, AR 385-10, *The Army Safety Program*, authorizes safety accident investigations but does not incorporate AR 15-6).

2) Function of an AR 15-6 Investigation

An AR 15-6 investigation is used to ascertain facts and report them to the appropriate appointing authority. It is the duty of the investigating officer or board to ascertain and consider the evidence on all sides of each issue, thoroughly and impartially, and to make findings and recommendations that are warranted by the facts and that comply with the instructions of the appointing authority.

2. TYPES OF INVESTIGATIONS AND BOARDS: FORMAL AND INFORMAL

A. Formal or Informal, Investigation or Board of Officers

When deciding whether to use formal or informal procedures, consider the purpose of the inquiry, seriousness of the subject matter, complexity of the issues involved, need for documentation, and desirability of providing a hearing for persons whose conduct is being investigated. Proceedings that involve a single investigating officer using informal procedures are called **informal investigations.** Proceedings that involve more than one investigating officer using formal or informal procedures or a single officer using formal procedures are called a **Board of Officers.**

B. Formal (Chapter 5)

Generally, formal boards are used to provide a hearing for a named respondent. The board offers extensive due process rights to respondents (notice and time to prepare, right to be present at all open sessions, representation by counsel, ability to challenge members for cause, to present evidence and object to evidence, to cross examine witnesses, and to make argument).

Formal boards include a president, voting members, and a recorder who presents evidence on behalf of the government. A Judge Advocate (JA) is normally appointed as recorder but is not a voting member. If a recorder is not appointed, the junior member of the board acts as recorder and is a voting member. Additionally, a non-voting legal advisor may be appointed to the board.

Formal AR 15-6 investigations are not normally used unless required by regulation. Examples: Officer and enlisted separation boards (AR 600-8-24 and AR 635-200) and Flying Evaluation Boards (AR 600-105).

C. Informal (Chapter 4)

Informal investigations may be used to investigate any matter, to include individual conduct. The fact that an individual may have an interest in the matter under investigation or that the information may reflect adversely on that individual does not require that the proceedings constitute a hearing for that individual. Even if the purpose of the investigation is to inquire into the conduct or performance of a particular individual, formal procedures are not mandatory unless required by other regulations or by higher authority.

Informal investigations provide great flexibility. Generally, only one investigating officer (IO) is appointed (though multiple officers could be appointed); there is no formal hearing that is open to the public; statements are taken at informal sessions; and there is no named respondent with a right to counsel (unless required by Art 31(b), UCMJ); right to cross-examine witnesses; etc.

3. APPOINTING AUTHORITY (PARA. 2-1)

A. Formal proceedings

The following people may appoint a formal investigation or board after consulting with the JA or legal advisor prior to appointing a formal board: any general court-martial or special court-martial convening authority; any general officer; any commander or principal staff officer in the grade of colonel or above at the installation, activity, or unit level; any state adjutant general; and any DA GS-14 or above civilian supervisor assigned as a division or department chief.

B. Informal proceedings

The following individuals may appoint an informal investigation or board: any officer or supervisor authorized to appoint a formal board; a commander at any level; a principal staff officer or supervisor in grade of major or above.

C. Special cases

Only a General Court-Martial Convening Authority (GCMCA) can appoint an investigation or board if there is property damage of $1,000,000 or more, the loss or destruction of Army aircraft or missile, an injury or illness likely to result in death or permanent total disability, the death of one or more persons, and the death of one or more persons by friendly fire.

D. Friendly Fire Mishaps

DoDI 6055.07 defines friendly fire as a circumstance in which members of a U.S. or friendly military force are mistakenly or accidentally killed or injured in action by U.S. or friendly forces actively engaged with an enemy or who are directing fire at a hostile force or what is thought to be a hostile force.

DoDI 6055.07 states that the Combatant Commander *or his or her designee* will convene a legal investigation for all incidents of friendly fire. US Central Command has delegated this authority to: Service Component Commanders, General Officer/Flag Officer in command of subordinate Joint Command or Joint Task Force, and General Officer/Flag Officer commanders with GCMCA. (CENTCOM Commander Policy - Friendly Fire Investigation, Reporting, and Dissemination of Information, 1 December 2008).

MILPER Message 07-236, dated 10 September 2007, and AR 600-8-1 require commanders to complete an AR 15-6 investigation of all friendly fire incidents that result in the death **or** wounding of a Soldier.

AR 600-8-1 requires all AR 15-6 investigations of friendly fire incidents be convened by the GCMCA. This includes injury cases as well as fatality cases. (NOTE: In practice, this does not conflict with DODI 6055.07 since the Combatant Commander will or has delegated authority to a GCMCA to convene the investigation.)

In May 2007, the Army Vice Chief of Staff published detailed guidance regarding the reporting and investigation requirements for all incidents of friendly fire. Units must follow the following procedures for all friendly fire incidents, whether resulting in death or injury, as soon as personnel on the ground suspect that a friendly fire incident has occurred:

- The unit must provide immediate telephonic notice through the Casualty Assistance Center to the Army Casualty and Mortuary Affairs Operation Center (CMAOC). For time sensitive assistance contact the CMAOC Operations Center at 800-626-3317 COMM: 502-613-9025. DSN: 983-9025. OCONUS dial country code 001 or OCONUS DSN code (312);
- Generate an initial casualty report IAW AR 600-8-1, approved by a field grade officer, through command channels to the Combatant Commander;
- Initiate an AR 15-6 investigation (Appointed by GCMCA; approved by Combatant Commander *or his or her designee* IAW DODI 6055.07 and AR 600-8-1. See discussion above);
- Contact the Combat Readiness/Safety Center (COMM: (334) 255-2660/3410, DSN: 558) and initiate safety investigation based upon CRC guidance;
- Contact the local Criminal Investigation Division. They will provide forensics assistance to the AR 15-6 Officer or conduct investigation if criminal action or negligence is suspected or substantiated;
- Submit supplemental casualty report when there is a substantial change to the initial report (i.e., when inflicting force is discovered);
- Once approved by the Combatant Commander *or his or her designee*, submit the AR 15-6 proceedings to the CMAOC;
- Continue coordination with the CMAOC to provide an AR 600-34 family presentation for fatality cases.

DODI 6055.07 also requires units to furnish the Commander, U.S. Joint Forces Command (USJFCOM), with completed privileged friendly fire safety investigations. USJFCOM is the lead agent for friendly fire mishap analysis. It maintains a joint database of pertinent causal factors and is responsible for developing plans designed to prevent or mitigate future friendly fire mishaps. DODI 6055.07 also authorizes combatant commanders to delegate their authority to subordinates. These delegations should be reviewed prior to any deployment.

E. Hostile Death Investigations

AR 600-8-1 requires AR 15–6 investigations for all hostile deaths. Hostile deaths are those resulting from a terrorist activity – such as by an IED or VBIED - or casualties caused "in action" – such as a direct-fire engagement with an opposing force.

The GCMCA may, in writing, delegate appointing/approval authority to a subordinate commander exercising SPCMCA for hostile death cases only. This authority may not be further delegated.

If evidence is discovered during a hostile death investigation, convened pursuant to this delegation, that indicates that the death(s) may have been the result of friendly fire, the investigating officer will immediately suspend the investigation and inform the appointing authority and legal advisor. At this time, the friendly fire reporting and investigation requirements must be followed. This requires the GCMCA to appoint a new investigation into the friendly fire incident. The GCMCA may appoint the same officer who was conducting the hostile death investigation if the officer is otherwise qualified. Any evidence from the hostile fire investigation should be provided to and considered by the investigating officer or board conducting the friendly fire investigation.

F. Suspected Suicides

Army Directive 2010-01 requires AR 15-6 investigations for all suspected suicides. This requirement does not apply to suicide attempts. The appointing authority is a GCMCA, as in most other investigations into deaths.

The investigation should focus on suicide prevention: "The purpose of an AR 15-6 investigation into a suspected suicide is to identify the circumstances, methods, and contributing factors surrounding the event. The investigations should examine the Soldier's behavior before the event; actions by the chain of command; and potential improvements to the unit's, installation's, or Army's suicide prevention program. The completed investigations should provide clear, relevant, and practical recommendation(s) to prevent future suicides."

The AR 15-6 investigation will serve as the basis for the Suicide Incident Family Brief that must be offered to the primary NOK (and to the parents of the decedent when they are secondary NOK, when practicable) for confirmed cases of suicide that occur on or after 15 April 2010. The Suicide Incident Family Brief should be conducted utilizing the procedures for Fatal Training/Operational Accident Presentations to Next of Kin described in AR 600-34.

4. METHOD OF APPOINTMENT – THE MEMORANDUM OF APPOINTMENT (PARA. 2-1)

Formal investigations or boards will be appointed in writing but, when necessary, may be appointed orally and later confirmed in writing. **Informal investigations** or boards may be appointed orally or in writing. A written memorandum of appointment is preferred.

The memorandum of appointment should specify purpose and scope of investigation and nature of findings and recommendations required. The appointing authority should include any special instructions or guidance for the investigating officer. AR 15-6 includes examples of memorandums of appointment but the examples provided are minimal. The memorandum of appointment is important and should include enough detail as is necessary to fully inform and guide the investigating officer. Any changes to the scope of the investigation should be documented in writing.

Those who may be appointment as investigating officers and board members shall be those persons who are best qualified for the duty by reason of education, training, experience, length of service, and temperament. Only commissioned officers, warrant officers, or Department of the Army civilian employees permanently assigned to a position graded as a GS–13 or above will be appointed as investigating officers or voting members of boards.

Investigating officers and voting board members must be senior to any individual whose conduct is under investigation, unless military exigencies make this impracticable. Non-voting members (i.e., legal advisor, judge advocate recorder) do not have to be senior. Specific regulations may require additional qualifications (i.e., officers, professionally certified, security clearance.)

5. CONDUCTING THE INFORMAL INVESTIGATION (CHAPTER 3/4)

Before starting an informal investigation, the Investigating Officer must review all written materials provided by the appointing authority and meet with the legal advisor prior to beginning an informal investigation. The legal advisor should explain the rules and legal concerns for AR 15-6 investigations and assist the Investigating Officer in developing an investigation plan. Make sure the Investigating Officer gets an Investigating Officer Guidebook with checklist and has access to AR 15-6 and other applicable regulations.

The Investigating Officer has an investigation plan and should ask the following questions which should be addressed in the appointment memorandum: What are the questions that need answering? What specific findings and recommendations must be made? What is the timeline? The memorandum of appointment should address these matters. The Investigating Officer should consider the facts known and gaps (and more importantly, how to fill the gaps); potential witnesses and order of interviewing; physical and documentary evidence required; possible criminal or counter-intelligence implications; Article 31 Uniform Code of Military Justice (UCMJ) warnings; Privacy Act requirements; regulations and laws involved; and chronology of the investigation as well as chronology of the incident under investigation.

Generally, an Investigating Officer is not bound by the Military Rules of Evidence (MREs). Anything that in the minds of reasonable persons is relevant and material to an issue may be accepted as evidence. All evidence is given such weight as circumstances warrant. For example, medical records, counseling statements, police reports, and other records may be considered, regardless of whether the preparer of the record is available to give a statement or testify in person.

Although an Investigating Officer is generally not bound by the Military Rules of Evidence, the following limitations, however, do apply:

- **Privileged Communications.** The rules in section V, part III, MCM, concerning privileged communications between lawyer and client (MRE 502), privileged communications with clergy (MRE 503), and husband-wife privilege (MRE 504) apply.
- **Polygraph Tests.** The person involved in the polygraph test must consent to the use of any evidence regarding the results, or regarding the taking or refusing of a polygraph.
- **"Off the record" statements are not allowed.** Findings and recommendations cannot be based on statements not contained in the report of investigation.

- **Statements regarding disease or injury.** A Soldier cannot be required to sign a statement relating to the origin, incurrence, or aggravation of a disease or injury. Any such statement against interest is invalid under 10 USC 1219 and may not be considered on the issue of the origin, incurrence, or aggravation of the disease or injury.

Investigating officers generally do not have subpoena power to compel **witnesses** to appear and testify. Commanders and supervisors may order military personnel and civilian employees to appear and testify. No military witness can be compelled to incriminate himself or herself (UCMJ Article 31) or to make a statement or produce evidence that is not material to an issue that might tend to degrade them.

No witness not subject to the UCMJ can be required to make a statement or produce evidence that would violate the 5th Amendment to the US Constitution. If a witness invokes UCMJ Article 31 or the 5th Amendment, the IO must stop questioning and contact the legal advisor. The legal advisor should assist the IO in determining if the invocation is well taken. This may require sending the witness to see a legal assistance or Trial Defense Service attorney for advice. If the IO, in consultation with the legal advisor, determines that the invocation is not well taken, the IO may order military and civilian employee witnesses to testify, or they may contact the witness's supervisor for assistance.

Weingarten rights may be necessary for bargaining unit member employees. If a civilian employee, who is a member of a certified bargaining unit represented by a labor organization, reasonably believes that he or she might be disciplined as a result of an interview, and requests union representation, then the employee is entitled to have a union representative present during the interview.

If a bargaining unit member requests union representation, the IO should consult with the legal advisor. The IO's options are to grant the request, discontinue the interview, or offer the employee the choice between continuing the interview unaccompanied by a union representative and having no interview at all.

A confession or admission obtained by unlawful coercion or inducement likely to affect its truthfulness will not be accepted as evidence.

If members of the Armed Forces acting in their official capacity conduct or direct a search that they know is unlawful, evidence obtained as a result of that search may not be accepted or considered against any respondent whose personal rights were violated by the search. Such evidence is acceptable only if it can reasonably be determined by the legal advisor or, if none, by the investigating officer or president that the evidence would inevitably have been discovered. In all other cases, evidence obtained as a result of any search or inspection may be accepted, even if it has been or would be ruled inadmissible in a criminal proceeding. This exclusionary provision is applicable only when a respondent is involved, in other words, during a formal investigation.

G. Findings and Recommendations (Para. 3-10 thru 3-13)

A **finding** is a clear and concise statement of fact directly established by evidence in the record. It includes negative findings (evidence does not establish a fact). In arriving at findings, the Investigating Officer should not exceed the scope of appointment. Each finding of fact should refer back to evidence gathered in the investigation.

The standard is preponderance of the evidence: findings must be supported by greater weight of evidence than supports a contrary conclusion. The weight is not determined by number of witnesses but by considering all evidence and factors such as demeanor, opportunity for knowledge, information possessed, ability to recall and relate events, and other indicators of veracity.

The investigating officer should work with the legal advisor to develop the findings based on the record of investigation facts, the commander's appointment memorandum, and any applicable regulation.

The **recommendations** must be consistent with the findings. They can be negative (e.g., no further action taken). The legal advisor should ensure that the recommendations make sense and are supported by the record of investigation.

Investigating officers and boards make recommendations according to their understanding of the rules, regulations, and customs of the service, guided by fairness both to the Government and to individuals.

H. Deliberations and Voting (Boards of Officers)

Deliberations are conducted in private. Only voting members of the board may deliberate and vote. If consultation with non-voting member is required, named respondent, if any, has right to attend consultation.

Board with more than one member reaches decisions by voting. Majority vote controls. In the event of a tie, president's vote determines.

I. Legal Review (Para. 2-3.b.)

Not all AR 15-6 investigations require a legal review. A legal review is required for serious or complex cases, such as death or serious bodily injury cases; or where findings and recommendations may result in adverse administrative action or will be relied upon by higher HQs.

The legal review determines whether the investigation complies with requirements in the appointing order and other legal requirements, the effects of any errors in the investigation, whether the findings (including findings of no fault, no loss, or no wrongdoing) and recommendations are supported by sufficient evidence (preponderance of the evidence), and whether the recommendations are consistent with the findings.

Appointing errors occur when the appointing authority does not have the authority to appoint the particular investigation. If that is the case, the proceedings are a nullity unless an appropriate authority ratifies the appointment.

Substantial errors are errors that have a material adverse effect on an individual's substantial rights.

Harmless errors are defects in the proceedings that do not have a material adverse effect on an individual's substantial rights.

There is no inherent conflict of interest or prohibition against the legal advisor conducting the legal review, however, the decision to do so should be a deliberate decision. It is recommended that a second attorney conduct the legal review in high-profile or complex cases.

If a judge advocate finds an investigation legally insufficient, he or she should work with the IO to try to remedy the error(s). Negotiation, good advice, and wise counsel should be used by the judge advocate to resolve the legal insufficiencies. Under no circumstances should the legal advisor or the judge advocate conducting the legal review rewrite any portion of the report of investigation without the IO's permission, or try to hide anything from the report from the appointing authority. If the legal insufficiencies cannot be resolved, the judge advocate should prepare an appropriate legal review describing the errors for the appointing authority. Just like the IO's report, however, the appointing authority is not bound by the legal review.

J. Action By Appointing Authority (Para. 2-3)

Unless otherwise provided by another directive, the appointing authority is neither bound nor limited by the findings or recommendations of an investigation or board. The appointing authority has the option to approve as is, disapprove, and/or return for additional investigation. The appointing authority may consider all relevant information, even information not considered by Investigating Officer. Unless otherwise provided by another directive (i.e., AR 635-200, appointing authority bound by board recommendation of retention), the appointing authority is not bound by findings or recommendations and may take action less favorable than recommended. The appointing authority may also substitute findings and recommendations.

The appointing authority's decision can be documented on DA Form 1574 (Report of Proceedings by Investigating Officer/Board of Officers) or can be documented in a separate memorandum. If documented in a separate memorandum, the DA Form 1574, if used, should still be annotated and signed by the appointing authority.

Once approved by the appointing authority, the report of investigation becomes an official agency decision and thus subject to the provisions of the Freedom of Information Act (5 USC § 552).

No adverse administrative action may be taken by a commander based on an informal AR 15-6 investigation until the following occurs unless another regulation that action is being taken under provides appropriate due process procedures. Notice is given to the subject of the investigation of the allegations against him or her. The subject is given a copy of the investigation subject to any required redactions. The subject is given a reasonable opportunity to rebut the allegations. The Commander must consider the subject's rebuttal to the investigation, if submitted in a timely manner, before taking any adverse action.

K. Release of AR 15-6 Investigative Reports and Materials (Para. 3-18)

AR 15-6 documents hold no special, automatic status under either the Privacy Act or the Freedom of Information Act. The individual parts of a report of investigation must be analyzed under both laws to determine suitability for release.

No part of a report should be released (unless specifically authorized by law or regulation such as a valid Freedom of Information Act request) without the approval of the appointing authority.

In accoridance with the Army Records Information Management System (ARIMS) and Record Retention Schedule – Army (RRS-A), investigations must be retained by the approving authority for five years, and then destroyed or shipped for permanent storage IAW ARIMS.

Chapter 16

ACCIDENT INVESTIGATIONS

This chapter provides an OVERVIEW of procedures for conducting accident investigations. Please consult your legal advisor early and often during the process of the investigation.

1. AR 385-10 ACCIDENT INVESTIGATIONS

A. APPLICABILITY

AR 385-10, The Army Safety Program applies to Active Army, the Army National Guard, and the U.S. Army Reserve. It also applies to Army civilian employees and the US Army Corps of Engineers and Civil Works activities and tenants and volunteers.

1) Purpose

AR 385-10 provides policy on Army safety management procedures. Chapter 3 provides policies and procedures for initial notification, investigating, reporting, and submitting reports of Army accidents and incidents.

2) Function of an AR 385-10 Accident Investigation (Chapter 3)

To determine the facts and causes of accidents in order to prevent future accidents, and to assess liability to determine the most likely organization to initiate corrective actions. The primary purpose of investigating and reporting Army accidents is prevention. A safety investigation cannot be used as the basis for disciplinary action.

B. WHAT IS AN ACCIDENT? (Para. 3-3)

An Army accident is defined as an unplanned event, or series of events, which results in one or more of the following: occupational illness to Army military or Army civilian personnel; injury to on–duty Army civilian personnel; injury to Army military on–duty or off–duty; damage to Army property; damage to public or private property, and/or injury or illness to non–Army personnel caused by Army operations.

Accident classes are used to determine reporting and investigation requirements. Class A is damage totaling $2M or more; accidents involving aircraft destroyed/missing/abandoned; injury/occupational illness resulting in fatality or permanent total disability. (Note: friendly fire fatalities must be reported and investigated as a Class A accident.) Class B is damage between $500k - $2M; injury/occupational illness resulting in permanent, partial disability; three or more personnel hospitalized in a single occurrence. Class C is damage between $50k - $500k; a nonfatal injury/occupational illness that causes one or more days away from work or training beyond the day or shift on which it occurred or disability at any time (that does not meet the definition of Class A or B and is a day(s) away from work case). Class D is damage between $2k - $50k; a nonfatal injury/occupational illness resulting in restricted work, transfer, medical treatment greater than first aid; needle sticks/cuts from contaminated objects; medical removal under OSHA standard; occupational hearing loss; work-related tuberculosis. Class E is an aviation accident in which there has been damage less than $2k. Class F is an aviation incident in which there has been damage to Army aircraft engines as a result of unavoidable internal or external foreign object damage.

C. INITIAL NOTIFICATION AND REPORTING (Para 3-5 and 3-8)

All Army accidents and incidents, including occupational illnesses and injuries, regardless of how minor, are reportable to the unit/local safety office. The unit/local safety office will determine the reporting and investigative requirements for the accident.

Notification to the US Army Combat Readiness/Safety Center. All Class A, Class B, and Class C Aviation accidents and incidents (includes in flight and on ground, and unmanned aerial systems.)

D. CATEGORIES OF ACCIDENT INVESTIGATION REPORTS (Para. 3-10)

The Army has two categories of safety accident investigation reports—limited use reports and general use reports.

1) Limited-Use Safety Accident Investigation Reports

These are close-hold, internal communications of DA whose sole purpose is prevention of subsequent DA accidents. To encourage open and frank discussion of the accident, the Army will use its best efforts to prevent disclosure of statements provided under a promise of confidentiality. They are required for all flight/flight related and friendly fire accidents. They also may be used for accidents involving other complex weapon systems, equipment, or military-unique items, and military unique equipment/operations/exercises when the determination of causal factors is vital to the national defense as determined by Cdr, US Army Combat Readiness/Safety Center .

These reports cannot be used as evidence or to obtain evidence for disciplinary action, in determining the misconduct or line-of-duty status of any person, before any evaluation board, or to determine liability in administrative claims for or against the government.

Witnesses may be given the option of making their statement under a promise of confidentiality if they are unwilling to make a complete statement without such a promise and the investigation board believes it is necessary to obtain a statement from a witness.

Findings, recommendations, and analysis are privileged. Only the Freedom of Information Act Initial Denial Authority for safety investigations, Cdr, US Army Combat Readiness/Safety Center, may release that information.

2) General-Use Safety Accident Investigation Reports

These reports prepared to record data concerning all recordable DA accidents not covered by the Limited-Use Safety Accident Investigation Report. They are intended for accident prevention purposes only. They may not be used as evidence in any disciplinary, administrative, or legal action (punitive). Promises of confidentiality cannot be made that information will be treated as exempt from mandatory disclosure in response to a request under the FOIA.

Both limited use and general use reports contain privileged information. Federal courts have recognized the need to protect certain information within these reports to further accident prevention within the military and to protect national security. In both types of accident reports, the board's findings, analysis, and recommendations are privileged and protected from release under FOIA. Within a Limited Use Accident

Report, the confidential witness statements are also protected from release. The Supreme Court upheld the privilege for confidential witness statements in U.S. v. Weber Aircraft Corp., 465 U.S. 792 (1984).

E. CONDUCTING THE ACCIDENT INVESTIGATION (Para. 3-12 thru 3-15)

The type and extent of the investigation depends upon the class and type of accident. The appointing authority is a Commander with general court-martial jurisdiction over the installation or unit responsible for the operation, personnel, or materiel involved in the accident; Commander, US Army Reserve Command, for US Army Reserve units; and State Adjutant General for National Guard units.

The following accidents must be investigated by a board consisting of at least three members:

- All on-duty Class A and B accidents. Upon notification of a Class A or B accident, the Cdr, United States Army Combat Readiness/Safety Center, will determine whether a Centralized Accident Investigation or a Local Accident Investigation will be conducted.
- Centralized Accident Investigation Board. Some members provided by Army Combat Readiness Center and some provided from the local command.
- Local Accident Investigative Board. Members provided from the local command.
- Any accident that an appointing authority, or Cdr, US Army Combat Readiness/Safety Center, believes may involve a potential hazard serious enough to warrant investigation by multimember board.

Class C Aircraft Accidents must be investigated by a board consisting of at least one member.

Single-Officer Investigations (does not require formal board appointment orders). The following accidents will be investigated by one or more officers, warrant officers, safety officers/NCOs, supervisors, or DA safety and occupational health specialists GS 9 or higher: all off-duty military accidents, Class C and D ground accidents, Aircraft Class D, E, and F accidents, and Class E and FOD incidents.

The board must be composed of must be Army officers or warrant officers, DA safety and occupational health specialist/manager/engineer GS-9 or higher, full-time technicians holding federally recognized officer or warrant officer status, DoD medical officer or DoD contracted medical officers, DoD maintenance personnel, subject matter expert senior NCOs, E-5 and above in MOS 93U, 33U, 52D (UAS accidents), DoD weather officers, any other personnel approved by Cdr, Combat Readiness/Safety Center.

For Class A and B accidents, board members will not be from the same unit that incurred the accident (battalion/ company/battery/troop or detachment.) Rank/grade/specialty requirement varies with type of accident.

Note special board member qualification requirements of AR 385-10, para. 3-15 (aviation accident boards will include qualified aviators; watercraft investigations will include Army marine warrant officer.)

The US Army Combat Readiness/Safety Center will review all accident reports.

F. LEGAL ACCIDENT INVESTIGATION (LEGAL INVESTIGATION) (Para. 3-10)

These investigations are **formerly known as the collateral investigation**. See also AR 600-34 for guidance.

Used to obtain and preserve all available evidence for use in litigation, claims, disciplinary action, or adverse administrative action. Such investigations are often conducted simultaneously but independently of the accident safety investigation. They are essential to protect the privileged information of safety reports as they ensure an alternate source of information.

Legal Accident Investigations are required for all Class A accidents, to include cases of friendly fire, as directed by the SJA IAW the claims regulation (AR 27-20); on accidents where there is a potential claim or litigation for or against the government or government contractor; or on accidents with a high degree of public interest or anticipated disciplinary or adverse administrative action against any individual.

Commanders may direct a legal investigation into any other accident. The investigation should use AR 27-20 procedures if applicable. If not, AR 15-6 informal procedures should be used.

Legal investigations into fatal training/operational accidents must be completed within 30 days of the accident. Upon written request, the appointing authority may grant delays in 10-day increments (AR 600-34, para 3-5).

G. PRIORITY AND SHARING OF INFORMATION (Para. 3-24 thru 3-27)

The safety investigation has priority (collection of evidence/access to scene) over the legal investigation and all other investigations except a criminal investigation conducted by military police or Criminal Investigation Command. The safety investigation may obtain all information collected by the legal or criminal investigation. Safety Accident Investigation Reports will not be enclosed in any other report unless the sole purpose of the report is accident prevention. Only factual information may be obtained by the legal investigation from the safety investigation.

Information that will not be given the collateral investigation include (punitive): witness statements taken by safety board members; preliminary or final, findings, analysis, and recommendations; voice recordings of intra-cockpit communications without Cdr, US Army Combat Readiness/Safety Center authorization.

H. RELEASE OF INFORMATION FROM ACCIDENT INVESTIGATION REPORTS (Para. 3-28 and 3-29)

AR 600-34, para. 4-2(f) makes unauthorized disclosure of privileged safety information punishable under Article 92, UCMJ. The Combat Readiness Center is the repository for Class A, B, C, D, and E accident reports, and Class E and F incident reports.

Freedom of Information Act requests for Class A, B, or C safety accident reports must be referred to the US Army Combat Readiness/Safety Center.

Local safety offices are authorized to release Class D and E general use reports if release otherwise appropriate under the Freedom of Information Act. Units wishing to withhold information from a Class D and E report should send it to the Commander, Combat Readiness Center, who is the initial denial authority for safety reports.

Chapter 17

LINE OF DUTY INVESTIGATIONS

1. AR 600-8-4, LINE OF DUTY POLICY, PROCEDURES, AND INVESTIGATIONS

A. Applicability

Applies to the Active Army, the Army National Guard, the US Army Reserve, ROTC Simultaneous Membership Program Cadets, US Military Academy Cadets, Senior ROTC Cadets, and applicants for enrollment while performing authorized travel to or from or while attending training or a practice cruise.

1) Purpose

Prescribes procedures governing line of duty determinations of Soldiers who die or sustain certain injuries, diseases, or illnesses.

2) Function of an AR 600-84 Line of Duty Investigation

To determine the duty status of Soldiers who die or sustain certain injuries, diseases, or illnesses, and to determine whether such death, injury, disease, or illness occurred in the line of duty.

B. Possible Outcomes & Impact of that Determination (Para. 2-2)

The possible outcomes are the following:

- In Line of Duty (ILD): the Soldier may be entitled to Army Disability Retirement or Separation Compensation, DVA Compensation and Hospitalization Benefits.
- Not in Line of Duty-Not Due to Own Misconduct (NLD-NDOM): If on active duty, Soldier denied disability retirement or separation compensation; If disabled after leaving AD, Soldier may be denied DVA disability or hospitalization benefits; may be denied civil service preference
- Not in Line of Duty-Due to Own Misconduct (NLD-DOM): days lost > 1 added to service obligation; days lost > 1 may be excluded from computations for pay and allowances; may result in loss of pay where disease (not injury) immediately follows intemperate use of drugs (includes alcohol).

C. Two-Step Analysis

1) Did the Soldier's misconduct proximately cause the injury, illness, or death?

Injury, illness, or death caused by Soldiers own misconduct can never be in line of duty. Violation of a regulation by itself is not misconduct, it is simple negligence. Regulatory violations should be considered in the analysis, however.

2) What was the Soldier's status?

Duty status refers to an authorized duty status – on leave, on pass, present for duty, versus unauthorized status – AWOL, deserter, DFR. It does not refer to worker's compensation or claim's theories of "performing military duties" or "job-related."

Example of Soldier found to be in Line of Duty. Soldier is injured in car crash while on leave. Crash is caused by another driver's negligence. Soldier is considered to be in the line of duty.

Example of Soldier found not in Line of Duty Not Due to Own Misconduct: Soldier is AWOL (while mentally sound), but otherwise doing nothing wrong. While walking down the street, Soldier is hit by a car that jumps the curve and is seriously injured. Soldier is considered to be not in the line of duty, but not due to own misconduct. NOTE: NLOD-NDOM may also be based on an EPTS condition, not aggravated by service.

Example of Soldier found not in Line of Duty Due to Own Misconduct: Soldier gets drunk at a party and attempts to drive home but is involved in an accident on the way. If the intoxication caused the accident, Soldier is considered to be not in the line of duty due to own misconduct.

D. Procedures

Presumptive Finding of In Line of Duty – No investigation is required when a disease does not involve a factor cited at paragraph 3 below; injury is clearly incurred as the result of enemy action or terrorist attack; or death by natural causes or death occurs while a passenger on a common commercial carrier or military aircraft..

1) Informal Investigation

An informal investigation is conducted when no misconduct is suspected, no negligence is suspected, formal investigation is not required. At a minimum, the MTF representative and commander must sign a DA Form 2173. Supporting exhibits should be attached.

Special court-martial convening authority (SPCMCA) is appointing and approving authority. (National Guard appointing authority is commander of at least battalion or squadron size unit). SPCMCA should approve informal investigation in writing "By Authority of the Secretary of the Army."

NOTE: Informal investigation can only result in an ILD determination except in the case where the MTF finds that a condition existed prior to service (EPTS). In that event, the status would be NLD-NDOM.

2) Formal Investigation

For a formal investigation, the appointing Authority is the SPCMCA. Final approving authority is the General court-martial convening authority (GCMCA). May be delegated to field grade officer on the GCMCA's staff.

The investigating officer must be senior in grade to the individual investigated. May be commissioned officer, warrant officer, or commissioned officer of another US military service in joint activities where Army has been designated as the executive agent.

Formal investigations are required when any of the following factors are present: strange or doubtful circumstances, injury or death involving alcohol or drug abuse, self-inflicted injuries or suicide, injury or death incurred while AWOL, training death of a USAR/ARNG Soldier, Injury or death of a USAR or ARNG member while traveling to or from authorized training or duty, injury or death occurring while en route to final acceptance in the Army, USAR/ARNG Soldier serving active duty tour of 30 days or less is disabled by disease, in connection with an appeal of an unfavorable finding of alcohol or drug abuse, a valid request for formal investigation is made (e.g., requested by the Physical Disability Agency).

E. Evidentiary standards and presumptions

Soldier is presumed ILD UNLESS refuted by substantial evidence contained in the investigation. A finding or determination must be supported by a greater weight of evidence than supports any different conclusion. A reasonable person must be convinced of the truth or falseness of a fact considering equally direct and indirect evidence. .

The general guidance contained in AR 15-6 applies unless AR 600-8-1 provides more specific or different guidance.

F. Timeline for Active Component Soldiers

- Informal: 40 calendar days after incident.
- Formal: 75 calendar days after incident.

G. Procedural Due Process Requirements

During Evidence Collection: Soldier not required to make a statement against interest. Soldier must be advised that he or she does not have to make a statement against interest. If Soldier is not informed of her right not to make statement, or is forced to make statement, the statement cannot be used in making the LOD determination (10 USC § 1219).

Regarding Adverse Findings: Investigating officer must provide Soldier with written notice of proposed adverse finding, a copy of the investigation, and the supporting evidence. Investigating officer must issue warning regarding making statements against interest. Investigating officer must give a reasonable opportunity to reply in writing and to offer rebuttal. If investigating officer receives a response, it must be considered before finalizing findings. If investigating officer does not receive a response, the investigating officer may proceed to finalize the findings.

Formal investigations must receive a legal review before a final determination is made. Informal investigations may receive a legal review but it is not required. (Para. 3-6 & 3-9)

H. Final Approving Authority (GCMCA Or Field Grade Designee) Decision

Final approving authority either approves or disapproves the finding under the authority of the Secretary of the Army. The report must be forwarded to the service member through his command. The transmittal letter must notify the service member of his right not to make a statement against interest and of his appellate rights.

I. Appellate Rights (Para. 4-17)

The service member may appeal in writing within 30 days after receipt of the notice of adverse finding. The service member's appeal is to the final approving authority. The final approving authority may only change the finding to "in line of duty," based on substantial new evidence.

J. Special Considerations

Always consult the Rules Governing Line of Duty and Misconduct Determinations at Appendix B, AR 600-8-4.

The regulation also discusses and provides direction regarding pregnancies, venereal disease, conditions existing prior to service, intoxication and drug use, etc. throughout chapter 4.

Mental responsibility, emotional disorder, suicide, and suicide attempts. Soldier may not be held responsible for acts if, as the result of, mental defect, disease or derangement, Soldier unable to comprehend or appreciate the nature of conduct. These disorders are presumed LD unless they existed prior to service.

Suicide and suicide attempt line of duty investigations must determine whether Soldier was mentally sound. Investigating officer must, therefore, inquire into the Soldier's background. A mental health officer must review the evidence and render an opinion whether the Soldier was mentally sound at the time.

Self-inflicted injuries by a mentally sound Soldier should be considered misconduct.

Cases Involving Death. Prior to 10 September 2001, deaths did not require a line of duty determination. Congress authorized the payment of Survivor benefit Plan benefits to Service members who die on active duty "in the line of duty" regardless of amount of time of service (FY 02 National Defense Authorization Act).

All active-duty deaths on or after 10 September 2001 require a line of duty determination. An investigation is required for all deaths except death by natural causes, or when death occurs while a passenger on a common commercial carrier or military aircraft, or death as the result of combat, attack by terrorists or other forces antagonistic to the interests of the United States, or in friendly-fire incidents, or while a prisoner of war.

2. PROCEDURES FOR SOLDIERS OF THE U.S. ARMY RESERVES AND ARMY NATIONAL GUARD

All LODs for RC Soldiers will be processed by using the electronic website, LOD module. Upon demobilization all LODs will be uploaded into the LOD module. A LOD must be completed promptly, as the determination will impact the Soldier's eligibility for benefits, such as military medical care and incapacitation pay.

Commanders, Medical Officers, S1s, SJAs, UA, Personnel NCOs, and RC Soldier's who learn of a Soldier's illness, injury, disease or death that occurred under circumstances that warrant a LOD investigation/determination shall take an active role in ensuring that an investigation/determination is initiated, completed and uploaded into the LOD module in a timely manner.

Casualty Assistance Centers are responsible for completing and forwarding LOD Investigations in all cases involving death when a Soldier is in an authorized duty status.

RC Soldiers will not be separated or retired while a LOD determination is pending.

Medical Evaluation Board (MEB) / Physical Evaluation Board (PEB) will also be completed prior to separation or retirement of the Soldier.

A formal LOD is required for any illness, injury, disease or death incurred while performing AT, IDT, or ordered to active duty for less than 30 days.

Refer to AR 600-8-1 to ensure the RC Soldier is being processed by the proper command, the correct procedures are followed, and the timelines are met.

Chapter 18

FATAL TRAINING/OPERATIONAL ACCIDENT PRESENTATIONS TO NEXT OF KIN

This chapter provides an OVERVIEW of procedures for conducting fatal training/operational accident presentations to next of kin.

1. APPLICABILITY: ACTIVE ARMY, ARMY NATIONAL GUARD, AND US ARMY RESERVE

A. Purpose

Prescribes mandated tasks that govern collateral investigations, as they apply to fatal training/operational accidents, and provides guidance and direction for preparing and delivering primary next of kin presentations. This regulation implements guidance published in DODI 1300.18 (14 AUG 09).

B. Function of an AR 600-34 Family Presentation

To provide a thorough explanation of releasable investigative results of fatal training/operational accidents to the deceased's primary next of kin; ensure the family understands the circumstances of the accident; and ensure the family is reassured of the Army's concern regarding the tragedy and is aware of the compassion of Army leaders.

2. CONGRESSIONAL REQUIREMENT

Pub. L. 102-484, § 1072, Oct. 23, 1992, 106 Stat. 2508 (10 U.S.C. § 113, note) requires the Service Secretaries to ensure that fatality reports and records pertaining to members of the Armed Forces who die in the line of duty are made available to family members.

Within a reasonable period of time after the family members are notified of the death, but not more than 30 days after the date of notification, the Secretary must:

In any case under investigation, inform the family members of the names of the agencies conducting the investigation and of the existence of any reports by such agencies that have been or will be issued; and

Furnish, if the family members desire, a copy of any completed investigative report to the extent such reports may be furnished consistent with the Privacy Act and the Freedom of Information Act.

3. ARMY IMPLEMENTATION

A. Key definitions

- Fatal training accidents include those accidents associated with non-combat military exercises or training activities that are designed to develop a Soldier's physical ability or to maintain or increase individual/collective combat and/or peacekeeping skills.

- Fatal operational accidents are those deaths associated with active duty military exercises or activities occurring in a designated war zone or toward designated missions related to current war operations or Military Operations Other Than War, contributing directly or indirectly to the death.
- Primary Next of Kin (PNOK). The legal next of kin. That person of any age most closely related to the individual according to the line of succession. Seniority, as determined by age, will control when the persons are of equal relationship.

B. Collateral Investigations

Collateral investigations are required for all on-duty Class A accidents resulting in a Soldier's death, anticipated litigation for or against the Government or Government contractor, anticipated disciplinary or adverse action against any individual, probable high public interest, and all suspected cases of friendly fire.

C. Presentations to PNOK

Presentations are required for all fatal training/operational accidents investigated under AR 15-6, AR 385-10, and AR 600-34; special interest cases or cases in which there is probable high public interest, as determined by The Adjutant General; all suspected cases of Friendly Fire; in general, fatal accidents that are hostile, but do not occur as a result of engagement with the enemy.

Though not required by AR 600-34, Suicide Incident Family Briefs utilizing the same procedures are required for confirmed cases of suicide that occur on or after 15 APR 10 (Army Directive 2010-01). Suicide Incident Family Briefs are not required regarding investigations into the suicides of Army Reserve or Army National Guard Soldiers whose deaths are not reportable casualties under AR 600-8-1 para 3-1.

D. Updates to PNOK

If the appointing/approval authority grants an extension of the 30-day requirement to complete the legal investigation, the approval authority is responsible for the release of information from the investigation to the PNOK.

The approving authority's legal office must review each update to ensure that it contains no admission of liability, waiver of any defense, offer of compensation or any statement that might jeopardize the Army's litigation posture.

The update is provided to the Casualty and Mortuary Affairs Operation Center (CMAOC) who will direct the Casualty Assistance officer (CAO) to provide the update to the family.

E. Preparing the presentation to the PNOK

Once the investigation is complete, the CMAOC contacts the Army command commander and the collateral investigation appointing/approval authority in order to coordinate appointment of the briefer who is "most often the deceased Soldier's colonel or brigade level commander."

The command is ultimately responsible to provide an O6 to present the briefing as the CMAOC does not provide briefing teams.

WITHIN 24-HOURS OF COMPLETION OF THE INVESTIGATION, THE CAO MUST NOTIFY THE PNOK THAT THE ARMY IS PREPARED TO DISCUSS THE RESULTS OF THE INVESTIGATION WITH THE FAMILY.

The CAO then follows up with the PNOK to arrange for the presentation date and forward the preferred dates (primary and secondary) to the CMAOC.

F. Briefing Team

At a minimum, the briefing team must consist of the briefer (an O6 from the chain of command), the family's CAO, and a chaplain from the mishap unit.

The briefer must consider including the SJA or legal advisor or PAO representative when it is apparent that a family has invited, or may invite, the local media or a family legal representative will attend the presentation.

The CAO must work with the PNOK to obtain a list of people the PNOK intends to invite to the presentation to enable the presentation team to determine the family's intent to invite media or legal representation.

NOTE: The Army is prohibited from putting conditions or limitations upon those whom the family wishes to invite to the presentation.

The briefer must also consider including an interpreter if the PNOK or other attending family members do not understand English.

G. Conducting the Family Presentation

The briefer's primary responsibility is to meet personally with the PNOK and deliver a thorough open explanation of the releasable facts and circumstances surrounding the accident. At a minimum, the briefer must provide the following:

An explanation of the unit's mission which highlights the Soldier's significant contributions to the mission and the Army; an accurate account of the facts and circumstances leading up to the accident, the sequence of events that caused the accident, and a very clear explanation of primary and contributing factors causing the accident as determined by the collateral investigation, actions taken at the unit level to correct any deficiencies.

The briefer should be prepared to answer questions related to benefits, entitlements, internment, and delivery of personal effects.

The preferred choice for the presentation is the PNOK's home.

H. Style of presentation

Dialogue with no notes but with maps and diagrams of training areas. This works best for a briefer who is intimately familiar with the accident and investigation.

Bullet briefing charts. These work well as they tend to help the briefer stay focused. Charts must be reviewed and approved in advance by the SJA.

Simple notes and an executive summary. Written materials must be reviewed and approved by the SJA and copies should be left with the PNOK if requested.

I. Completion of Family Presentation

Within two weeks of the presentation, the briefer must submit an AAR through the appointing authority and MACOM to the TAG.

J. SJA Requirements

The OSJA is required to review the presentation to ensure that it contains no admission of liability, waiver of any defense, offer of compensation, or any other statement that might jeopardize the Army's litigation posture. This may include review of briefing charts, notes, and executive summaries.

The SJA or legal advisor must provide a non-redacted copy of the collateral investigation report to CMAOC.

The regulation is not intended to provide the PNOK with information not otherwise releasable under the Privacy Act or the Freedom of Information Act.

The SJA must redact the collateral investigation report and prepare the required number of copies. At a minimum, the briefer, each team member, and each PNOK will be given a redacted copy.

The SJA also must prepare a letter to accompany the redacted version of the report delivered to the family and will explain, in general terms, the reasons for the redactions.

More detailed guidance concerning redaction of reports of investigation related to deaths is contained in Army Directive 2010-02.

K. Release of the Collateral Investigation

The investigation will be released in the following order: Interested offices within DOD and DA; PNOK and other family members designated by the PNOK; Members of Congress, upon request; and Members of the public and media.

Chapter 19

FINANCIAL LIABILITY INVESTIGATIONS

This chapter provides an OVERVIEW of procedures for financial liability investigations.

1. REFERENCES

- AR 735-5, Policies and Procedures for Property Accountability, 28 February 2005.
- DA Pam 735-5, Financial liability Officer's Guide, 9 April 2007.

2. FINANCIAL LIABILITY INVESTIGATIONS OF PROPERTY LOSS (FLIPL)

A. Applicability

Applies to the Active Army, the Army National Guard, and the US Army Reserve.

1) Purpose

Prescribes the basic policies and procedures in accounting for Army property.

2) Tools

Financial liability officers should use DA Pam 735-5, Financial Liability Officer's Guide, during their investigation. Units must use DA Form 7531, Checklist and Tracking Document for Financial Liability Investigations of Property Loss, to track investigations.

B. Function of an AR 735-5 Financial Liability Investigation of Property Loss

A FLIPL is used to document the circumstances concerning the loss, damage, or destruction (LDD) of Government property and serves as, or supports a voucher for adjusting the property from accountable records. It also documents a charge of financial liability assessed against an individual or entity, or provides for the relief from financial liability.

It is used to enforce property accountability and is not intended as corrective action or punishment. Commanders, however, are not precluded from using administrative or disciplinary measures, such as reprimand, Article 15, if appropriate as the result of LDD of Government property.

3. ALTERNATIVES TO FINANCIAL LIABILITY INVESTIGATIONS

- **Statement of Charges/Cash Collection Voucher** when liability is admitted and the charge does not exceed one month's base pay. (These two functions have been combined on DD Form 362)
- **Cash sales** of hand tools and organizational clothing and individual equipment.
- Unit level commanders may **adjust losses** of durable hand tools up to $100 per incident, if no negligence or misconduct is involved.
- **Abandonment order** may be used in combat, large-scale field exercises simulating combat, military advisor activities, or to meet other military requirements.

- **Damage statement.** Approval authority may sign damage statement when there is no evidence of negligence or misconduct.
- **Recovery of property** unlawfully held by civilians is authorized — show proof it is U.S. property and do not breach the peace.
- **AR 15-6 investigations** and other collateral investigations can be used in conjunction with the DD Form 200 (replaced DA Form 4697) as a substitute for financial liability investigation investigations.

4. MANDATORY FLIPLS (PARA. 13-3). A UNIT MUST INITIATE TO ACCOUNT FOR LDD OF GOVERNMENT EQUIPMENT WHEN...

- An individual refuses to admit liability and negligence or misconduct is suspected.
- Property is lost by an outgoing accountable officer, unless voluntary reimbursement is made for the full value of the loss.
- The amount of loss or damage exceeds an individual's monthly base pay, even if liability is admitted.
- The damage to government quarters or furnishings exceeds one month's base pay.
- The loss involves certain bulk petroleum products.
- A sensitive item is lost or destroyed (requires AR 15-6 investigation).
- A higher authority or other DA regulation directs a financial liability investigation.
- Loss involves public funds or other negotiable instruments and individual does not voluntarily reimburse Army.
- Loss or damage involves GSA vehicle and responsible party not relieved of liability.
- Loss resulted from fire, theft. Or natural disaster.
- Loss involves certain recoverable items.
- Certain ammunition losses require AR 15-6 investigation (See AR 190-11, Appendix E).

5. JOINT FINANCIAL LIABILITY INVESTIGATIONS

Absent a loan agreement stating otherwise, the regulation of the Service that owns the property (property is located on that service's property account) is the appropriate regulation to apply.

The Army and Air Force have a reciprocal agreement outlined in paragraph 14-36 of AR 735-5 that explains the process for processing financial liability investigations that find Air Force personnel liable for the loss, damage, or destruction of Army property. Upon completion of the investigation, it should be forwarded to the appropriate Air Force approval authority for final action and possible collection.

For all other situations where non-Army personnel are found to be liable for the loss, damage, or destruction of Army property, the procedures of AR 735-5, paragraph 14-35 should be followed. Upon completion of the investigation, the respondent will be formally notified and requested to make payment in full. If after 60 days, the respondent fails to pay, the investigation should be sent to the respondent's servicing finance office for processing.

Financial liability investigations that find contractors liable should be processed IAW the applicable contract.

6. INITIATING THE FLIPL (PARA. 13-7 AND 13-8)

Upon discovering the LDD of Government equipment, the hand receipt holder, accountable officer, or person with most knowledge of the incident will initiate a FLIPL within: Active Army: 15 calendar days; Army Reserve: 75 calendar days; National Guard: 45 calendar days.

Certain losses (sensitive items, items identified in AR 190-11, App E) require an AR 15-6 investigation as the underlying investigative mechanism. A DD Form 200 (FLIPL) will be completed as the adjustment document, but the appointing or approving authority should not conduct a separate FLIPL.

Initiation of a FLIPL is complete when forwarded to the appointing/approving authority for appointment of a financial liability officer (investigating officer).

The approving authority is an Army officer, or DA civilian employee authorized to appoint a financial liability officer and to approve financial liability investigations "by authority of the Secretary of the Army." The approving authority does not have to be a court-martial convening authority.

Per ALARACT 124/2006 dated 28 June 2006, the following personnel are approving authorities for FLIPLs. For final loss or damage less than $100,000 the first colonel or supervisory GS-15 in the rating chain is the approval authority. For final loss or damage $100,000 or greater, or any final loss of a controlled item, the first general officer or senior executive service civilian in the rating chain is the approval authority.

The appointing authority is an officer or civilian employee designated by the approving authority with responsibility for appointing financial liability investigation investigating officers. The approving authority may designate, in writing, a Lieutenant Colonel (05) (or major in a lieutenant colonel billet) or DOD civilian employee in the grade of GS-13 (or a GS-12 in a GS-13 billet) or above as an appointing authority.

Regardless of who initiates the financial liability investigation, it is processed through the chain of command of the individual responsible for the property at the time of the incident, provided the individual is subject to AR 735-5. AR 735-5, para. 13-5.

In order for the financial liability officer to be qualified, he/she must be senior to the person subject to possible financial liability, "except when impractical due to military exigencies." The financial liability officer can be an Army commissioned officer; warrant officer; or enlisted Soldier in the rank of Sergeant First Class (E-7), or higher; a civilian employee GS-07 or above; or a Wage Leader (WL) or Wage Supervisor (WS) employee. In joint commands or activities, any DOD commissioned or warrant officer or non-commissioned officer E-7 or above assigned to the activity or command can be the financial liability officer.

7. CONDUCTING THE INVESTIGATION

The financial liability officer's primary duty is the investigation. He/she will receive a briefing from prior to beginning the investigation. The regulation does not mandate who provides the briefing. It should be provided by the unit S4 or a judge advocate.

The financial liability officer must complete the investigation within: Active Army: 30 calendar days (55 cumulative days from discovery of LDD); Army Reserve: 60 calendar days. (160 cumulative days from discovery of LDD); National Guard: 60 calendar days. (120 cumulative days from discovery of LDD).

The financial liability officer must seek out all the facts that surround the LDD and conduct a thorough and impartial investigation; physically examine damaged property and release it for turn-in or repair; interview and obtain statements from individuals with useful information; resolve conflicting statements and confirm self-serving statements; organize investigation in accordance with the regulation; determine the cause and value of the LDD of Government property and determine if assessment of financial liability is warranted.

8. ASSESSMENT OF FINANCIAL LIABILITY (PARA. 13-29)

Individuals may be held financially liable for the LDD of Government property if they were negligent or have committed willful misconduct, and their negligence or willful misconduct is the proximate cause of that LDD. Before a person may be held liable, the facts must show that a loss to the Government occurred. There are two types of losses which can result in financial liability: (1) Actual loss. Physical loss, damage or destruction of the property; and (2) Loss of accountability. Due to loss of circumstances, it is impossible to determine if there has been actual physical loss, damage, or destruction because it is impossible to account for the property.

The actual value at the time of the loss is the preferred method of valuing the loss. Determine the item's condition item at the time of the loss or damage. Determine a price value for similar property in similar condition sold in the commercial market within the last 6 months.

Depreciation is the least preferred method of determining the loss to the government. Compute charges according to AR 735-5, App. B, para. B-2b.

The type of responsibility a person has for property determines the obligations incurred by that person for the property. The type of obligation a person has toward property is relevant when determining whether a person was negligent. There must be a finding of either negligence or willful misconduct before an individual may be held liable.

The commander has an obligation to insure proper use, care, custody, and safekeeping of government property within his or her command. Command responsibility is inherent in command and cannot be delegated. It is evidenced by assignment to command at any level.

The obligation of a supervisor for the proper use, care, and safekeeping of government property issued to, or used by, subordinates. It is inherent in all supervisory positions and not contingent upon signed receipts or responsibility statements. If supervisory responsibility is involved, also consider the following factors: The nature and complexity of the activity and how it affected the ability to maintain close supervision; The adequacy of supervisory measures used to monitor the activity of subordinates; The extent supervisory duties were hampered by other duties or the lack of qualified assistants.

The obligation to ensure the proper use, care, custody, and safekeeping of all government property for which the person has receipted. Direct responsibility is closely related to custodial responsibility (discussed below).

Custodial Responsibility is an individual's obligation regarding property in storage awaiting issue or turn-in to exercise reasonable and prudent actions to properly care for and ensure property custody and safekeeping of the property. Who has custodial responsibility? A supply sergeant, supply custodian, supply clerk, or warehouse person who is rated by and answerable directly to the accountable officer or the individual having direct responsibility for the property.

Responsibilities include: Ensuring the security of all property stored within the supply room and storage annexes belonging to the supply room or SSA is adequate; Observing subordinates to ensure they properly care for and safeguard property; Enforcing security, safety and accounting requirements; If unable to enforce any of these, reporting the problems to their immediate supervisor.

Personal Responsibility is an individual's obligations to properly use, care, and keep safe government property in their possession, with or without a receipt.

A person can only be held liable if the facts show that she acted negligently or engaged in willful misconduct.

Simple negligence is the failure to act as a reasonably prudent person would have acted under similar circumstances. Remember, a reasonably prudent person is an average person, not a perfect person. Also consider: What could be expected of the person considering their age, experience, and special qualifications? The type of responsibility involved. The type and nature of the property. More complex or sensitive property normally requires a greater degree of care. The nature, complexity, level of danger, or urgency of the activity ongoing at the time of the LDD of the property.

Examples of simple negligence are failure to do required maintenance checks, leaving weapon leaning against a tree while attending to other duties, driving too fast for road or weather conditions, or failing to maintain proper hand receipts.

Gross negligence is an extreme departure from the course of action expected of a reasonably prudent person, all circumstances being considered, and accompanied by a reckless, deliberate, or wanton disregard for the foreseeable consequences of the act. Reckless, deliberate, or wanton. These elements can be express or implied. Does not include thoughtlessness, inadvertence, or errors in judgment.

Foreseeable consequences do not require actual knowledge of actual results. You do not need to foresee the particular loss or damage that occurs, but you must foresee that some loss or damage may occur.

Examples of gross negligence are: Soldier drives a vehicle at a speed in excess of 40 mph of the posted speed limit. Intentionally tries to make a sharp curve without slowing down. Soldier lives in family quarters and has a child who likes to play with matches. Soldier leaves matches out where child can reach them.

Willful misconduct is any intentional or unlawful act. Willfulness can be express or implied. Includes violations of law and regulations such as theft and misappropriation of government property. A violation of law or regulation is not negligence per se.

Examples of willful misconduct. A violation of law or regulation is not negligence per se. Soldier throws a tear gas grenade into the mess tent to let the cooks know what he thought about breakfast, and as a result, the tent burns to the ground. Soldier steals a self-propelled howitzer, but he does not know how to operate it. Accordingly, his joy ride around post results in damage to several buildings.

Before a person can be held liable, the facts must clearly show that a person's conduct was the proximate cause of the LDD. Proximate cause is based upon whether the LDD was foreseeable. If the LDD of property was a reasonably foreseeable consequence of the respondent's misconduct or negligence, and LDD to property actually occurred, then that misconduct or negligence is the proximate cause of the LDD.

The cause which, in a natural and continuous sequence, unbroken by a new cause, produces the loss or damage, and without which the loss or damage would not have occurred. It is the immediate or direct cause of the LDD, without which the LDD would not have occurred. Use common sense and good judgment to determine proximate cause.

Examples of proximate cause are the following: Soldier driving a vehicle fails to stop at a stop sign and strikes another vehicle after failing to look. Proximate cause is the Soldier's failure to stop and look.

Soldier A illegally parks his vehicle in a no parking zone. Soldier B backs into A's vehicle. B did not check for obstructions to the rear of his vehicle. A's misconduct is not the proximate cause of the damage. Instead, B's negligent driving is the proximate cause.

Independent intervening cause is an act which interrupts the original flow of events or consequences of the original negligence. It may include an act of God, criminal misconduct, or negligence.

9. CONCLUDING THE INVESTIGATION

Liability not recommended by the financial liability officer. (Para. 13-33) If financial liability is not recommended, the investigation is forwarded through the appointing authority, if any, to the approving authority for action.

If the approving authority concurs and does not assess liability, the investigation is complete.

If the approving authority does not concur and decides to assess liability, the individual against whom liability will be imposed (respondent) must be given notice and an opportunity to rebut the decision (same procedure as if the financial liability officer initially recommended liability).

Liability recommended by the financial liability officer. (Para. 13-34 & 13-35) If financial liability is recommended against an individual, the individual is referred to as the respondent. Respondents have certain rights. The financial liability officer will notify the respondent by memorandum of the proposed recommendation of financial responsibility. The notification includes:

- The right to inspect and copy the report of investigation. A copy of the investigation is normally sent with the notification.
- The right to obtain free legal advice (military and DA civilians).
- The right to submit a statement and other evidence in rebuttal to the recommendation

Time limits for submitting rebuttal evidence to the financial liability officer are as follows: 7 calendar days—when investigation is hand delivered to the respondent; 15 calendar days—when respondent is unavailable but in the same country and the investigation is mailed; 30 calendar days—when respondent is unavailable and in a different country and the investigation is mailed.

The financial liability officer must consider the respondent's rebuttal. Regardless of whether the financial liability officer changes the recommendation, the investigation is forwarded through the appointing authority, if any, to the approving authority for decision.

The approving authority is not bound by the recommendation of the financial liability officer. The approving authority may decide not to impose liability or to impose liability.

Note: If financial liability officer recommended no liability and therefore did not provide the individual with notice and opportunity to rebut, the approving authority must do so before he can assess liability.

When the approving authority decides to impose liability, the approval authority must notify the respondent of that collection efforts will commence in 30 days (NOTE: ARNG affords 60 days). In the memorandum the approval authority must also notify the respondent of the following rights:

- The right to inspect and copy the file.
- The right to legal advice.
- The right to request reconsideration based on legal error.
- The right to a hearing (for DOD civilians only).
- The right to request remission of indebtedness. Is Available for enlisted Soldiers only. Only to avoid extreme hardship. Only unpaid portions can be remitted. Suspend collection action long enough for the Soldier to submit his request for remission of the debt. Must request reconsideration before submitting request for remission of indebtedness.
- The right to request extension of collection time.
- The right to petition Army Board for the Correction of Military Records (ABCMR) IAW AR 15-185. Based on unjustness. Can only be made after appeal authority acts on request for reconsideration (see below).
- Civilian employees may avail themselves of the grievance/arbitration procedures.

Request for reconsideration, a hearing, or remission or cancellation of debt stops all collection action pending outcome of request.

Before the approving authority approves a recommendation of liability, a judge advocate MUST review the survey for legal sufficiency of the evidence and propriety of the findings and recommendations. Although AR 735-5 states that the legal review is conducted after the approving authority makes his or her decision regarding liability, in practice the legal review is most often conducted prior to review by the approving authority. The financial liability officer's or judge advocate's recommendations do not bind the approving authority.

10. DECISION BY APPROVING AUTHORITY WITHOUT INVESTIGATION (SHORT FLIPL) (PARA. 13-22 & 13-23)

When initial information indicates there was no negligence involved in the LDD of Government property, the approving authority may relieve all individuals from liability.

When initial information indicates that negligence or willful misconduct was the proximate cause of the LDD of Government property, the approving authority may assess liability by:

- Notifying the respondent of the intent to hold him/her liable. Notification must include all the facts upon which the decision is based and must include notice of all the respondent rights as outlined above. The respondent has the right to submit a rebuttal.
- The approving official must consider the rebuttal if submitted and make a determination.
- The information and rebuttal must receive a legal review.

The approving authority makes a final decision and notifies the respondent accordingly.

11. RELIEF FROM LIABILITY

Request for reconsideration & appeal must be submitted within 30 days of liability notification and can only be based on legal error.

Submitted to approving authority. If approving authority does not reverse the decision, the request becomes an appeal, which is forwarded to the appeal authority by the approving authority.

Appeal authority is the next higher commander or DA civilian in the chain of command or supervision. The decision of appeal authority is final. Only further recourse is application to ABCMR. The investigation must receive a legal review by the legal advisor prior to appeal authority action.

Reopening financial liability investigations is not an appeal. The authority to reopen rests with the approval authority. It may occur as part of an appeal of the assessment of financial liability; when a response is submitted to the surveying officer from the person charged subsequent to the approving authority having assessed liability; when a subordinate headquarters recommends reopening based upon new evidence; when the property is recovered; or when the approving authority becomes aware that an injustice has occurred.

12. LIMITS ON FINANCIAL LIABILITY

The general rule is that an individual will not be charged more than one month's base pay. The amount charged is based upon the Soldier's base pay at the time of the loss.

For ARNG and USAR personnel, base pay is the amount they would receive if they were on active duty.

For civilian employees it is 1/12 of their annual pay.

Exceptions to the general rule are when there are times when personnel are liable for the full amount of the loss. AR 735-5, para. 13-41a. Any Soldier is liable for the full loss to the Government (less depreciation) when they lose, damage, or destroy personal arms or equipment. Any person is liable for the full loss of public funds. Accountable officers will be liable for the full amount of the loss. Any person assigned government quarters is liable for the full amount of the loss to the quarters, furnishings, or equipment as a result of gross negligence or willful misconduct of the responsible individual, his guests, dependents, or pets.

Collective financial liability: Two or more persons may be held liable for the same loss. There is no comparative negligence. Financial loss is apportioned according to AR 735-5, Table 12-4. Each respondent pays a percentage of the loss in accordance with their percentage of pay when all respondent's pay is totaled. If one of the collective liability respondents is not federally employed, divide the total amount of the loss by the total number of respondents. Each respondent is liable for that amount or their monthly pay, whichever is less.

13. INVOLUNTARY WITHHOLDING OF CURRENT PAY

- Members of the armed forces may have charges involuntarily withheld. 37 U.S.C. § 1007.
- Involuntary withholding for civilian employees. 5 U.S.C. § 5512, AR 37-1, Chapter 15.

14. TOTAL PROCESSING TIME

- The Active Army Component: 75 days (2 1/2 months).
- The U.S. Army Reserve component: 240 days (8 months).
- The Army NG: 150 days (5 months).

STANDARDS OF ETHICAL CONDUCT

Section 3

THIS PAGE IS INTENTIONALLY BLANK

Chapter 20

STANDARDS OF ETHICAL CONDUCT IN THE ARMY

1. INTRODUCTION

This chapter contains the most common guidelines, rules, restrictions, and prohibitions contained in the Joint Ethics Regulation. It is not all inclusive. Commanders should exercise caution when applying these rules and are encouraged to contact their supporting judge advocate or ethics counselor when these issues arise.

2. GIFTS

A. General

Federal regulations and the Department of Defense (DoD) Joint Ethics Regulation (JER) place several restrictions on DoD employees when it comes to soliciting and accepting gifts. There are, however, several exceptions and exclusions.

B. Gift Exclusions And Exceptions

A gift is defined as any gratuity, favor, discount, entertainment, hospitality or any other item having monetary value. It includes services as well as gifts of training, transportation, local travel, lodging and meals. It does not include:

- Coffee, donuts & modest refreshments not intended as a meal;
- Greeting cards, plaques, trophies, and other items with little intrinsic value intended solely for presentation;
- Rewards & prizes for contests open to public;
- Commercial discounts available to the public or military; or
- Anything for which an employee pays market value

C. Rules for Gifts between Employees

In general, a DoD employee may not accept a gift from a lower paid employee or solicit or give a gift to a superior. There are two major exceptions.

First, an employee may accept a gift on a traditional gift giving occasion as long as the gift is valued at less than $10.00 (no cash). Examples would include birthdays or holidays.

Second, an employee may accept a gift on a special, infrequent occasion. Examples of a special, infrequent occasion would include marriage, change of command, PCS, or retirement. When accepting a gift based on a special, infrequent occasion, the following rules apply.

- The gift must be valued at $300.00 or less per donating group;
- The employee may not "buy down" the value of the gift;
- All contributions must be voluntary;

- Employees may solicit for contributions for the gift as long as the solicitation does not exceed $10.00. Solicitation must be free from coercion.

D. Rules for Gifts from Foreign Governments

Members of the military may accept a gift from a foreign government that is valued at $350.00 or less. The General Services Administration periodically adjusts this amount. The value of the gift must be based on its fair market value in the United States, not the market value in the donor nation. A gift from a foreign government to your spouse is treated as a gift to you.

E. Rules for Gifts from Outside Sources

DoD employees are prohibited from accepting gifts from a prohibited source. In addition, DoD employees cannot accept a gift offered because of the employee's official position. There are, however, several general exceptions:

- **$20/$50 Rule.** A DoD employee can accept a gift from an outside source valued at $20 or less, per source, per occasion, not to exceed $50 in a calendar year.
- **Personal Relationship.** Gifts from outside sources based on a preexisting personal relationship.
- **Widely Attended Gathering.** For information about the possibility of accepting a gift of free attendance at a widely attended gathering consult your ethics counselor.

3. TRAVEL

Chapter 4 of the Joint Ethics Regulation (JER) and the Secretary of the Army Policy for Travel by Department of the Army Officials contains the key rules associated with travel benefits.

A. Air Travel

Service members are authorized to wear **uniforms** when travelling in coach class. However, service members should not wear their uniforms when traveling in any class of travel above coach.

B. Frequent Flyer Miles

Frequent flyer miles accrued during official travel belong to the traveler and not the government. Travelers can use their frequent flyer miles to upgrade a government purchased ticket or for any other purpose.

C. On-the-Spot Upgrades

Travelers may accept an unsolicited offer from the airline to upgrade their government ticket to a premium class of travel even if they are in uniform. However, senior officers must always consider the potential appearance of impropriety.

D. Airline "Bump" Rules

You may not volunteer to take a later flight in exchange for travel benefits offered by the airline if it will interfere with your mission. If there is no impact on the mission you may accept the travel benefits offered by the airline in exchange for taking a later flight.

A traveler who is involuntarily bumped from a seat is considered to be "awaiting transportation" for per diem and miscellaneous expense reimbursement; therefore, any monetary compensation from the airline (including meal and/or lodging vouchers) for the denied seat belongs to the government. The service member must turn in all such items with the travel voucher on return.

4. USE OF NON-TACTICAL VEHICLES

A. Duty to Domicile

AR 58-1 and federal law provide extremely narrow exceptions for the use of an NTV between the place of duty and private domicile. Commanders should consult with an ethics counselor prior to using their NTV to travel to or from their domicile.

B. Travel to Commercial Air Terminals

AR 58-1 limits the circumstances under which a commander can use an NTV to travel to a commercial air terminal. Consult with your ethics counselor

C. Space Available Travel

Spouses may travel in an NTV to an official function as long as space is available.

5. USE OF GOVERNMENT RESOURCES

Federal Government resources shall be for official use and authorized purposes only. Official use is any use that is necessary to accomplish the mission. Under limited circumstances, a commander can authorize the use of a government resource for personal use. When authorizing the use of an official government resource for personal use the commander must ensure that the personal use meets the following criteria:

- No adverse effect on duty performance
- Reasonable duration and frequency
- Legitimate public interest served
- Does not overburden Government communications
- No Adverse Reflection on DOD
- *No significant additional cost*

Examples of acceptable personal use of a government resource would be short (local) phone calls home, limited personal use of the internet, making a few personal photocopies. Government resources may never be used to operate a private business.

6. FINANCIAL DISCLOSURE

The DoD currently uses two different financial disclosure forms, the OGE 450 and the OGE 278. Which form an individual must use depends on the rank or grade and responsibilities of that individual; therefore, commanders should contact their servicing judge advocate or ethics counselor to determine whether they are required to file a financial disclosure form.

A. Confidential Financial Disclosure Report (OGE 450)

Persons required to file this form include: All military members (O-6 and below) and all civilian employees (GS/GM-15 and below) when the official position of such employees or members requires them to participate personally and substantially in taking an official action for contracting or procurement, or if the supervisor of such employee or member determines the position requires such a report to avoid an actual or apparent conflict of interest.

B. Public Financial Disclosure Report (OGE 278)

Persons required to file this form include: Regular and Reserve officers whose grade is O-7 or above (The requirement begins when a Reserve General Officer reaches 60 active duty days in a calendar year); members of the Senior Executive Service; and civilian employees whose positions are classified above GS/GM-15 or whose rate of basic pay is fixed at or above 120% of the minimum rate of basic pay for a GS/GM-15.

7. CONFLICTS OF INTEREST

Under federal law, Army Regulations, and the Joint Ethics Regulation, personnel shall not engage in any personal business or professional activity that places them in a position of conflict between their private interests and the public interest of the United States. In order to preserve the public confidence in the Army, even the appearance of a conflict of interest must be avoided. The following general rules apply:

A. Inside Information

Army personnel shall not use inside information to further a private gain for themselves or others if that information was obtained by reason of their position and is not generally available to the public.

B. Commercial Solicitation

Active duty members shall not engage in commercial solicitations or solicited sales to DoD personnel junior in rank at any time.

C. Fundraising

Although there are exceptions for the Combined Federal Campaign and the Army Emergency Relief Fund, fundraising is not allowed in the federal workplace. For rules and exceptions on fundraising see AR 600-29 and consult your ethics counselor.

D. Endorsement

DoD employees are prohibited from using their grades, titles or positions in connection with any commercial enterprise or for endorsing a commercial product. DOD employees must not use their official capacities and titles, positions, or organization names to suggest official endorsement or preferential treatment of any non-Federal entity.

E. Outside Employment

DoD employees are prohibited from accepting employment outside of the Army if it interferes with or is not compatible with the performance of government duties, or if it might discredit the government. Commanders typically approve outside employment.

There are several service restrictions that apply when a DoD employee is presented with an offer to speak at an event, lecture, or write on a particular topic. Commanders are highly encouraged to consult with their servicing judge advocate or ethics counselor prior to accepting an offer to teach, speak, or write.

Chapter 21

COMMANDERS COINS

1. REFERENCES

- 10 U.S.C. § 1125
- AR 37-47, Representation Funds of the Secretary of the Army, dtd 12 March 2004
- AR 600-8-22, Military Awards, dtd 11 December 2006

2. OVERVIEW

HQDA scrutinizes the purchase and presentation of commanders' coins. Commanders must recognize fiscal rules that affect their purchase and distribution. Coins may be purchased, depending on circumstances, using appropriated funds, non-appropriated funds (NAFs), official representation funds (ORF) or private funds. Many Army Commands and Army Service Component Commands either place dollar limits, or create formulas based upon the number of Soldiers in a unit, to limit the purchase of commander's coins.

A. Purchase with Appropriated Funds (APFs)

Commanders may present coins purchased with appropriated funds only to reward Soldiers and DA civilians for outstanding duty performance or to recognize unique achievements. Commanders may not present coins purchased with appropriated funds as merely gifts, mementos or tokens of appreciation (e.g., as a "farewell" gift or during a visit to a unit). Coins purchased with appropriated funds may not be presented to contractor employees, family members, members of a private organization (POs), or to Soldiers as an award for participating in a PO activity. Coins intended for presentation to certain dignitaries may be purchased with ORF, if the recipients qualify as "authorized guests" IAW AR 37-47. Though individual commands may require it, Commanders presenting coins purchased with APFs should keep a register detailing the circumstances of each presentation.

B. Purchase with NAFs

Commanders may present coins purchased with NAFs only to award Soldiers and DoD civilians for excellence in athletic or nonathletic competitions, proficiency in recreational programs, or unusual accomplishment in supporting special events.

C. Private Funds

Commanders wishing to present coins to anyone for any reason may purchase them with their own private funds. Commanders should keep receipts for all such purchases.

THIS PAGE IS INTENTIONALLY BLANK

Chapter 22

SUPPORT TO NON-FEDERAL ENTITIES

1. REFERENCES

- DoD Regulation 5500.7-R (Joint Ethics Regulation)
- DoD Directive 5410.18, Public Affairs Community Relations Policy, dtd 20 November 2001, certified current as of 30 May 2007
- DoD Instruction 1000.15, Procedures and Support for Non-Federal Entities Authorized to Operate on DoD Installations, dtd 24 October 2008
- DoD Instruction 5410.19, Public Affairs Community Relations Policy Implementation, dtd 13 November 2001
- 5 C.F.R. §§ 2635.704; 2635.705; 2635.808

2. AR 360-1, THE ARMY PUBLIC AFFAIRS PROGRAM, DTD 25 MAY 2011

A. Basic Ethics Principles Regarding Official Support to Non-Federal Entities (NFEs)

1) Use Government Property Only for Authorized Purposes

The Government's performance of services for most NFEs is an improper use of funds and resources. This applies even if the Government is compensated or reimbursed. Federal law entitles some NFEs to particular types of support (e.g., CFC, Red Cross, Boy Scouts, Girl Scouts).

Official communications channels may be used to notify DoD personnel of NFE-sponsored events of common interest that support the goal of enhancing morale, welfare, or professional education.

Logistical support and DoD speakers may be provided to NFE-sponsored events (Other than Fundraisers) if the support:

- Does not interfere with official duties;
- Serves official interests;
- Is appropriate for DoD involvement;
- Benefits DoD or the local community;
- Does not offer preferential treatment;
- Is incidental to the event, or the event's admission fee does not exceed the event's cost; **and**
- Does not violate federal law or regulations.

DoD personnel may speak or otherwise participate in NFE events when 1) over 20% of the audience is military personnel, and 2) the primary purpose is to train DoD personnel. See DA SOCO Advisory 23 March 2009.

Support to NFE fundraisers is limited to **logistical support** only. *The Army may not Endorse or otherwise Sanction NFEs, Even if Otherwise Permissible Support is Provided:*

- NFE fundraisers may not be supported through the use of a DoD employee's official position or title.
- Receiving or presenting awards, giving other-than-official speeches, and serving in honorary positions at NFE fundraising events in an official capacity is prohibited.
- DoD personnel may not be the "star attraction" at NFE fundraisers.

2) No NFE may Receive Preferential Treatment.

B. Management of NFEs in an Official Capacity

Management in an Official Capacity is Limited to "Designated" Organizations Only:

- Army Emergency Relief.
- Air Force Aid Society.
- Navy-Marine Corps Relief Society.
- Coast Guard Mutual Assistance.
- Entities regulating and supporting service academy athletics programs.
- Entities regulating international athletic competitions.
- Entities accrediting service academies and other DoD schools.

DoD Personnel Serving in a "Management" Position may not Participate in the Internal Management or Day-to-Day Operations of the NFE. Compensation is NOT Permitted.

C. Personal Participation in NFEs

Management may be in a Personal Capacity, Only. Generally, DoD personnel may not serve in a personal capacity, if the position was offered because of the DoD employee's official position.

- **Active Duty** General Officers generally may not accept compensation for their service in their personal capacities as officers or members of NFE boards.
- **Reserve** Personnel, not in Title 10 status, may receive compensation from NFEs as part of their civilian employment. Conflict of Interest, Representation, and Appearance restrictions still apply.

Personnel Personally Participating in NFEs **<u>may not</u>**:

- Take Official Action on Matters Involving those NFEs.
- Solicit Funds from their Subordinates.
- Use their Official Titles or Positions to endorse an NFE.
- Use Government Resources and Time in Support of Personal Participation in NFEs (Generally).

Chapter 23

GOVERNMENT MOTOR VEHICLE TRANSPORTATION

1. REFERENCES

- DoD Regulation 5500.7-R (Joint Ethics Regulation)
- Joint Federal Travel Regulation
- Joint Travel Regulation
- DoD Directive 4500.36, DoD Policy on Management, Acquisition, and Use of Motor Vehicles, dtd 3 August 2004
- Army Regulation 58-1, Management, Acquisition, and Use of Administrative Motor Vehicles, 10 August 2004

2. GOVERNMENT MOTOR VEHICLE TRANSPORTATION

A. The use of Army motor vehicles (including NTVs) is restricted to official purposes only

Changes of command, promotions, retirements, unit activations/deactivations are considered official business internal to the Army community. Attendance by the Army community is encouraged. For that reason, the use of a GOV or GOVs to attend such activities should be managed and not discouraged. However, transportation will begin and end at the transported individual's normal place of duty, NOT a personal residence or domicile.

Official non-DoD persons invited to take part in a DA function may be provided free transportation between commercial transportation terminals and residence or visitation points.

Army NTVs may be used for trips between home or place of duty and commercial or military transportation terminals only when:

- Required for emergencies or for security reasons.
- Terminals are located where other means of transportation are not available or cannot meet mission requirements.
- Justified by cost analysis AND approved by SECARMY.

B. Domicile-To-Duty(D-T-D) Transportation

Except for certain extremely limited exceptions prescribed by statute, D-T-D transportation is not transportation for official purposes, and use of government vehicles for this purpose is prohibited.

Authorized exceptions to the D-T-D prohibition are outlined in AR 58-1, Chapter 4-3. Note that all exemptions require Secretary of the Army approval, except 4-3(e) pertaining to overnight retention of a Government vehicle for next day departure pursuant to temporary duty orders.

C. Official After-Hours Functions

Transportation to official after-hours functions will be treated as an exception to policy for which prior approval is required. All transportation to after-hours functions will begin and end at the individual's normal place of duty.

Official motor vehicle transportation requirements do not include: transportation to private social functions; personal errands or side trips for unofficial purposes; transportation of dependents or visitors without an accompanying official; or in support of non-DoD activities unless specifically approved under the provisions of Army Regulations.

Chapter 24

FAMILY READINESS GROUPS

1. REFERENCES

- AR 608-1, Army Community Service Center, Appendix J, 21 December 2010
- AR 600-20, Army Command Policy, 4 August 2011
- AR 210-22, Private Organizations on Department of the Army Installations 22 October 2001
- AR 600-29, Fund-Raising Within the Department of the Army, 7 June 2010

2. OVERVIEW

A Family Readiness Group (FRG) is an organization created to foster a climate of mutual support within the unit. FRG goals include supporting the military mission through provision of support, outreach, and information to family members. A Family Readiness Group (FRG) is a volunteer group governed by DA Pam 608-47. IAW AR 608-1, paragraph J-2a, the FRG mission is to: "(1) Act as an extension of the unit in providing official, accurate command information; (2) Provide mutual support between the command and the FRG membership; (3) Advocate more efficient use of available community resources; [and] (4) Help families solve problems at the lowest level."

3. FUNDRAISING

A. Establishment of an FRG Fund

FRG mission-essential activities are supported using a unit's appropriated funds (APFs). Therefore, FRG mission-essential activities may not be augmented with private money, and any such augmentation may violate the Anti-Deficiency Act. AR 608-1, paragraph J-7a, allows Commanders to authorize their FRG to maintain one informal fund in accordance with AR 600-20. Informal funds are private funds generated by FRG members that are used to benefit the FRG membership as a whole. Currently an informal fund may not exceed more than $10,000 net worth (total assets less total liabilities) during a calendar year. In addition, an FRG is prohibited from raising more than $10,000 in a calendar year. For instructions on how to handle a situation where your FRG exceeds the $10,000 cap, commanders should consult their servicing judge advocate or ethics counselor. The FRG informal fund must have a Standard Operating Procedure (SOP) memorializing the FRG members' determination of the purpose of the FRG informal fund. The following statement must be included in the FRG informal fund SOP: "This FRG informal fund is for the benefit of the FRG members only and is established exclusively for charitable purposes and to provide support to Soldiers and Family members as the Soldiers and Families adapt to Army life. It is not a business and is not being run to generate profits. It is not an instrumentality of the United States Government." The FRG SOP must be approved by the unit commander and a majority of the FRG members. Informal funds may not be deposited or mixed with appropriated funds, unit MWR funds, unit cup and flower funds, or personal funds. Use of informal funds is limited to expenses consistent with the purpose and function of the fund and the fund's SOP, and must benefit the FRG membership as a whole. Examples include FRG newsletters that contain mostly unofficial information, parties, social outings, volunteer recognition, and picnics.

B. Pre-Approval Requirements for Fund Raisers

Joint Ethics Regulation (JER), paragraph 3-210a(6), exempts "organizations composed primarily of DoD employees or their dependents" from the general prohibition against fundraising "when [the organization is] fundraising among their own members for the benefit of welfare funds for their own members or their dependents [and] when [the fundraising has been] approved by the head of the DoD Component command or organization after consultation with the DAEO or designee."

Therefore, an FRG may conduct a fundraiser on an installation, from its own community members or dependents, and from all persons benefiting from the FRG, if:

- The commander approves of the fundraising effort after consultation with the commander's servicing Staff Judge Advocate (SJA) or ethics official;
- The fundraising purpose is consistent with the approved SOP; and
- The manner of fundraising must be consistent with the JER and AR 600-29.

For the Army Reserve commander, USAR Reg. 608-1, paragraph 4-4g, requires the commander to approve the FRG Informal Fund Account and all FRG fundraising activities prior to planning and executing the event. Additionally, USAR Reg. 608-1, paragraph 4-18b, states that: "The FRG may conduct a fundraising activity at the Army Reserve Center and use unit equipment, if available, with the unit commander's approval. The fundraising activity must NOT interfere with mission requirements. **Fundraising activities are only authorized at the unit's Reserve Center, NOT outside in the community**" (emphasis added).

Approval by the appropriate authority is required before conducting a fundraiser. The approval authority is dependent on installation policy and where the fundraiser will be held, but can range from company commander to installation commander. Additionally, coordination with other agencies may be necessary. For example, if food is sold, local policy may require prior coordination with preventive medicine.

C. Taxes

FRG's must comply with all Federal, State, and local tax laws, including state excise taxes. FRG's must seek private counsel or contact proper tax officials to ensure compliance with all tax laws.

D. Insurance

FRG's often overlook liability for injuries or even death caused by their fund raising activities. Finding insurance coverage may be difficult. Nevertheless, FRG's and their members face the possibility of personal liability for damages caused by their activities. The best course is to select safe activities and, in some cases, to include Army safety experts in the planning process. Insist that private vendors, who may assist you with a fundraiser, carry appropriate insurance coverage.

E. Raffles, Lotteries & Games of Chance

Raffles and lotteries are subject to state law, local installation policy, and AR 600-29.

F. Money Accountability

Money raised by FRG's must be guarded carefully. The fund custodian and the alternate custodian are responsible for maintaining, accounting for, and documenting expenditures. This does not mean that only one signature is required to spend money, however. Custodians of FRG money are liable to the FRG if they lose it. The custodian should open a non-interest-bearing checking account (interest-bearing accounts may be liable for local, State, or Federal taxes, and responsible to file tax returns). Although FRG's may qualify for exemption from Federal income tax, pursuant to section 501 of the Internal Revenue Code, the savings to be achieved may not equal the time and effort required to obtain an exemption.

The informal fund custodian will provide informal fund reports to the unit commander monthly and as requested. An annual report on the FRG informal fund activity will be provided to the first colonel (O–6) commander or designee in the unit's chain of command no later than 30 days after the end of the calendar year. Detailed records should be maintained on how money is raised and how it is spent. The FRG membership should make spending decisions. The FRG membership should determine the amount of money the FRG leadership may spend without consulting the entire membership. Commanders must review FRG financial records annually in accordance with local installation policy. Fidelity bonding must also be purchased by an organization for members or employees handling monthly cash flows exceeding $500. (Bonding will be equal to the normal maximum amount of cash handled.)

G. How FRG's May Spend Money

FRG funds should be used for activities that support the entire group rather than for specific individuals. Thus, inviting third party representatives for the purpose of sales, such as Tupperware or Longaberger baskets does not support the entire group or the broad goals of an FRG. The use of funds should not duplicate what other agencies provide (i.e., establishing a loan fund or emergency food locker when other agencies such as ACS, AER, ARC already have programs established). Finally, FRG monies may not be spent in a way that appears improper or contrary to Army interests.

4. AUTHORIZED SUPPORT

Appendix J of AR 608-1 outlines the types of support authorized to FRGs. They include: **(1) Official mail:** The requirements are that it must be for an official, mission-related purpose and be approved by the commander. Official mail cannot be used to support private organization activities, fundraisers, or commercial ventures. **(2) FRG Newsletters:** Newsletters can be printed with appropriated funds (APFs) provided information is considered official and approved by the commander. To qualify for use of APFs, the newsletter cannot contain any personal or social information, or information regarding private organizations, fund raisers or commercial ventures. **(3) Use of Government Facilities:** FRG volunteers may use government facilities to include dedicated office space, desks, equipment, supplies, and telephones needed to accomplish their assigned duties. **(4) Use of military vehicles:** Requirements for the use of military vehicles are outlined in AR 58-1, Management, Acquisition, and Use of Administrative Vehicles. Government vehicles may also be used when several criteria are met, as provided for in AR 608-1, Paragraph J-3.

THIS PAGE IS INTENTIONALLY BLANK

Chapter 25

ACCOMPANYING SPOUSAL TRAVEL

1. REFERENCES

- Joint Travel Regulation, Appendix E
- Department of Defense Directive 4500.56, DoD Policy on the Use of Government Aircraft and Air Travel 14 April 2009
- Secretary of the Army Policy Memorandum, 25 January 2007, Policy for Travel By Department of the Army Officials
- AR 58-1, Management, Acquisition, and Use of Motor Vehicles, 10 August 2004

2. OVERVIEW

As a general rule, spouses or other family members may not accompany DA personnel, either military or civilian, on official business at government expense. Rather, spouse travel on either military or commercial aircraft is accomplished as an exception to policy. These exceptions are normally limited to the spouses of senior officials, and other family members or dependents are not permitted to travel at government expense.

- Accompanying spouses traveling on commercial aircraft at government expense will fly coach-class (unless otherwise authorized IAW SA Policy memo, section 3, Commercial Air Travel).
- Accompanying spouses traveling on MILAIR will travel in a noninterference (non-reimbursable) status. MILAIR must be independently authorized IAW SA Policy memo, section 5.
- Spouses traveling in an accompanying spouse status are NOT permitted per diem.

3. EXCEPTIONS TO POLICY

A. As an exception to policy, spouses may accompany their sponsors on military or commercial aircraft at government expenses only

- To attend an unquestionably official function in which the spouse is actually to participate in an official capacity. Actual participation is not mere attendance at a meeting or conference, even if hosted by the DoD on a matter related to official business. The meeting or conference must include a sufficiently substantive spouse agenda requiring the spouses' active participation for a sufficient duration of time to warrant travel at government expense. **Or,**
- If such travel is deemed in the national interest because of diplomatic or public relations benefit to the United States. Representatives of foreign governments must also be attending the event.

B. Spouses traveling at government expense will be in the company of their sponsors

Spouses may only travel unaccompanied when such travel is justified due to unusual circumstances. Under these circumstances, the spouse must travel in the most cost-effective manner, which may include travel on a previously scheduled military or civilian aircraft. Unusual circumstances may include, but are not limited to:

- Unplanned or unanticipated schedule changes or compelling requirements of the DoD sponsor (e.g. deployment), or
- The sponsor will be attending the unquestionably official event, and due to other official business requirements, it is more economical for the sponsor to meet the spouse at the destination point and/or depart directly from the destination point for additional official business while the spouse returns home.

4. APPROVAL AUTHORITIES

Each occurrence of spouse travel is approved on a case-by-case basis. Blanket travel orders for spouses are not permitted. All requests will be reviewed by the servicing legal counsel prior to submission for approval through the normal chain of command. Each request will include the following supporting documentation, and will be retained by the requesting organization for two years:

- Request signed by the sponsor;
- Name, grade, and position/title of the sponsor;
- Purpose of the spouse's travel;
- Travel date and destination;
- Type of conveyance, to include cost if commercial flight;
- Agenda or itinerary for spouse that indicates either actual participation or a diplomatic benefit to the United States.

5. OTHER SPOUSE TRAVEL

Travel by spouses is usually accomplished in an "accompanying" status as provided above. However, spouses may also travel independent of their sponsors when travel is authorized IAW the JTR/JFTR (other than Appendix E). When traveling pursuant to an independent basis, spouses are authorized per diem. For example, travel and per diem for spouses is authorized when:

- The spouse will attend a service-oriented training course or briefing and provide subsequent volunteer service incident to such training, (e.g., Pre-Command Course, anti-terrorist training course) as specified by HQDA.
- The spouse will confer with DoD officials on DoD matters as a subject matter expert. Under this authority, the spouse may be issued invitational travel orders through normal procedures without obtaining special approval for spousal travel. It is generally DA policy, however, that spouses traveling to participate in discussions on Army Family Programs and/or Quality of Life issues shall travel in an accompanying spouse status (per diem not authorized), unless travel is for an excepted program listed in the following paragraph.

When the spouse or other qualified individual has been selected to serve as a member of the delegation to an official conference concerning Army Family Programs or Quality of Life issues, then the activity that is sponsoring the conference may authorize the sending command to issue an ITO (per diem authorized) for that spouse's travel. In order to qualify for this exception, the activity that is sponsoring the conference must be commanded by an official in the rank of Major General (or civilian equivalent) or above. The conference must also have a substantive agenda and require full-time participation of the spouse. In no case, however, will the spouse of a Soldier or DA employee be entitled to separate reimbursement for lodging if the Soldier or employee is on TDY to the same conference, is concurrently on TDY in the same commuting area of the conference, or resides within commuting distance to the conference site.

- The Yellow Ribbon Program has been determined to be a mission of the Army Reserve. Spouses can travel at government expense to Army Reserve Yellow Ribbon Events.

6. MOTOR VEHICLE TRANSPORTATION

Spouses of DA officials may be authorized transportation in government vehicles only when accompanying their DA sponsor, the use of the vehicle has already been authorized to accomplish official business, and there is **space available**. Such transportation must be provided at no additional cost to the government, and the spouse's presence may not require a larger vehicle than that already authorized.

THIS PAGE IS INTENTIONALLY BLANK

Chapter 26

ANNUAL FILING OF FINANCIAL DISCLOSURE FORMS

1. REFERENCES

- DoD Regulation 5500.7-R (Joint Ethics Regulation)
- Website: www.fdm.army.mil

2. CONFIDENTIAL FINANCIAL DISCLOSURE – OGE FORM 450

A. Purpose of Filing

OGE Form 450s are filed in order to ensure DoD employees do not engage in official financial transactions or decision-making in which, due to their private interests, they may have a conflict of interest.

B. Who Must File

Personnel in "covered positions" including:

- All Army installation commanders, unless they are an OGE 278 filer.

- Special Government Employees (SGE) defined at 18 U.S.C. § 202(a), generally defined as employees performing temporary duty for 130 days or less in any 365 day period. Consult with an ethics counselor to determine whether an SGE, including a Reserve or National Guard members, are required to file.

- Civilian employees at grade GS-15 and below, and military personnel below grade O-7, when they participate personally and substantially in taking official action for:

    - Contracting or procurement
    - Administering or monitoring grants, subsidies, licenses, or other Federal benefits
    - Activities in which the final decision may have a direct and substantial economic impact on the interests of a non-federal entity.
    - Regulation or auditing of non-federal entities.
    - Administering or monitoring grants, subsidies, licenses, or other federal benefits.

C. Who is Excluded from Filing

Personnel not employed in contracting or procurement, who have authority to make purchases of less than $2,500 per purchase, and less than $20,000 cumulatively per year. Pursuant to a memorandum signed by the Secretary of the Army on 11 October 2001, the following personnel are presumptively excluded from filing:

- Officers in the grade of O-3 and below, enlisted Soldiers in the grade of E-6 and below, and civilians in the grade of GS-6 and below. Warrant officers are not included in this category. These exclusions do not extend to officers in the Acquisition Corps.

- Government purchase card holders with authority up to the simplified acquisition threshold, currently $150,000.

- None of these exclusions preclude supervisors from requiring subordinates to file the form when, in the supervisor's judgment, the subordinate has duties involving the exercise of significant independent judgment over matters that will have a substantial impact on the integrity of Army operations and relationships with non-Federal parties. Further, these exclusions do not apply to individuals who hold contracting warrants, or otherwise fall within categories defined in the Code of Federal Regulations or the Joint Ethics Regulation. Commanders are advised to consult with an ethics counselor before granting an exclusion.

In addition, personnel excluded by the head of an agency because:

- The possibility that the employee will be involved in a real or apparent conflict of interest is remote.
- The effect on the integrity of the federal government is inconsequential.
- There is a substantial degree of supervision and review.

D. When Must One File?

The OGE 450s are due by February 15 of each year. Personnel who move into a "covered" position must file a new entrant report within 30 days of doing so. If that person filed an annual OGE 450 as part of their previous duty position, a new entrant report is not required.

3. PUBLIC FINANCIAL DISCLOSURE – OGE 278

A. Purpose of Filing

To report the personal financial holdings of DoD employees holding certain status.

B. Who Must File

Military personnel in the grade of O-7 or higher. Army Reserve General Officers are required to initially file upon reaching 60 active duty days in a calendar year.

C. Filing and Reporting Requirements

- Transactions only for calendar year reported.
- Assets with fair market value of more than $1,000.
- Mutual Funds and IRAs.
- Employment by or ownership of a business.
- Assets gained or lost from one year to the next.
- Underlying assets of an investment or broker's account.

D. When Must One File?

The OGE 278 is due by 15 May of each year. If it is more than 30 days overdue, a $200 fine is assessed to the filer.

4. FINANCIAL DISCLOSURE ONLINE

All financial disclosure statements, both OGE 450 and OGE 278, are now filed online at **www.fdm.army.mil.**

ADMINISTRATIVE LAW & PERSONNEL ACTIONS

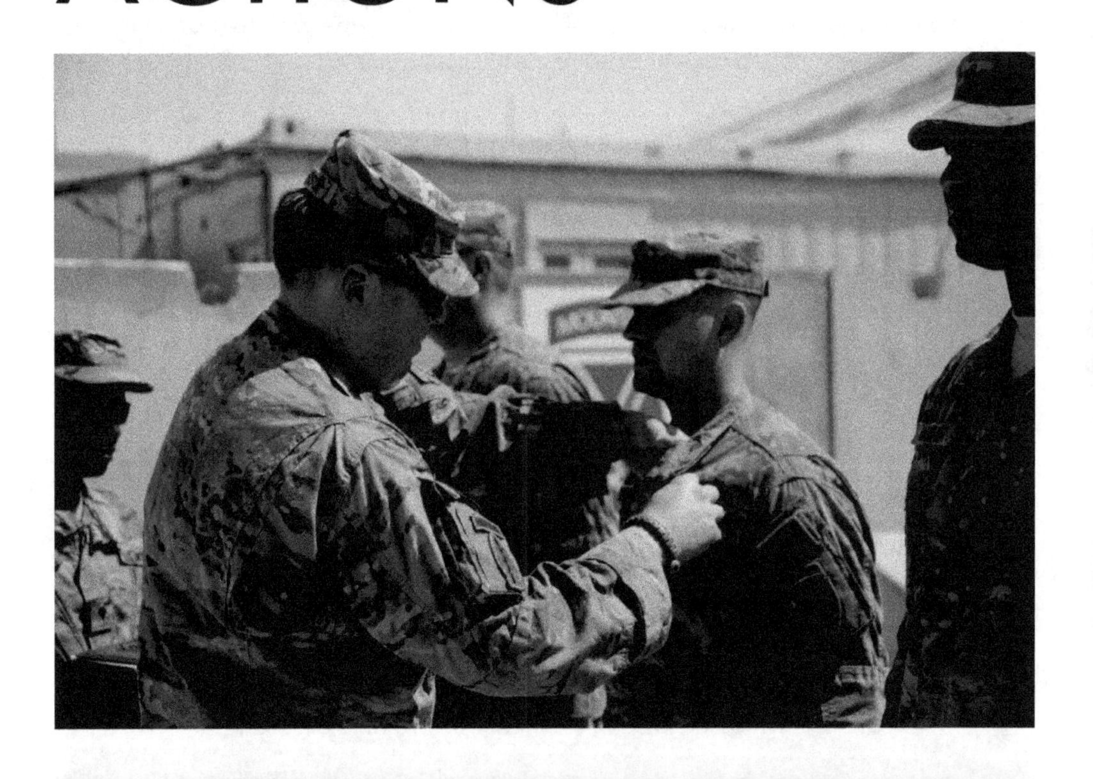

Section 4

THIS PAGE IS INTENTIONALLY BLANK

Chapter 27

"FLAGGING" SOLDIERS FROM POSITIVE PERSONNEL ACTIONS

1. REFERENCES

- AR 600-8-2, Suspension of Favorable Personnel Actions (FLAGS), 23 December 2004
- ALARACT 386/2011, Suspension of Favorable Personnel Actions (FLAGS), 191831Z Oct 11

2. FLAG MANAGEMENT ISSUE

Command teams are challenged with flag management. Poor flag management is detrimental to the Army's morale and negatively impacts our collective ability to manage the force by making timely and informed decisions. ALARACT 386/2011 191831Z OCT 11, paragraphs 2c and 8.

3. FLAG POLICY

A. Initiate Immediately

Do not take a "wait and see" approach before imposing flags. A flag will be initiated immediately when a Soldier's status changes from favorable to unfavorable. ALARACT 386/2011 191831Z OCT 11, paragraphs 2b; AR 600-8-2, paragraph 1-10a.

B. Flag Mandatory

Suspension of favorable personnel actions is mandatory if an investigation (formal or informal) is initiated on a Soldier by military or civilian authorities. Regardless of the reason for an arrest by civilian authorities, an arrested Soldier must be immediately flagged. AR 600-8-2, paragraphs 1-11, 1-12a(1).

C. Effective Date

The effective date of the flag will be the date of the incident triggering the investigation or arrest, not the date the command became aware of the incident or arrest. AR 600-8-2, paragraph 2-1c.

D. Removal of Flag

A flag based on an arrest, investigation, court-martial, or Article 15 will not be removed until the Soldier is released without charges, the charges are dropped, or the punishment (confinement, probation, restriction, extra duty, etc.) or adverse action is completed (including any term of suspension). A flag for a Soldier on a HQDA promotion list can only be removed by HQDA. AR 600-8-2, paragraph 1-12a.

THIS PAGE IS INTENTIONALLY BLANK

Chapter 28

ENLISTED SEPARATIONS

1. REFERENCES

- Department of Defense Directive (DoDD) 1332.14, Enlisted Administrative Separations
- Department of Defense Instruction (DoDI) 1332.29, Eligibility of Regular and Reserve Personnel for Separation Pay
- Army Regulation (AR) 15-6, Procedures for Investigating Officers and Boards of Officers
- AR 135-178, Enlisted Administrative Separations [USAR]
- AR 600-8-2, Suspension of Favorable Personnel Actions (FLAGS)
- AR 600-9, The Army Weight Control Program
- AR 600-20, Army Command Policy
- AR 600-85, Army Substance Abuse Program (ASAP)
- AR 601-280, Army Retention Program
- AR 635-200, Active Duty Enlisted Administrative Separations
- National Guard Regulation (NGR) 600-200, Enlisted Personnel Management
- U.S. Army Reserve Command Memorandum, Delegation of Involuntary Separation Authority Under AR 135-178, dtd 14 October 2008

2. INTRODUCTION

The topic of enlisted administrative separations covers both *favorable* and *unfavorable* separations. Examples of favorable separations include retirement and honorable discharge separations at the expiration of a Soldier's service obligation. Examples of unfavorable separations include separation based on misconduct and unsatisfactory performance. Additionally, enlisted administrative separations are either *involuntary* (initiated by the chain-of-command) or *voluntary* (initiated by the Soldier). This outline does not contain all bases for administrative separation, but attempts to identify the most common separation actions encountered by Commanders, including unique issues when the separation involves Reserve Component Soldiers.

When analyzing enlisted administrative separations, consider:

A. What is the reason for the separation action (e.g., overweight, misconduct)? Is the separation voluntary or involuntary?

The various bases for enlisted administrative separations are generally found in AR 635-200, AR 135-178 for Reserve Component (RC) personnel, and NGR 600-200 for Army National Guard (ARNG) personnel under different chapter headings (e.g., Chap. 14, AR 635, 200 covers misconduct separations for AC Soldiers). Hence, separation actions are often called "chapters."

B. *Who has the authority* to order (i.e., direct or approve) the separation?

Only certain commanders can direct or approve separations.

C. What kind of discharge can the Soldier receive?

There are different types of administrative discharges, and often the type of discharge a Soldier can receive is contingent upon the reason for separation and the authority approving the separation. Characterizations may affect benefits eligibility and can carry a social judgment. Consequently, the contemplated characterization of service may dictate whether the Soldier is entitled to an administrative separation board.

D. What procedural steps are required to separate the Soldier?

Various factors (e.g., the reason for the separation, the number of years the Soldier has in the Army, and the type of discharge) determine the procedural requirements for the separation action.

3. THE AUTHORITY TO ORDER SEPARATIONS

NOTE: Citations without reference to a regulation will be to AR 635-200.

A. Secretary of the Army (SA)

Virtually unlimited authority to separate a Soldier.

B. General Court-Martial Convening Authority (GCMCA)

May approve all separations, except: SA plenary authority cases (para. 5-3); reduction in force (RIF), strength limitations, and budgetary constraints (para. 16-7); Qualitative Management Program (QMP) (Ch. 19); voluntary separations of Soldiers serving indefinite enlistments (para. 4-4); conviction by a foreign court (paras. 1-41a and d, and 14-9a), and early release from active duty (AD) of RC personnel serving Active Guard Reserve (AGR) tours under Title 10 (para. 5-15).

C. General officer (GO) in command with a legal advisor

Same separation authority as a GCMCA *except* lack of jurisdiction (para. 5-9) and discharge in lieu of court-martial (Ch. 10).

The USARC CG has delegated authority to take final action on enlisted separations to USARC General Officer Commands with full-time Judge Advocate support available via a policy memo published 14 October 2008. This authority only extends to Troop Program Unit (TPU) Soldiers and the USARC CG has still retained authority to take final action on Soldiers with more than 18, but less than 20 years of qualifying service for retired pay. This authority includes directing retention, suspending the discharge, or forwarding the case to HQDA for approval. (See below).

D. Special Court-Martial Convening Authority (SPCMCA)

A SPCMCA may not convene an administrative separation board contemplating an under other than honorable conditions (OTH) discharge or approve such a discharge, but may take other action under the following chapters:

- Ch. 5, Convenience of the Government (except para. 5-9, Lack of Jurisdiction);
- Ch. 6, Dependency or Hardship;
- Ch. 7, Defective Enlistments, Reenlistments, and Extensions;
- Ch. 8, Pregnancy;
- Ch. 9, Alcohol or Other Drug Abuse Rehabilitation Failure;

- Ch. 10, Discharge in Lieu of Court-Martial (if delegated for Absent Without Leave (AWOL) reasons at an installation with a personnel confinement facility (PCF), and may only approve before trial, but may never disapprove);
- Ch. 11, Entry Level Performance and Conduct;
- Ch. 12, Retirement;
- Ch. 13, Unsatisfactory Performance;
- Ch. 14, Misconduct;
- Ch. 16, Selected Changes in Service Obligations, and
- Ch. 18, Failure to Meet Body Fat Standards.

E. Lieutenant Colonel (LTC)-level commander with a legal advisor (includes MAJ(P) assigned to LTC position, but does not include MAJ or MAJ(P) acting commander)

A LTC-level commander may not take action on an OTH discharge. A LTC-level commander may take action with regard to the following chapters:

- Separation of Personnel Who Did Not Meet Procurement Medical Fitness Standards (para. 5-11);
- Separation of Enlisted Women-Pregnancy (Ch. 8);
- Alcohol or Other Drug Abuse Rehabilitation Failure (Ch. 9);
- Entry Level Performance and Conduct (Ch. 11);
- Separation for Unsatisfactory Performance (Ch. 13);
- Selected Changes in Service Obligations (paras. 16-4 through 16-10), and
- Failure to Meet Body Fat Standards (Ch. 18).

F. Commander, Human Resources Command

May order the separation of enlisted Soldiers serving in an Individual Mobilization Augmentee (IMA), Individual Ready Reserve (IRR), Standby Reserve, or Ready Reserve status.

G. Headquarters, Department of the Army (HQDA)

Only HQDA may involuntarily discharge a Soldier with 18 or more years of active federal service. Only the Secretary or his designee may order the involuntary separation a USAR Soldier with more than 18, but fewer than 20 years of qualifying service for retired pay.

H. Separation Authority's Determinations

In making their decision, the separation authority must consider:

- Is there sufficient evidence? Government's burden, not the Soldier (or "respondent"). Preponderance (a greater weight of evidence than that which supports a contrary conclusion) of evidence standard.
- Retain or separate?
- If separation, what characterization of service?

I. Waivers of Boards

A Soldier entitled to an Administrative Board may submit a conditional waiver to a hearing by a board after a reasonable opportunity to consult with counsel. The conditional waiver is a memorandum submitted by a Soldier waiving the right to a hearing by a board on the condition characterization of service on separation will be higher than the least favorable characterization or description of service authorized for the basis of the separation reason listed in the notification memorandum. The separation authority will be the same as if the Soldier had not submitted the conditional waiver.

Under a circumstance where a Soldier offers to waive the right to a board hearing authorized to recommend an OTH discharge in exchange for a more favorable discharge, the separation authority remains the GCMCA or GO in command with a legal advisor (despite a SPCMCA or LTC-level commander's authorization to approve a discharge under the relevant chapter).

When the Soldier waives her right to separation board, the separation will be process under the Notification Procedure discussed above.

A SPCMCA or lower authority may not approve a waiver or discharge in a case where the chain of command initiated or recommended an OTH, or in a case where a board is appointed to consider a separation with a possible OTH discharge.

4. CHARACTERIZATION OF SERVICE OR TYPE OF DISCHARGE

> *Characterization of service will be based on the quality of the [S]oldier's service, including the reason for separation . . . subject to the limitation under the various reasons for separation. The quality of service will be determined according to standards of acceptable personal conduct and performance of duty for military personnel. These standards are found in the UCMJ, directives and regulations issued by the Army, and the time-honored customs and traditions of military service.*
>
> -- AR 635-200, para. 3-5a, AR 135-78, para. 2-8a.

A. Honorable Discharge

- "[A]ppropriate when the quality of the Soldier's service generally has met the standards of acceptable conduct and performance of duty for Army personnel . . . ." AR 635-200, para. 3-7a.; AR 135-178, para. 2-9a.
- Look at the pattern of behavior, not isolated incidents.
- Soldier receives DD Form 256A, Honorable Discharge Certificate.
- Usually required if the Government introduces limited use information from the Army Substance Abuse Program (ASAP) during discharge proceedings.

B. General Discharge (Under Honorable Conditions)

- AC: "[I]ssued to a Soldier whose military record is satisfactory but not sufficiently meritorious to warrant an honorable discharge." AR 635-200, para. 3-7b(1).
- USAR: "If a Soldier's service has been honest and faithful, it is appropriate to characterize that service as under honorable conditions. Characterization of service as general (under honorable conditions) is warranted when significant negative aspects of the Soldier's conduct or performance of duty outweigh positive aspects of the Soldier's military record." AR 135-178, para 2-9b.

- Only permitted if the reasons for separation (chapter) specifically authorize, and not permitted for expiration of term of service (ETS).
- Soldier receives DD Form 257A, General Discharge Certificate.
- Impact on benefits.
  - No civil service retirement credit for time spent on active duty.
  - No education benefits. Money paid in to Montgomery GI Bill is forfeited (subject to vesting of the benefit due to previous honorable discharge).
  - Many states will not pay unemployment compensation.
  - "I understand that I may expect to encounter substantial prejudice in civilian life." This statement is generally included in separation counseling to inform the Soldier that there may be negative impacts resulting from a general discharge.
- No automatic upgrading of discharges. Upgrading requires application to the Army Board for Correction of Military Records (ABCMR) or the Army Discharge Review Board (ADRB).

C. Under Other Than Honorable (OTH) Conditions Discharge

- Authorized under certain chapters for a pattern of behavior, or one or more acts or omissions, "that constitutes a significant departure from the conduct expected of [S]oldiers." AR 635-200, para. 3-7c(1); AR 135-178, para. 2-9c..
- Board hearing is generally required, unless waived by the Soldier or the separation is voluntary (i.e., Ch. 10).
- No discharge certificate issued (but Soldier still receives DD Form 214 with characterization of service annotated).
- The Soldier must indicate that "I . . . understand . . . I may be ineligible for many or all benefits as a veteran under both Federal and State laws and . . . I may expect to encounter substantial prejudice in civilian life."
- When approved by a separation authority, automatically reduces an enlisted Soldier to Private, E-1, by operation of law.
- No automatic upgrading of discharges; upgrading requires application to the ABCMR or the ADRB.

D. Entry Level Status (ELS) (Uncharacterized) Separation

- For "unsatisfactory performance and/or conduct while in entry-level status" (first 180 days of creditable service, or first 180 days of creditable service after a break in service of over 92 days for active duty (AD) Soldiers). See AR 635-200, Glossary, Section II.
- Service will be described as uncharacterized if separation processing is initiated while a Soldier is in an entry level status.
- "Entry level status" for a USAR Soldier generally terminates 180 days after beginning training if the Soldier is ordered to ADT for one continuous period of 180 days or more, or 90 days after the beginning of the second period of ADT if the Soldier is ordered to ADT under a program that splits the training into two or more separate periods of active duty.
- Counseling and rehabilitation essential before separation.
- Not a per se bar to veteran's benefits, but has the effect of disqualifying the Soldier for most federal benefits, since most require service of over 180 days to qualify.

E. Order of Release from Custody and Control of the Army

- Usually no characterization of service, because the person never acquired military status. There is an exception for constructive enlistment.
- Very rare, used only for void enlistments.
- Since no "service," no veteran's benefits.

F. Punitive Discharges

Dishonorable and Bad Conduct discharges may only result from an approved court-martial sentence, not an administrative separation. A common mistake by leaders conducting counseling for misconduct or unsatisfactory performance is the threat of a punitive discharge if the behavior continues. Such counseling is ineffective and fails to meet counseling requirements under AR 135-178; your Judge Advocate or paralegal NCO can provide a template for counseling that includes the lawful characterizations of service a Soldier could receive for various misconduct or unsatisfactory performance.

5. PROCEDURAL REQUIREMENTS AND ADMINISTRATIVE CONSIDERATIONS

A. Counseling

Counseling and rehabilitative transfer requirements apply to many separations. Commanders must make reasonable efforts to identify Soldiers who may be candidates for separation as early as possible, on order to improve their chances for retention.

1) Counseling is always required for

- Involuntary separation due to parenthood
- Other designated physical or mental conditions, para. 6-7 (if separation considered for a Personality Disorder, DoD policy also requires counseling the Soldier that diagnosis of a personality disorder does not qualify as a disability)
- Entry level performance and conduct
- Unsatisfactory performance
- Minor disciplinary infractions or a pattern of misconduct
- Failure to meet Army body composition standards

2) Rehabilitative transfer is generally required for separations under Chaps. 11, 13, 14-12a, and 14-12b.

Recycle trainees between companies or platoons at least once. Recycle Soldiers between battalion-sized units or larger at least once, with at least 3 months at each unit. Permanent Change of Station (PCS) is only for "meritorious cases" where the Soldier is a "distinct asset" to the Army. Waiver is authorized if transfer would serve no useful purpose, would not produce a quality Soldier, or is not in the best interest of the Army.

USAR Soldiers may also be reassigned at least once if within commuting distance, with a minimum of two months at each USAR unit. If no unit within commuting distance, commanders should conduct other rehabilitative measures such as retraining or reassignment of duties. The separation authority may waive the rehabilitation requirement based on the facts of the case. A transfer to another unit, for example, could simply invite more serious misconduct or affect the readiness of the Soldier's new unit.

B. Medical Examination

Commanders will ensure that Soldiers initiated for separation under this regulation who are required to obtain a physical examination per 10 U.S.C. 1145 obtain such. Physical examinations and mental health evaluations will comply with AR 40-501and other policy guidance issued by the Surgeon General and U.S. Army Medical Command. In addition to medical examinations, mental status evaluations conducted by a psychologist, or master-level, licensed clinical social worker, are required for Soldiers being processed for separation under chapters 13 or 14.

C. Written Notification

The Commander notifies the Soldier in writing that separation is recommended. The Soldier must sign acknowledgment of receipt. Notice will include: Specific allegations and provisions of regulation that authorize separation; Least favorable characterization of service Soldier could receive; Right to consult with counsel; Right to submit statements; Right to obtain copies of all matters going to separation authority, and Right to a hearing if Soldier has 6 years or more of combined active and reserve service on date separation is initiated.

D. Soldier may consult with counsel

They may also submit matters within 7 duty days (or request an extension justified with good cause). For USAR Soldiers, must consult with counsel and submit matters within the deadline set which must be no fewer than 30 calendar days from the date of notice. USAR Soldiers may also request an extension for good cause.

E. Action forwarded through command channels to separation authority for final action.

F. Legal review

No requirement for legal review unless ASAP limited use evidence (typically, Ch. 9, and possibly some Chaps. 13 and 14) involved. As a practical matter, most Staff Judge Advocate (SJA) offices try to do a legal review twice: before the packet is presented to the Soldier, and before final action goes to the separation authority.

6. NOTIFICATION PROCEDURE

A. Notification procedure alone may be used when

- Soldier has less than 6 years of combined active and reserve service on date separation is initiated;
- Command does not seek to impose an OTH discharge.

B. The Regulation *permits* Notification Procedure for

- Some provisions of Ch. 5
- Convenience of the Government. Ch. 7
- Defective Enlistments/Reenlistments and Extensions. Ch. 9
- Alcohol or Other Drug Abuse Rehabilitation Failure. Ch. 11
- Entry Level Performance and Conduct. Ch. 13
- Unsatisfactory Performance. Ch. 14, Misconduct, but only when service should be characterized as General. Ch. 18, Failure to Meet Body Fat Standards.

7. BOARD HEARING CASES

Used if required by the governing chapter of the regulation, if the Soldier elects a board and has 6 or more years of total active and reserve military service, or if the command is contemplating discharge with an Other Than Honorable Discharge.

The Board must be composed of at least three commissioned, warrant, or noncommissioned officers; at least one of the voting commissioned officers must be a Reserve officer if the Soldier being separated is in the Reserve Component. Enlisted members of the board must be sergeants first class or above and senior in grade (per DoD policy) to the respondent. At least one member of the board must be a Major or above, and all members of the board must be commissioned officers if an Under Other Than Honorable Conditions characterization of service is authorized for the basis of separation.

The board is conducted under the provisions of AR 15-6, with the government and respondent presenting evidence, witnesses, and arguments to the board for deliberation. A verbatim record of findings and recommendations is made, as is a summary of the proceedings and testimony for the separation authority's review.

The respondent's rights include testifying on their own behalf to the board, submission of a written or recorded matter, obtaining military counsel to represent them at the board, questioning witnesses at the board and personal appearance at the board. Failure to invoke these rights, including failure to appear at the board, does not bar the board from meeting and making findings and recommendations.

The board must make a finding as to each allegation mentioned in the notification of separation, as well as a recommendation to either retain or separate the Soldier. If separation is directed, the board must recommend a characterization of service. Finally, the board may also recommend suspension of the separation for a period not to exceed 12 months.

SEPARATION ACTIONS

	SECRETARIAL AUTHORITY	PARENTHOOD	PHYSICAL OR MENTAL CONDITIONS	PERSONALITY DISORDER	FAILURE TO MEET BODY FAT STANDARDS
Grounds for action.	Best interest of the Army; may apply to reason not covered by other, more specific provision.	Parental obligations interfere with military responsibilities; e.g., repeated absenteeism, late for work, unavailable for field exercises, CQ, SDO, world-wide deployment or assignment.	Conditions that potentially interfere with assignment or duty, but not disability or paras. 5-11 or 5-13 conditions. Diagnosed by psychiatrist or licensed clinical psychologist w/ PhD.	Long term, deeply ingrained, maladaptive pattern of behavior that interferes with duty performance, diagnosed by psychiatrist or licensed clinical psychologist.	Failure to meet body fat standards in AR 600-9. Overweight condition must be only basis for discharge.
Counseling and rehab required?	No.	Yes.	Yes.	Yes.	Comply w/ AR 600-9.
Who initiates?	Soldier or any commander, including separation authority if board recommends retention.	Immediate or any higher commander.			
Board hearing?	No. If command initiated, use notification procedure only, even if Soldier has more than 6 years service.	Use notification procedure. Entitled to board if Soldier has 6 or more years of active and reserve service.			
Regulation.	AR 635-200, para. 5-3.	AR 635-200, para. 5-8.	AR 635-200, para. 5-17	AR 635-200, para. 5-13.	AR 635-200, para. 18.
SJA Review?	Maybe. See AR 635-200, paras. 2-6a & e(4)(c).				
Separation Authority.	Secretary of the Army.	SPCMCA.	SPCMCA or GCMCA if Soldier has been in imminent danger pay area.	SPCMCA or GCMCA if Soldier has been in imminent danger pay area.	LTC cdr (or MAJ(P) in LTC cmd) if no board; SPCMCA if board used.
Characterization of service.	Hon, Gen, or ELS.	Hon, Gen, or ELS.	Hon, Gen, or ELS. See para. 5-1.	Hon, Gen, or ELS. See para. 5-13h for Gen.	Hon or ELS.

	Release for Minority (16 or younger)	Release for Minority (17 Years Old)	Erroneous Enlistment	Defective or Unfulfilled Enlistment	Fraudulent Entry
Grounds for action.	Enlisted when under age 17 and still under age 17.	Enlisted under age 18 w/o parental consent, and still under 18, not facing court-martial (CM) charges, serving CM sentence, or in military confinement.	Enlistment would not have occurred had government known the relevant facts or had appropriate directives been followed.	Eligible for enlistment but not option for which enlisted; or received promise that Army can't fulfill. Soldier must identify w/in 30 days of discovery.	Material misrepresen-tation, omission, or concealment of information that if known by Army might have resulted in rejection.
Counseling and rehab required?	No.	No.	No.	No.	No.
Who initiates?	Immediate or higher commander.	Parents w/in 90 days of enlistment.	Immediate or higher commander.	Immediate or higher commander.	Immediate or higher commander.
Board hearing?	No.	No.	Use notification procedure. Entitled to board if Soldier has 6 or more years of active and reserve service.	No.	Yes, but may be waived. No board if OTH not warranted and Soldier has less than 6 years service.
Regulation.	AR 635-200, Ch. 7, Sec. II.	AR 635-200, Ch. 7, Sec. II.	AR 635-200, Ch. 7, Sec. III.	AR 635-200, Ch. 7, Sec. III.	AR 635-200, Ch. 7, Sec. IV.
Entitled to counsel?	Counsel for consultation.	Counsel for consultation.	Counsel for consultation. Counsel for representation if board.	Counsel for consultation (possibly legal assistance).	Counsel for consultation. Counsel for representation if board.
SJA Review?	No.	No.	Maybe. See AR 635-200, paras. 2-6a & e(4)(c).	No.	Maybe. See AR 635-200, paras. 2-6a & e(4)(c).
Separation Authority.	SPCMCA.	SPCMCA.	SPCMCA.	SPCMCA.	OTH: GCMCA If OTH not warranted and notification procedure used: SPCMCA.
Characterization of service.	Release from custody & control of the Army.	ELS.	Hon, ELS, or Release from C&C of Army.	Hon or ELS.	Hon, Gen, OTH, or ELS.

	ALCOHOL OR DRUG ABUSE REHABILITATION FAILURE	IN LIEU OF TRIAL BY COURT-MARTIAL	ENTRY LEVEL PERFORMANCE AND CONDUCT	UNSATISFACTORY PERFORMANCE
Grounds for action.	Soldier enrolled in ASAP and (1) lacks potential for service and rehab is not practical or 2) long-term civilian rehab required.	Preferral of charges for which punitive discharge authorized OR referral to court-martial authorized a punitive-discharge UP RCM 1003(d).	Unsat performance or minor disciplinary infractions in first 180 days of service. Inability, lack of effort, failure to adapt, or pregnancy which prevents MOS training.	Unsatisfactory duty performance.
Counseling and rehab required?	No.	No.	Yes.	Yes.
Who initiates?	Immediate or any higher commander.	Soldier.	Immediate or any higher commander.	Immediate or any higher commander.
Board hearing?	Use notification procedure. Entitled to board if Soldier has more than 6 years active and reserve service.	No.	Use notification procedure.	Use notification procedure. Entitled to board if Soldier has more than 6 years active and reserve service.
Regulation	AR 635-200, Ch. 9.	AR 635-200, Ch. 10.	AR 635-200, Ch. 11.	AR 635-200, Ch. 13.
Entitled to counsel?	Counsel for consultation. Counsel for representation if board used.	Counsel for consultation (performed by trial defense counsel).	Counsel for consultation.	Counsel for consultation. Counsel for representation if board used.
SJA Review?	Maybe. See AR 635-200, paras. 2-6a & e(4)(c).	Yes.	Maybe. See AR 635-200, paras. 2-6a & e(4)(c).	
Separation Authority	No board: LTC Cdr or MAJ(P) in LTC cmd. Board: SPCMCA.	GCMCA in most cases	No board: LTC Cdr or MAJ(P) in LTC cmd.	No board: LTC Cdr or MAJ(P) in LTC cmd. Board: SPCMCA.
Characterization of service	Hon, Gen, or ELS. Hon required in Limited Use Evidence used.	Normally OTH. Hon, Gen possible.	ELS.	Hon, Gen.

	Conviction by Civilian Court	Minor (Military) Disciplinary Infractions	Pattern of Misconduct	Commission of a Serious Offense
Grounds for action.	Civilian conviction for offense that authorizes punitive discharge under UCMJ, or any civilian sentence to confinement for more than 6 months.	Pattern of misconduct consisting solely of minor military disciplinary infractions.	Discreditable involvement with civil **or** military authorities, or conduct prejudicial to good order and discipline.	Commission of any offense (military or civilian) for which punitive discharge authorized under UCMJ.
Counseling and rehab required?	No.	Yes.	Yes.	No.
Who initiates?	Immediate or any higher commander.	Immediate or any higher commander.	Immediate or any higher commander.	Immediate or any higher commander.
Board hearing?	Yes. May be waived. No appearance if in confinement. No board if OTH not warranted and Soldier has less than 6 years service.	Yes. May be waived. No board if OTH not warranted and Soldier has less than 6 years active and reserve service.	Yes. May be waived. No board if OTH not warranted and Soldier has less than 6 years active and reserve service.	Yes. May be waived. No board if OTH not warranted and Soldier has less than 6 years active and reserve service.
Regulation.	AR 635-200, para. 14-5.	AR 635-200, para. 14-12a.	AR 635-200, para. 14-12b.	AR 635-200, para. 14-12c.
Entitled to counsel?	Counsel for consultation. Counsel for representation if board used.	Counsel for consultation. Counsel for representation if board used.	Counsel for consultation. Counsel for representation if board used.	Counsel for consultation. Counsel for representation if board used.
SJA Review?	Maybe. *See* AR 635-200, paras. 2-6a & e(4)(c).			
Separation Authority.	OTH: GCMCA If OTH not warranted and notification procedure used: SPCMCA.	OTH: GCMCA If OTH not warranted and notification procedure used: SPCMCA.	OTH: GCMCA If OTH not warranted and notification procedure used: SPCMCA.	OTH: GCMCA If OTH not warranted and notification procedure used: SPCMCA.
Characterization of service.	Hon, Gen, OTH, or ELS.	Hon, Gen, OTH, or ELS.	Hon, Gen, OTH, or ELS.	Hon, Gen, OTH, or ELS.

Chapter 29

OFFICER SEPARATIONS

1. REFERENCES

- AR 600-8-24, Officer Transfers and Discharges, dtd RAR 19 November 2008
- Secretary of the Army Directive Type Memorandum, Involuntary Separation of Reserve Component Officers for Final Denial or Revocation of Secret Security Clearance or Failure to Apply for a Security Clearance, dtd 29 August 2011
- AR 135-175, Separation of Officers, dtd RAR 27 April 2010

2. OVERVIEW

Numerous conditions may justify the initiation of an elimination action against an officer. Elimination of "probationary" officers may be expeditious, while "non-probationary" officers are afforded more due process prior to final action. Troop Program Unit (TPU) and Individual Mobilization Augmentee (IMA) officers are separated UP AR 135-175. Active Guard Reserve (AGR) officers must be separated under the provisions of AR 600-8-24, the same regulation applicable to Active Army (AA) officers.

3. REASONS FOR ELIMINATION

Officers may be eliminated for, among other reasons, substandard performance of duty, misconduct, or the existence of adverse or derogatory information in their official records. AR 600-8-24, para 4-2 (AR 135-175, paras. 2-10 thru 2-13 for USAR Officers), contains a list of specific, but nonexclusive, reasons that may lead to elimination. Moreover, probationary officers may be eliminated for additional reasons, as set forth in paragraph V. below.

A. Substandard Performance of Duty

Officers discharged exclusively for one of the following or similar conditions will be issued an Honorable Discharge Certificate. Given that the characterization of service is limited under this paragraph to the most favorable certificate given to officers leaving the service, commanders should carefully consider the reasons for separation cited in the officer's notification memorandum. If evidence of misconduct or professional dereliction exists, consider separation under that basis.

- Downward trend in overall performance resulting in an unacceptable record of efficiency or a consistent record of mediocre service indicating the officer has reached the peak of his potential.
- Failure to keep pace or to progress with contemporaries, such as successive promotion failure or a low record of efficiency when compared with other officers of the same grade, branch, and length or service.
- Failure to exercise necessary leadership or command required of an officer of his grade.
- Failure to perform with the technical proficiency required by the grade held.
- Failure to meet standards in a course of instruction at a service school due to academic or leadership deficiencies.

- Failure to properly discharge assignments commensurate with his grade and experience.
- Apathy, defective attitudes, or other character disorders, including inability or unwillingness to expend effort.
- Failure of a dual component member to be recommended for promotion in enlisted status, or to be selected for retention under the Active component enlisted Qualitative Retention Program.
- Failure to achieve satisfactory progress after participation in a medically established weight control program (see AR 600–9).

B. Moral or Professional Dereliction

Officers discharged for one of the following or similar conditions may be issued an Honorable, General (Under Honorable Conditions), or Other Than Honorable Discharge Certificate. For USAR Officers, the most frequently cited reason for officer elimination is failure to satisfactorily participate in required Ready Reserve training. This basis is included as a reason for elimination in this category.

- Discreditable, intentional failure to meet personal financial obligations.
- Mismanagement of personal affairs to the discredit of the service.
- Mismanagement of personal affairs detrimentally affecting the performance of duty of the officer concerned.
- Intentional omission or misstatement of facts in official statements or records for the purpose of misrepresentation.
- Acts of personal misconduct (including, but not limited to, acts committed while in a drunken or drug-intoxicated state).
- Intentional neglect or failure to—
  - Perform assigned duties.
  - Participate satisfactorily in required Ready Reserve training (AR 135–91, chap 6).
  - Comply with applicable directives to include but not be limited to—
    - Furnishing a current address of record. (The officer cannot be located through the address furnished.)
    - Maintaining a permanent residence, for mailing purposes, in the United States or its territories while traveling or residing in a foreign country other than one within the jurisdiction of an oversea commander (AR 140–1).
  - Having the medical examination required by AR 40–501.
  - Replying to official correspondence or completing administrative forms. When the follow-up action prescribed in AR 135–133 fails to locate the officer or clearly evidences willful neglect to complete the required forms or to reply to official correspondence, the appropriate commander will initiate involuntary separation action.
- Conviction by civil court of a felony when no sentence to confinement results
- Conviction by a foreign court, resulting in confinement or other restriction of the officer's freedom which significantly diminishes that individual's usefulness to the Army.
- Entry into a military service of a foreign government.
- Special derogatory evaluation report.
- Failure to meet the standards in a course of instruction at a service school due to disciplinary reasons.
- Conduct unbecoming an officer.

C. In the Interest of National Security

Existence of acts or behavior not clearly consistent with the interests of National security requires the involuntary separation of an officer. AR 380-67, Personnel Security Program, details the procedures under which an officer might lose their security clearance, and these underlying reasons, usually determined during a personnel security investigation, can be used to justify separation. A directive-type memorandum issued by the Secretary of the Army on 29 August 2011 also allows for the separation of officers for denial of a security clearance or failure to apply for a clearance or reinvestigation.

4. NON-PROBATIONARY OFFICERS

Non-probationary officers have more time in service than probationary officers. They include Regular Army (RA) and USAR (OTRA) officers with more than 5 years commissioned service, and Warrant Officers with more than 3 years service since appointment. They therefore are entitled to more due process prior to final elimination. The specific procedures for eliminating non-probationary officers are contained in AR 600-8-24, Table 4-1.

The U.S. Army Reserve Command (USARC) Commanding General has delegated the authority to initiate separations under AR 135-175 to General Officer Show Cause Authorities (GOSCAs), which includes every General Court-Martial Convening Authority (GCMCA) and any general officer commander who has a (typically AGR) judge advocate or legal advisor available. Unit commanders from company to brigade-level units should forward requests for separation, with substantiating documents attached as enclosures, to their full-time supporting Office of the Staff Judge Advocate (OSJA). The show cause authority may return the action for further evidence, close the case and disapprove the recommendation, appoint an investigating officer under AR 15-6 to investigate the matter further, or notify the officer concerned that he has been identified for separation. Officer promotion boards may also identify officers who are deemed unfit for continued service, and recommend to the USARC CG that they be required to "show cause," or appear before an administrative separation board.

In particular, commanders should be aware of the following tasks that must be accomplished:

A. Notification of Elimination

Either a General Officer Show Cause Authority or the CG, Human Resources Command normally notifies in writing the affected officer of the intent to eliminate him. This notification will identify, among other things, the provision under which the officer has been identified for separation, a contemplated characterization of service, and information on obtaining counsel. AR 600-8-2 also requires imposition of a flag suspending favorable actions against an officer identified for separation.

B. Notification of Rights

The notification memorandum will inform the officer of the right to submit a written statement in his behalf, and to tender his resignation in lieu of elimination, retire in lieu of elimination, or appear before a board of inquiry ("Show Cause" Board) that will hear his case and decide whether to recommend his separation or retention.

C. Board of Inquiry

If the officer elects to have his case heard by a board of inquiry, a board (consisting of 3 senior officers and at least one 0-6) will convene and recommend whether or not to separate the officer. At this board, the officer will have the right to present matters in his behalf and to cross-examine witnesses against him, with the aid of a military defense counsel or, in his discretion, the assistance of a civilian attorney of his choosing (at no cost to the Government). Boards must be completed no later than 90 days from the date that the initiating General Officer directs them to convene.

D. Action on Board Results

If the board recommends retention, the officer will be advised and the action will be closed. If the board recommends the officer's separation, the board's report will be forwarded through command channels (the officer's MACOM), to the Secretary of the Army (SECARMY). SECARMY is the final approval authority regarding whether to retain or eliminate the officer.

E. Officer's Options

After the board of inquiry, and at any time before final elimination action by SECARMY, the officer may tender his resignation, request discharge (if he is a RA officer), or apply for retirement if he otherwise is eligible.

F. Discharges

Officers eliminated from the Army may receive an Honorable, General, or Other than Honorable Discharge. Officers discharged solely on the basis of substandard duty performance will receive an Honorable Discharge.

5. PROBATIONARY OFFICERS

Probationary officers are either RA or USAR (OTRA) officers with less than 5 years commissioned service, or Warrant Officers with less than 3 years service since original appointment. Probationary officers receive less due process in the elimination process.

A. Elimination Bases

In addition to the other bases for elimination contained in para 4-2 of AR 600-8-24, probationary officers may be eliminated for failing a service school, failing to resign for medical reasons existing at the time of their appointment, or the discovery of other conditions that would have precluded their original appointment or that do not warrant their continued retention.

B. Elimination Procedures

Elimination procedures for probationary officers are contained in AR 600-8-24, Table 4-2. The procedures generally are the same as for non-probationary officers, except that probationary officers are not entitled to have their cases heard by a board of inquiry, unless an Other Than Honorable Discharge is recommended.

6. UNSATISFACTORY PARTICIPATION (RC OFFICERS)

One of the most vexing problems facing USAR commanders is the issue of Soldiers failing to meet their Reserve obligations. Under AR 135-91, a USAR officer may be deemed an "unsatisfactory participant" if they accrue within a one year period a total of nine unexcused absences (nine missed Multiple Unit Training Assembly, or MUTAs) or fail to attend or complete annual training (AT). MUTAs are usually 4-hour blocks of training, with 4 MUTAs comprising a typical weekend battle assembly. Thus, while a Soldier missing three two-day battle assemblies would accrue twelve unexcused absences, any combination of nine MUTAs in a year, beginning the date of the first absence, could justify separation.

A. Documentation Requirements

Commanders must ensure every MUTA missed by their Soldiers is documented by their servicing unit administrator or S/G-1. AR 135-91, paragraph 4-15 details documentation requirements to substantiate separation, including delivery of a notice of unexcused absence either in person or by first-class mail (with the first notice required to be sent by certified mail, return receipt requested) and the filing of such notices into the Soldier's personnel file. When unexcused absences are noted using the USAR's RLAS system, certain bonus and benefit payments are suspended upon the ninth missed MUTA; again, commanders must be diligent in ensuring their support personnel are properly documenting absences. When separation is based on failure to complete annual training (AT), no notices are required beyond notifying the Soldier via AT orders send to their address on record. If the Soldier cannot be personally delivered the AT order, the order should be sent via certified mail, return receipt requested.

B. Verification of Officer's Address

Commanders should also ensure their support personnel are inputting officer requests to change their mailing addresses. When an officer simply stops coming to battle assemblies, the main means of communicating with them regarding accumulating absences and pending separation action is via U.S. mail. Proper notice to the officer of his absences, service requirements, AT obligations, and pending administrative separation board is crucial in ensuring the final separation packet passes legal scrutiny by USARC and HQDA. To assist in locating absentees and thus avoid repeated mailings to the wrong address, the commander's staff should coordinate with their servicing OSJA to request a report (generated by Westlaw or other means) which lists an officer's last known address, real estate transactions, and other information. Finally, commanders should request personnel working administrative actions to verify their Soldier's addresses via HRC's Soldier Management System and their DA Form 2A.

7. SUSPENSION OF FAVORABLE PERSONNEL ACTIONS

The HQDA Inspector General recently conducted a review of the Army's "flagging" process, and the results were identified in an ALARACT message published 18 October 2011. The review found that commanders at all levels were not properly administering the suspension of personnel actions process due to a lack of training and knowledge of the correct procedures. Immediately upon the change of a Soldier's status from favorable to unfavorable, a flag should be imposed on that officer's file. This includes administrative separation, and the flag should not be lifted until either HQDA has made a final determination of retention or the officer has been separated/assigned to a transition point for separation. AR 600-8-2 leaves no room for a commander's discretion on imposing a flag for elimination; so ensuring a flag is imposed as early as possible will prevent favorable action (including promotion) and make certain that the Army's flag requirements are being met.

THIS PAGE IS INTENTIONALLY BLANK

Chapter 30

BARS TO REENLISTMENT – FIELD INITIATED

1. REFERENCES

- AR 601-280, Army Retention Program, dated 31 January 2006
- AR 140-111, U.S. Army Reserve Reenlistment Program, dated 9 May 2007

2. OVERVIEW

Bars to reenlistment often serve a useful purpose as a "probationary period," enabling a Soldier to show signs of rehabilitation following acts of misconduct or substandard performance that lead to the bar. Bars are rehabilitative, not punitive, tools. This Chapter addresses bars initiated in the field (as opposed to by HQDA). HQDA-initiated bars to reenlistment under the Qualitative Management Program (QMP) are discussed in Chapter XVI of this Guide.

3. DEFICIENCIES TRIGGERING A BAR

A. Discretionary Grounds for Imposing Bars

Generally, commanders should consider bars to reenlistment against Soldiers who are un-trainable or unsuited for military service, when immediate separation is not warranted. Acts of misconduct or substandard performance may trigger a bar to reenlistment. A non-inclusive list of examples of such deficiencies is contained in Paragraph 8-4 of AR 601-280.

B. Mandatory Grounds for Imposing Bars

On 1 March 2012, Army Directive 2012-03 became effective and requires commanders to impose a bar to reenlistment for the following grounds.

- Loss of primary military occupational specialty qualification due to fault of the Soldier;
- Soldier denied Command List Integration for promotion by unit commander;
- An incident involving the use of illegal drugs or alcohol within the current enlistment/reenlistment period resulting in an officially filed reprimand; a finding of guilty under Article 15, UCMJ; a civilian criminal conviction; or a conviction by court-martial;
- Two or more separate proceedings under Article 15, UCMJ resulting in a finding of guilty by a field grade commander during the Soldier's current enlistment or period of service; and
- Soldier absent without a leave more than 96 hours during the current enlistment/reenlistment period.

4. SPECIAL RULES

A. Bars will not be initiated when

Administrative Separation is pending UP AR 635-200 or AR 135-178; Solely because a Soldier Refuses to Reenlist; In lieu of Courts-Martial, Article 15s, or other Adverse Actions; Against Soldiers with an Approved Retirement; Against Soldiers with 18 Years or More of Active Duty.

B. Bars should not be initiated Against Soldiers Assigned to the Unit for Less than 90 Days

If this occurs, the DA Form 4126-R (Commander's Certificate) must state why a bar is warranted.

C. Against Soldiers During the Last 30 Days Before ETS

If this occurs, the Commander's Certificate must explain why no action was taken at an earlier date.

D. For USAR Soldiers, during the last 90 days (30 days for an AGR Soldier) before the Soldier is discharged, transferred from the command, or released from active duty (REFRAD)

If initiated during this period, the commander must provide a complete explanation as to why the action was not taken earlier. This explanation will be entered on DA Form 8028–R (U.S. Army Reserve Bar to Reenlistment Certificate).

5. PROCEDURES FOR INITIATING AND IMPOSING BARS ON AC SOLDIERS

AR 601-280, Paragraph 8-5, details procedures for initiating a bar. Commanders should take special note of the following:

A. Initiating Commander

Any commander in the Soldier's chain of command may initiate the bar.

B. Commander's Certificate

DA Form 4126-R is the form on which bars are initiated. A sample is reproduced at Appendix N to this Guide.

C. Referral to Soldier

Soldiers will be afforded an opportunity to respond to the proposed bar, in writing. They will be provided a copy of the Commander's Certificate, and given at least 7 days to submit a response. Each commander in the chain of command up to the approval authority (see subparagraph D5, below) must personally endorse the Soldier's comment.

D. Forwarding to Higher Commander

The Commander's Certificate and the Soldier's rebuttal, if submitted, must be forwarded to the next higher commander in the normal chain, up to the proper Approval Authority.

E. Approval Authority

Final approval authority must be at least one approval level higher than the initiating commander.

- Soldiers with Less than 10 Years' Active Service at Date of Bar Initiation. The approval authority is the first commander in the grade of O-5 or above in the Soldier's chain of command, or the commander exercising Special Court Martial Convening Authority, whichever is in the most direct line to the Soldier; personal signature is required.
- Soldiers with More than 10 Years' Active Service at Date of Bar Initiation (Soldier Not on Indefinite Reenlistment Status). The approval authority is the first general officer in the Soldier's chain of command or the commander exercising General Court Martial Convening Authority (GCMCA), whichever is in the most direct line to the Soldier; personal signature is required.
- Bar Initiated by a Commander Above Company Level. The approval authority is the first general officer in the Soldier's Chain of Command, the GCMCA, or HQDA (CDR, HRC-Alexandria, Attn: AHRC-EPR); personal signature is required.
- Commanders do not have the authority to prevent a Soldier's retirement by barring the Soldier from reenlistment once the Soldier attains 18 years or more of active duty in order to preclude the Soldier from attaining retirement eligibility.

F. Placement in Soldier's Local Unit File

Approved bars will be placed in the Soldier's local unit file.

G. Continued Evaluation of Soldier

After placing an approved certificate in Soldier's local unit file, the company commander will continue documented evaluation of the Soldier.

H. Review by Company Commander

Company commanders will review bars at least every 3 months after the approval date, and 30 days before the Soldier's scheduled departure from the unit or separation from the Army. Commanders may recommend that the bar remain in place, or that it be removed, per AR 601-280, Paragraph 8-5h.

I. Mandatory Initiation of Separation

Commanders will initiate separation proceedings under AR 635-200 upon completion of the second 3-month review, unless a recommendation for removal is submitted and approved by proper authority. Initiation of separation action is not required for Soldiers who, at the time of the second 3-month review, have more than 18 years of active federal service but less than 20 years - these Soldiers will be required to retire on the last day of the month when retirement eligibility is attained. (Initiation of separation is not required but should be considered after a Soldier fails to overcome the bar at the first 3-month review.)

J. Mandatory Flagging

Imposing a bar to re-enlistment is an unfavorable action requiring the Soldier to be flagged. (AR 601-280, Paragraph 8-5b and AR 600-8-2, Paragraph 1-12.)

6. PROCESSING APPEALS TO BARS TO REENLISTMENT ON AC SOLDIERS

Soldiers have a right to appeal approved bars to reenlistment within 7 days of notification of the bar. Commanders should process Soldiers' appeals as follows:

A. Endorsements

Each commander in the chain of command up to the Appeal Authority must endorse the appeal, and may include statements in the endorsement regarding whether they recommend approval or disapproval of the appeal.

B. Appeal Authorities

1) Soldiers with Less than 10 Years Active Service at Time Bar was Initiated

The Appeal Authority is the first General Officer in the Soldier's chain of command, or the commander exercising GCMCA, whichever is in the most direct line to the soldier. The personal signature of the approving or disapproving authority is required.

2) Soldiers with More than 10 Years Active Service at Time Bar was Initiated

The Appeal Authority is the CG, HRC-Alexandria. Unless the authority who approved the bar directed, appeals will not be forwarded through the MACOM Commander en route to HRC-Alexandria.

7. PROCEDURES FOR INITIATING AND IMPOSING BARS ON USAR TPU AND AGR SOLDIERS

AR 140-111, paragraphs 1-27 through 1-36, detail policies and procedures for initiating bars to reenlistment. Commanders should take special note of the following:

A. Initiating Commander

Any commander in the Soldier's chain of command may initiate the bar.

B. Commander's Certificate

DA Form 8028-R (U.S. Army Reserve Bar to Reenlistment Certificate) is the form on which bars are initiated. The data requested on DA Form 8028–R, Section I, Commander's Recommendation, will be entered as appropriate, and the initiating officer will summarize the basis for his or her intent to initiate bar to reenlistment procedures. This must include all other factual and relevant data supporting the initiating officer's recommendation.

C. Referral to Soldier

The initiating officer will refer the certificate to the concerned Soldier for a statement on his or her own behalf. If the Soldier is serving on AGR status, he or she will be given 7 days to respond. All other Soldiers will be given 30 days to respond.

D. Forwarding to Higher Commander

Upon receipt of the Soldier's comments (DA Form 8028–R, Section II, Soldier's Review) the certificate will be endorsed personally by each commander in the chain of command. After proper endorsements recommending approval of a bar have been completed, the certificate will be sent to the appropriate approval authority. Note, however, that an endorsing officer who does not believe the bar is warranted, will disapprove the action and return it to the initiating officer. *An endorsing officer may also recommend a change in the severity of the bar (bar from AGR service versus bar from USAR service).* The bar to reenlistment will not be forwarded to a higher authority for consideration without a recommendation for approval.

E. Approval Authority

Final approval authority must be at least one approval level higher than the initiating commander.

1) Soldiers with Less than 10 Years of Qualifying Service for Retired Pay (or AS for AGR Soldiers)

The approval authority is the first commander in the grade of O-5 or above in the Soldier's chain of command, or the commander exercising Special Court-Martial Convening Authority, whichever is in the most direct line to the Soldier; personal signature is required.

2) Soldiers with More than 10 Years of Qualifying Service (or AS for AGR Soldiers), and Who Are Not on Indefinite Reenlistments

The approval authority is the first general officer in the Soldier's chain of command or the commander exercising General Court-Martial Convening Authority (GCMCA), whichever is in the most direct line to the Soldier; personal signature is required.

3) Approval of a bar on Soldiers having 18, but less than 20, years of qualifying service for retired pay (or AS for AGR Soldiers)

The Bar does not serve to deny the Soldier of attaining retirement eligibility (see 10 USC 1176). Commanders do not have the authority to deny such Soldiers from extending under the provisions of this regulation to attain retirement eligibility.

4) Final approval authority

For any bar to reenlistment the final approval authority must be at least one approval level of command higher than the initiating authority. A bar initiated by any commander above the company, battery, or troop level must be approved by the first general officer in the chain of command, the GCMCA, or commander, Human Resources Command, as appropriate.

F. Placement in Soldier's Local Unit File

Approved bars will be placed in the Soldier's local unit file.

G. Review by Unit Commander

Approved bars to reenlistment will be reviewed by the proper unit commander in 3–month intervals, and 30 days before the Soldier's scheduled departure from the unit, REFRAD, or discharge from the USAR for TPU or IMA Soldiers. Upon completion of the first 6–month review, the commander will inform the Soldier that the bar has been reviewed and will remain in effect unless recommended for removal.

H. Mandatory Initiation of Separation.

Upon completion of the second 6–month review, proceedings will be initiated leading to REFRAD, discharge, or reassignment to the IRR, as appropriate, unless the Soldier has demonstrated that the bar should be removed.

8. PROCESSING APPEALS TO BARS TO REENLISTMENT FOR USAR TPU AND AGR SOLDIERS

From the time he or she is informed that a bar to reenlistment was approved, a Soldier serving on AGR status will be allowed 7 days to submit an appeal. All other USAR Soldiers will be allowed 30 days to submit an appeal. Commanders should process Soldiers' appeals as follows:

A. Endorsements

Each commander in the chain of command up to the Appeal Authority must endorse the appeal, and may include statements in the endorsement regarding whether they recommend approval or disapproval of the appeal.

B. Appeal Authorities

For Soldiers with less than 10 years of qualifying service for retired pay (or AS for AGR Soldiers) at ETS, the approval or disapproval authority is the first general officer in the Soldier's normal chain of command, or the commander exercising GCMCA, whichever is in the most direct line to the Soldier. The personal signature of the approving or disapproving authority is required.

For Soldiers with more than 10 years of qualifying service for retired pay (or AS for AGR Soldiers) at ETS, the approval and/or disapproval authority is the commander, HRC–St. Louis. Unless specifically directed by the proper commander, appeals will not be sent through major or area commanders en route to HRC–St. Louis.

Bars to reenlistment approved by the CAR under this regulation may not be appealed.

Chapter 31

QUALITATIVE SERVICE PROGRAM (QSP)

1. REFERENCE

- AR 635-200, Active Duty Enlisted Administrative Separations, dated 6 June 2005

2. OVERVIEW

Effective 1 April 2012, the Army will employ the enlisted QSP to identify NCOs for involuntary early separation from active duty. The QSP consists of a series of centralized enlisted selection board processes designed to support the Army Leader Development Strategy and retain the highest quality NCOs.

3. THE THREE BOARD PROCESSES

A. Qualitative Management Program (QMP) Board

IAW AR 635-200, Chapter 19, the QMP board considers Senior NCOs (E7 through E9) for denial of continued service whose performance, conduct, and/or potential for advancement may not meet Army standards.

B. Over-Strength Qualitative Service Program (OS-QSP) Board

IAW AR 635-200, paragraph 16-7, the OS-QSP board will consider NCOs (E6 through E9) for denial of continued service in select MOSs/skill levels where the 12 month operating strength projections exceed 100%.

C. Promotion Stagnant Qualitative Service Program (PS-QSP) Board

IAW AR 635-200, paragraph 16-7, the PS-QSP board will consider NCOs (E6 through E9) for denial of continued service who are in select MOSs/skill levels where promotion stagnation exists at NCO levels within an MOS.

THIS PAGE IS INTENTIONALLY BLANK

Chapter 32

REMOVAL OF ENLISTED SOLDIERS FROM PROMOTION LISTS

1. REFERENCE

- AR 600-8-19, Enlisted Promotions and Reductions, dtd 30 April 2010

2. OVERVIEW

Removal from a promotion list may be directed either by commanders in the field ("local") or at HQDA level.

3. REMOVAL FROM LOCAL PROMOTION LISTS

Local promotion lists include those Soldiers recommended for promotion to the ranks of Sergeant and Staff Sergeant.

A. Mandatory Removal (AR 600-8-19, Paragraph 3-24)

Commanders must immediately request removal of Soldiers from promotion lists when:

- Soldier fails to qualify, for cause, for a security clearance required for their MOS.
- Soldier is subject to a local or DA imposed bar to reenlistment imposed after attaining recommended list status.
- Soldier was erroneously placed on a local promotion list.
- Soldier is enrolled in the Army Weight Control Program in accordance with AR 600-9.
- Soldier fails a record APFT.
- Soldier is subject to adverse action, as indicated by a suspension of favorable personnel action.
- Soldier is subject to mandatory reclassification as a result of inefficiency or misconduct.
- Soldier fails to complete training required for MOS for cause or academic reasons.
- Soldier refuses, in writing, to attend required NCOES course.

This list is non-inclusive; other conditions requiring mandatory removal are contained in AR 600-8-19, (see Table 3-10).

B. Procedures for Mandatory Removal

AR 600-8-19, Table 3-11, contains these procedures. The Soldier must be informed of the removal action in writing not later than 5 duty days after removal.

C. Procedures for Removal Board

AR 600-8-19, Table 3-12, contains these procedures. Commanders may conduct removal boards when a Soldier's substandard performance or inefficiencies warrants action (AR 600-8-19, Paragraph 3-26). The Soldier must be provided written notification of the removal board at least 15 duty days prior to the date of the board.

4. REMOVAL FROM HQDA PROMOTION LISTS

HQDA selects and recommends enlisted Soldiers for promotion to the ranks of Sergeant First Class through Sergeant Major. HQDA can administratively remove a Soldier's name from the recommendation list based on information provided by the commander. Commanders may also recommend a Soldier's removal from an HQDA promotion list.

A. Administrative Removal

Commanders must provide to HQDA documentation pertaining to Soldiers on an HQDA recommended list who meet any of the following criteria:

- Soldier is reduced
- Soldier has an approved retirement
- Soldier is dropped from the rolls as a deserter
- Soldier is in a promotable status and loses their security clearance for cause or is permanently disqualified from receiving a security clearance.

This list is non-inclusive; other conditions requiring command notification to HQDA for removal are contained in AR 600-8-19, Paragraph 4-15a.

B. Command Initiated Removal

Commanders must recommend the removal of Soldiers from HQDA promotion lists that are flagged for noncompliance with AR 600-9. The Commander must submit a recommendation for removal on a Soldier who has not met the weight requirements within the time prescribed in AR 600-9, provided no underlying or associated disease is found to be the cause of the overweight condition.

Commanders may also recommend that a Soldier's name be removed from an HQDA recommended list at any time for substandard performance or any other substantiated reason warranting removal.

Commanders will, when recommending removal, evaluate circumstances to ensure that all other appropriate actions have been taken (training, supervision, and formal counseling have not helped) or the basis for considering removal is serious enough to warrant denying the Soldier's promotion.

C. Removal from Centralized Promotion List by HQDA

AR 600-8-19, Paragraph 4-17, governs procedures for HQDA initiated removals from centralized promotion lists. HRC-Alexandria will continuously review promotion lists against all information available to ensure that no Soldier is promoted where there is cause to believe that a Soldier is mentally, physically, morally, or professionally unqualified to perform duties of the higher grade. In addition, Soldiers may be referred to a Standby Advisory Board (STAB) for the following reasons:

- Article 15 directed for filing in the OMPF.
- A memorandum of reprimand placed in the OMPF.
- Adverse documentation filed in the OMPF.
- Soldiers who are flagged IAW AR 600-8-2 and have not met the requirements in the time prescribed by that regulation.
- Other derogatory information received by HQDA, but not filed in the OMPF, if it is substantiated, relevant, and might reasonably and materially affect a promotion recommendation.

- Relief-for-cause NCOER.

D. Procedures

AR 600-8-19, Paragraph 4-15, governs procedures for initiating removal from HQDA promotion lists. Commanders should note the following provisions, in particular:

1) Full Documentation Required

Commanders should include all adverse documentation supporting their recommendation to remove a Soldier. Such documentation includes, for example, records of nonjudicial punishment, reprimands, and reports of law enforcement or other investigations.

2) Referral to Soldier

The Soldier will be provided a copy of the recommendation for removal, along with all supporting documents, and allowed to respond in writing within 15 days of receipt of the documents.

3) Submission Through Chain of Command

The removal action and all supporting documents will be submitted through command channels to the Soldier's General Court-Martial Convening Authority (GCMCA), or to the first Army General Officer in the chain of command who has a Judge Advocate on his staff.

4) Disapproval

Either HQDA or a commander at any level of command may disapprove the recommendation to remove a Soldier. Disapprovals will be returned to the originator with the reason for disapproval.

THIS PAGE IS INTENTIONALLY BLANK

Chapter 33

REMOVAL OF COMMISSIONED AND WARRANT OFFICERS FROM PROMOTION LISTS

1. REFERENCES

- AR 600-8-29, Officer Promotions, dtd 25 February 2005

2. OVERVIEW

Commanders may recommend the removal of an officer from a HQDA promotion list where there is cause to believe he is mentally, physically, morally or professionally unqualified to perform the duties of the higher grade. A Promotion Review Board (PRB), convened by the Commander, HRC, determines whether or not to remove the officer. The Secretary of the Army (SECARMY) is the approval authority for all determinations.

3. INSTANCES TRIGGERING REFERRAL TO A PRB

Such reasons include, but are not limited to Referred Officer Evaluation Report (OER) or Academic Evaluation Report (AER); Article 15 Punishment; Court-Martial Conviction; Memorandum of Reprimand Filed in Officer's OMPF; Other reasons contained in AR 600-8-29, Paragraph 8-2.

4. PROCEDURES

AR 600-8-29, Chapter 8, governs the procedures for processing an officer's removal from a promotion list. Commanders should note the following provisions, in particular:

A. Submission Through Command Channels

Commanders should submit all recommendations and accompanying documents through command channels to the Commander, Army Human Resources Command.

B. Detailed Justification

Commanders must indicate whether an OER has been submitted regarding the justification for requesting removal, and include detailed justification for the officer's removal from the promotion list.

C. Flag from Positive Personnel Actions

Upon referral of a case to a PRB for review, HQDA will flag the officer concerned, and lift the flag upon SECARMY's determination whether or not to remove the officer from the promotion list.

D. Notice to Officer Concerned

Before the PRB convenes, the officer concerned will be informed of the reason for the action. He will be provided copies of all information that the PRB will consider, and be permitted to submit comments within 14 days.

5. RESULTS OF PRB

Officers will be notified in writing, through their chain of command, of the results of PRB determinations and after SECARMY acts on the PRB's recommendation. This notice normally will be within 180 days after HQDA determines that a PRB will consider the officer's case.

Chapter 34

SECURITY CLEARANCES – SUSPENSION AND REVOCATION

1. REFERENCE

- AR 380-67, Personnel Security Program, (dated 9 Sep 88)(rapid action revision date issue date 4 Aug 11)

2. OVERVIEW:

When commanders learn of derogatory information on a Soldier, civilian employee, contractor or consultant in his command who holds a security clearance or has access to classified information, the commander must: (a) report the derogatory information to CCF using a DA Form 5248-R (when the derogatory information is credible) and (b) decide whether to informally or informally suspend access to classified information (when the derogatory information is significant). (AR 380-67, Paragraphs 8-2 and 8-3). Suspension may be "informal" (e.g., taking away access to classified repositories) or formal (e.g., compliance with the security regulation procedures for suspension). Commanders should coordinate suspension and revocation actions with their servicing S-2s.

3. DEROGATORY INFORMATION

Information that qualifies as derogatory is listed in AR 380-67 Paragraph 2-4 and includes, but is not limited to, incidents of criminal or dishonest conduct; unauthorized disclosure of classified information; and acts that indicate poor judgment, unreliability or untrustworthiness.

4. PROCEDURES FOR SUSPENSION

AR 380-67, Chapter 8, governs these procedures. In particular, commanders should ensure the following:

A. Informal Procedures

Follow AR 380-67, paragraph 8-3a.

B. Formal Procedures

Follow AR 380-67, Paragraph 8-3b, which includes removing the Soldier's DA form 873 and forwarding it to CCF.

NOTE: While a commander can later restore access if it was informally suspended, he cannot do so if it was formally suspended.

C. Notify the Special Security Officer

This is required if the Soldier whose clearance has been suspended was indoctrinated for Sensitive Compartmented Information.

D. Ensure the Suspension is Documented

The suspension is document in the Field Determined Personnel Security Status data field of the Standard Installation/Division Personnel System personnel file.

5. PROCEDURES FOR REVOCATION

Chapter 8 of AR 380-67 governs these procedures, and requires providing the subject individual due process before final action is taken to revoke his clearance. In particular, commanders should be aware of the following:

A. Written Statement of Reasons

The subject individual must receive a written statement of the reasons why the revocation is contemplated.

B. Opportunity to Respond

The subject individual must receive an opportunity to submit a written response regarding the proposed revocation.

C. Written Explanation in Response to the Subject Individual's Rebuttal

The subject individual must receive a written response to his own response.

D. Opportunity to Appeal

The subject individual must be afforded an opportunity to appeal to a higher authority any determination against him.

Chapter 35

SEXUAL HARASSMENT

1. REFERENCES

- DOD: DoD Dir. 1350.2 (18 Aug 95)
- Army: AR 600-20, Chapter 7 and Appendix D
- Guard: NGR 600-21; NGR 600-22/ANGI 36-3

2. SEXUAL HARASSMENT

A. Defined

Conduct that involves unwelcome sexual advances, requests for sexual favors, and deliberate or repeated offensive comments or gestures of a sexual nature when— submission to such conduct is made either explicitly or implicitly a term or condition of a person's job, pay, or career; submission to or rejection of such conduct by a person is used as a basis for career or employment decisions affecting that person; or such conduct has the purpose or effect of unreasonably interfering with an individual's work performance or creates an intimidating, hostile, or offensive working environment; and is so severe or pervasive that a reasonable person would perceive, and the victim does perceive, the work environment as hostile or offensive.

Any use, or any implicit or explicit approval, by any person in a supervisory or command position, of any form of sexual behavior to control, influence, or affect the career, pay, or job of a member of the armed forces or a civilian employee of the Department of Defense.

Any deliberate or repeated unwelcome verbal comment or gesture of a sexual nature in the workplace by any member of the armed forces or civilian employee of the Department of Defense.

B. AR 600-20, chapter 7, defines two types of sexual harassment

1) Quid Pro Quo

(meaning "this for that") sexual harassment occurs when an employee suffers or is threatened with some kind of employment injury for refusing to grant sexual favors or is promised some sort of tangible job benefit in exchange for sexual favors. Examples include demanding sexual favors in exchange for a promotion, award, or favorable assignment; disciplining or relieving a subordinate who refuses sexual advances; and threats of poor job evaluation for refusing sexual advances.

2) Hostile Environment

Hostile environment occurs when a supervisor, co-worker, or someone else with whom the victim comes in contact on the job creates an abusive work environment or interferes with the employee's work performance through words, actions, or conduct that is perceived as sexual in nature Some examples include: discussing sexual activities, unnecessary touching, commenting on physical attributes, displaying sexually suggestive pictures or pornography, using demeaning or inappropriate terms such as "babe", using unseemly or profane gestures, granting job favors to those who participate in consensual sexual activity, using sexually crude, profane, or offensive language.

C. Three methods for filing a complaint

1) Equal Opportunity (EO) complaint process. (AR 600-20, Appendix D)

A Commander's Program that requires Command involvement. Available to Soldiers, Family members, and civilian employees, but primarily used by military personnel who believe they have been sexually harassed. DA civilian employees will generally use more specific means; see paragraph C. below (EEO complaint process). Fact-gathering usually done by AR 15-6 investigation. Filing and processing of sexual harassment complaints follow the same procedures as outlined in appendix D for EO complaints. Charges of sexual misconduct are to be processed through legal/ law enforcement channels, not EO channels.

2) Equal Employment Opportunity (EEO) complaint process

Available only to civilian employees, not military personnel. Civilian employees may use the EEO process even if the alleged sexual harasser is military. This is NOT a Commander's Program and Commanders should let this process run without interference.

Fact-gathering done by EEO counselor (informal complaint) and DoD Investigations Resolutions Division (formal complaint).

3) 10 U.S.C. § 1561 complaint process

The National Defense Authorization Act for fiscal year 1998 added section 1561 to Title 10 of the U.S. Code. It applies to complaints of sexual harassment by a member of the armed forces or a civilian employee of the DoD received by a commanding officer or officer in charge from a member of the command or a civilian employee under the supervision of the officer. 10 U.S.C. § 1561 established new requirements for processing sexual harassment complaints.

Establish a separate Point of Contact ("1561 POC") to handle 10 USC §1561 complaints. That person should be separate from the Equal Employment Opportunity (EEO) Officer to avoid any perceived conflict-of-interest issues.

AR 600-20 implements 10 U.S.C. § 1561 when a **military member** alleges sexual harassment.

Implementation of 10 U.S.C. § 1561 for complaints filed by civilian employees is found in a directive-type memorandum from Assistant Secretary of Defense for Force Management (SUBJECT: Interim Policy for DoD Implementation of 10 U.S.C. 1561: Sexual Harassment Investigations and Reports for Civilian Employees of the Military Services, dated February 9, 1999).

3. SANCTIONS AGAINST HARASSERS

Regardless of the forum in which a complaint is filed, Commanders always have an obligation to take reasonable steps to protect people from sexual harassment. Such steps can include no-contact orders, change of workplace location, bars from the installation, etc.

A. Military members

- Administrative action.

- Action under the Uniform Code of Military Justice (UCMJ)

B. Civilian employees

- May be subjected to administrative discipline in accordance with the current Army Table of Penalties (AR 690-700, chap 751, Table 1-1).
- No requirement for victims to file EEO complaints. A victim may seek redress or not, as he or she sees fit, but the right of the service to discipline employees who harass or discriminate is not affected in either event.
- Turner v. United States, 595 F. Supp. 708 (W.D. La. 1984) (National Guard recruiter found to be acting outside the scope of his employment in conducting complete physical examinations of female applicants).

THIS PAGE IS INTENTIONALLY BLANK

Chapter 36

DOMESTIC VIOLENCE AMENDMENT TO THE GUN CONTROL ACT (LAUTENBERG AMENDMENT) & FAP

1. REFERENCE

- Message, 221927Z Oct 03, Headquarters, Dep't of Army, DAPE-MPE, Subject: HQDA Message on Final Implementation of the Lautenberg Amendment (22 Oct 03)

2. OVERVIEW

The Lautenberg Amendment, 18 U.S.C. § 922(g)(9), (hereinafter "the Amendment") makes it a felony for any person convicted of a misdemeanor crime of domestic violence to ship, transport, possess, or receive firearms or ammunition. Because the Amendment applies to both military service members and civilians, HQDA published guidance in October 2003 regarding implementation of the Amendment.

3. GENERAL PROVISION AND DEFINITIONS

The Amendment bans the possession of firearms by any person who has been convicted of a misdemeanor crime of domestic violence (MCDV). Therefore, it is unlawful for any person who has been convicted of a MCDV to ship, transport, possess, or receive firearms or ammunition. For the purposes of this provision, the following definitions apply:

A. "Conviction"

This includes convictions either by a civilian court or by Special or General (but not Summary) Court-Martial. It does NOT include nonjudicial punishment or deferred civilian prosecutions. For a conviction to qualify, the offender must have been represented by counsel or knowingly and intelligently waived the right to counsel. If he was entitled to have the case tried by a jury, it must have been tried by a jury or the offender must have waived the jury trial knowingly and intelligently. Convictions do not qualify under the Amendment if they were expunged or set aside, or if the offender was pardoned for the offense or had his civil rights restored, unless the pardon, expungement, or restoration of civil rights expressly provides that the person may not ship, transport, possess, or receive firearms. Although the Amendment itself applies only to misdemeanor convictions, by DoD Policy, a felony conviction after 27 Nov 02 for a crime of domestic violence is also considered a qualifying conviction and triggers application of the Army's implementation of the Amendment.

B. "Misdemeanor Crime of Domestic Violence"

This includes any crime that contains an element of the use or attempted use of physical force or threatened use of a deadly weapon, and in which the convicted offender was, at the time of the offense, any of the following: Current or former spouse, parent or guardian of the victim; Person who had a child in common with the victim; Person who was Cohabitating or Did Cohabitate with the Victim as a Spouse, Parent or Guardian; Person who is living with another in an intimate, spouse-like relationship with the intent to make that place their home.

C. "Firearms and Ammunition"

This includes all Army-issue and privately-owned weapons, excluding Army-issue major weapons systems and crew-served weapons, such as tanks, missiles, and aircraft.

4. COMMAND RESPONSIBILITIES IN RESPONSE TO OCTOBER 2003 HQDA GUIDANCE

Periodically Inform All Soldiers of the Amendment's Provisions and Prohibitions: Commanders may either accomplish this by verbally briefing their Soldiers or by having their Soldiers read the provisions and acknowledge that they understand them. If commanders verbally inform their Soldiers of the provisions, it is recommended that they maintain a "sign-in" roster of all Soldiers who received the briefing, for unit record-keeping purposes. (Sample verbal and written briefing formats are enclosed at Appendices P and Q to this Guide, respectively).

Notify Soldiers with Qualifying Convictions that it is Unlawful to Possess, Ship, Transport or Receive Firearms or Ammunition as Stated in the Amendment. Display the DA Message Prominently Outside All Unit Arms Rooms and Facilities in which Government Arms and Ammunition are Stored, Issued, Disposed or Transported. Detail Soldiers Whom the Command Has Reason to Believe, or Knows to Possess, Qualifying Convictions to Meaningful Duties not Requiring the Soldier to Bear Weapons or Ammunition.

Soldiers with qualifying convictions may not hold leadership, supervisory or property accountability positions affording them access to firearms or ammunition. Soldiers with qualifying convictions may not attend any service school in which instruction with individual weapons or ammunition is part of the curriculum. Soldiers with qualifying convictions must be informed that their inability to complete service schools may impact adversely on their future promotion potential, as well as on their career length.

Company Level Commanders will Collect DD Form 2760 and File Them Locally IAW AR 600-8-104 and AR 25-400-2. If a Commander Knows or has Reasonable Cause to Believe a Soldier has a Qualifying Conviction, the Commander Should Take all Reasonable Steps to Investigate, to Include Ordering the Soldier to Complete a DD Form 2760. In Addition, the Commander will Retrieve all Government Issued Firearms and Ammunition and Refer the Soldier to a Legal Assistance Attorney.

5. ADVERSE ADMINISTRATIVE ACTION

Commanders may initiate separation for the conduct that led to the conviction or for the conviction itself. However, commanders may take reasonable steps to accommodate Soldiers with qualifying convictions, prior to initiating separation (such as granting a reasonable time – up to one year) to seek expungement or a pardon of the qualifying conviction. A commander may, but is not required to, defer administrative action for up to one year to allow the soldier to get the qualifying conviction expunged in civilian court. The Army will supply an attorney to assist in this process.

6. REPORTING TO HQDA

All Soldiers identified with qualifying convictions are required to be reported to HQDA using the Assignment Consideration Code (ASCO) L9 (LAUTENBERG AMENDMENT).

Chapter 37

ARTICLE 138 COMPLAINTS

1. REFERENCE

- AR 27-10, Military Justice, dated 03 October 2011

2. OVERVIEW

A member of the Armed Forces may submit a complaint under UCMJ, Art. 138 complaint for any act or omission by the member's commanding officer that the member believes to be a wrong, and for which the member has requested redress and been refused. Commanders will not restrict the submission of such complaints or retaliate against a Soldier for submitting a complaint.

3. DEFINITIONS

- Wrong – A discretionary act or omission by a commanding officer, under color of Federal military authority that adversely affects the complainant personally and that is in violation of law or regulation, beyond the legitimate authority of that commander, arbitrary, capricious, an abuse of discretion, or materially unfair.
- Redress – Any authorized action by any officer in the complainant's chain-of-command to effect the revocation of a previous official action or otherwise to restore to the complainant any rights, privileges, property, or status lost as a result of the wrong

4. PROCEDURES

A. Request for Redress

Before submitting a complaint under UCMJ, Art. 138, a member of the Armed Forces must make a written request for redress of the wrong to the commanding officer the member believes has wronged the member. The request for redress generally should be prepared in memorandum format and must clearly identify the commanding officer against whom it is made, the date and nature of the alleged wrong, and if possible, the specific redress desired.

B. Response by the Commanding Officer

A commanding officer receiving a request for redress submitted under this regulation will respond, in writing, in a timely manner so that the complainant will receive the response within 15 days. If a final response within 15 days is not possible, an interim response will be provided that indicates the estimated date of a final response. The regulation defines a failure to respond as a refusal for redress.

C. Refusal of Redress and Submission of Article 138 Complaint

If the commander committing the alleged wrong responds with a refusal to redress, the complainant may now submit an Article 138 complaint. The complainant will deliver the complaint to the complainant's immediate superior commissioned officer within 90 days of the date of complainant's discovery of the wrong, excluding any period during which the request for redress was in the hands of the respondent. A superior commissioned officer who receives a complaint under the provisions of UCMJ, Art. 138, will promptly forward it to the officer exercising GCM jurisdiction. Any other person receiving a complaint (except the officer exercising GCM jurisdiction) will forward it to the complainant's immediate superior commissioned officer or to the officer exercising GCM jurisdiction. The person receiving the complaint, or through whom it is forwarded, may add pertinent material to the file or grant any redress within that person's authority. If either action is taken, it will be noted in the transmittal.

Chapter 38

RELIEF FROM COMMAND

1. REFERENCE

- AR 600-20, Army Command Policy, dated 18 March 2008, RAR 4 August 2011

2. OVERVIEW

When a senior commander loses confidence in a subordinate commander's ability to command due to misconduct, poor judgment, the subordinate's inability to complete assigned duties, or for other similar reasons, the senior commander has the authority to relieve the subordinate commander.

3. PROCEDURES

A. Formal Counseling

Relief is preceded with formal counseling by the commander or supervisor unless such action is not deemed appropriate or practical under the circumstances.

B. General Officer Written Approval

Although any commander may temporarily suspend a subordinate from command, final action to relieve an officer from any command position will not be taken until after written approval by the first general officer (to include one frocked to the grade of brigadier general) in the chain of command of the officer being relieved is obtained. If a general officer (to include one frocked to the grade of brigadier general) is the relieving official, no further approval of the relief action is required; however, AR 623–3 concerning administrative review of relief reports remain applicable.

C. Basis for Relief Stems from an AR 15-6 Investigation

If a relief for cause is contemplated on the basis of an informal investigation under AR 15–6, the referral and comment procedures of that regulation must be followed before initiating or directing the relief. This does not preclude a temporary suspension from assigned duties pending completion of the procedural safeguards contained in AR 15–6.

THIS PAGE IS INTENTIONALLY BLANK

INDIVIDUAL SOLDIER RIGHTS

Section 5

THIS PAGE IS INTENTIONALLY BLANK

Chapter 39

BODY PIERCING & TATTOO POLICY

1. BODY PIERCING POLICY

A. References

- AR 670-1, Wear and Appearance of Army Uniforms and Insignia, dtd 3 February 2005

B. Overview

AR 670-1 requires Soldiers to uphold a certain military appearance on and off duty. Both the wear of piercings and earrings while in uniform detracts from a soldierly appearance.

1) Soldierly Appearance

When on any Army installation or other places under Army control, Soldiers may not attach, affix, or display objects, articles, jewelry, or ornamentation to or through the skin while they are in uniform, in civilian clothes on duty, or in civilian clothes off duty (this includes earrings for male Soldiers). The only exception is for earrings for females. (The term "skin" is not confined to external skin, but includes the tongue, lips, inside the mouth, and other surfaces of the body not readily visible). Females may wear any type of earring(s) off duty, on or off military installations.

2) Actions Upon Discovery of a Policy Violation

Commanders may order the Soldier to remove any such object placed through the skin on his or her body. Commanders encountering Soldiers who refuse to have the object removed should consider the following actions:

- Ensure the Soldier understands the policy.
- Counsel the Soldier in writing that he is not in compliance with Army policy, and that his decision not to remove the piercing could result in adverse action, to include discharge from the Army, the types of discharge authorized, and the consequences of a discharge characterized as less than honorable.

2. TATTOO POLICY

A. References

- AR 670-1, Wear and Appearance of Army Uniforms and Insignia, dtd 3 February 2005
- ALARACT (19 Dec 05)

B. Overview

AR 670-1 requires Soldiers to wear their uniforms in a fashion that does not detract from overall military appearance. The regulation references both tattoos and brands. The standards set forth in AR 670-1 prohibiting tattoos and brands that are visible in the Class A uniform were modified by an unnumbered, 19 Dec 05 ALARACT. Per the ALARACT, any tattoo or brand anywhere on the head or face is prohibited, except for permanent make-up. Tattoos that are not extremist, indecent, sexist, or racist are allowed on the hands and neck.

C. Soldierly Appearance

Tattoos or brands that violate DA policy even if covered by the Class A uniform or on the hands or neck include those that are:

1) Extremist

Affiliated with, depicting, or symbolizing extremist philosophies, organizations, or activities.

2) Indecent

Are grossly offensive to modesty, decency, or propriety and those that are vulgar, filthy, or disgusting in nature.

3) Sexist

Advocate a philosophy that degrades or demeans a person based on gender.

4) Racist

Advocate a philosophy that degrades or demeans a person based on race, ethnicity, or national origin.

D. Command Responses to Violations of Tattoo Policy

Commanders should not order Soldiers to have tattoos or brands removed. Commanders encountering Soldiers who refuse to have a tattoo or brand removed voluntarily should:

- Ensure the Soldier understands the policy.
- Ensure the Soldier has the opportunity to seek medical advice regarding removal of the tattoo or brand.
- Counsel the Soldier in writing that he or she is not in compliance with Army policy, and the Soldier's decision not to remove the tattoo or brand will result in discharge from the Army.

E. Exceptions to Policy

A request for an exception to policy is submitted through the chain of command to the MACOM for approval. Appeals to the MACOM decision will be submitted to the Army Deputy Chief of Staff, G-1 for decision.

Chapter 40

CONSCIENTIOUS OBJECTION

1. REFERENCE

- DoD Instruction 1300.6, Conscientious Objectors, dtd 5 May 2007
- AR 600-43, Conscientious Objection, dtd 21 August 2006

2. OVERVIEW

Any Soldier with a firm, fixed, and sincere objection to participation in any form of war, or to the bearing of arms because of religious training or belief may apply for separation from the Army as a conscientious objector. Applicants must establish by clear and convincing evidence that the objection is sincere and based on beliefs that either did not exist, or did not become fixed until after entry into the service. Applicants must consent to interviews and to an investigation into their status. Final decisions on many applications are made by HQDA.

3. CLASSES OF CONSCIENTIOUS OBJECTORS

The two classes of conscientious objectors are detailed below:

A. Class 1-A-0:

This class includes Soldiers who, by reason of conscientious objection, sincerely object to participation as combatants in war in any form, but whose convictions permit military service in a non-combatant status.

B. Class 1-0:

These Soldiers, by reason of conscientious objection, sincerely object to participation of any kind (whether in a combatant or non-combatant role) in war in any form. Applicants claiming this status will not be granted 1-A-0 status, as a compromise.

4. PROCEDURES FOR PROCESSING APPLICATIONS

AR 600-43 governs the procedures for processing conscientious objection claims. In particular, commanders should be aware of the provisions detailed below. Additionally, Appendix C of the regulation contains a checklist for processing these applications.

- A military chaplain and psychiatrist must interview applicants.
- The Special Court-Martial Convening Authority (normally, the Soldier's brigade commander) must appoint an officer to investigate the claim.
- The Record of Investigation will be forwarded to the General Court-Martial Convening Authority (GCMCA) and his Staff Judge Advocate for Review.
- Soldiers may withdraw their application at any time prior to final action on the case.

5. APPROVAL AUTHORITIES

The following authorities act as final approval authorities for applications.

A. Category 1-A-0:

Approval authority for applications submitted by Active component, and Reserve component Soldiers on active duty or ADT, is the Active Army commander having GCMCA over the Soldier concerned. If the GCMCA does not approve the application, HQDA acts as the approval authority.

B. Category 1-0:

Approval authority is HQDA (Conscientious Objector Review Board).

6. USE AND ASSIGNMENT OF APPLICANTS

Applicants pending final action on their cases must be retained in their unit and assigned duties providing minimum practicable conflict with their asserted beliefs. Applicants remain subject to all military orders, discipline, and regulations to include those on training. Some training exceptions exist for trainees.

7. ADMINISTRATIVE SEPARATION OF CONSCIENTIOUS OBJECTORS:

Soldiers separated from the Army for conscientious objection are entitled to receive either an Honorable or a General Discharge. Soldiers classified 1-A-0 are not eligible for discharge under AR 600-43. Personnel classified 1-A-0 will be reassigned IAW AR 600-43, paragraph 3-1 to an assignment that qualifies as noncombatant service or training.

Chapter 41

BEHAVIORAL HEALTH EVALUATIONS

1. REFERENCES

- DoD Directive 6490.1, Mental Health Evaluations of Members of the Armed Forces, dtd 1 October 1997 (Certified Current as of November 24, 2003)
- DOD Instruction 6490.4, Requirements for Mental Health Evaluations of Members of the Armed Forces, dtd 28 August 1997

2. OVERVIEW

A Soldier has certain rights when referred for a mental health evaluation and additional rights when admitted to a treatment facility for an emergency or involuntary mental health evaluation. The procedures outlined in the Directive / Instruction are designed to ensure Commanders do not use the mental health system as a means of "reprisal" or to control "whistleblowers."

IMPORTANT NOTE: **THESE PROCEDURES ARE VERY COMPLEX; WHEN POSSIBLE, COMMANDERS SHOULD CONSULT WITH THEIR SERVICING JUDGE ADVOCATE AND BEHAVIORAL HEALTH PROFESSIONAL BEFORE PROCEEDING WITH A REFERRAL. WHEN POSSIBLE, JUDGE ADVOCATES SHOULD PREPARE OR REVIEW ALL PAPERWORK INVOLVED IN INITIATING OR CONTINUING AN INVOLUNTARY MENTAL HEALTH EVALUATION.**

3. WHEN THE DIRECTIVE DOES NOT APPLY

- Voluntary self-referrals.
- Referrals that are a function of routine diagnostic procedures and made by health care providers not assigned to the service member's command.
- Interviews as part of the family advocacy programs.
- Interviews as part of the drug and alcohol rehabilitation programs.
- Referrals to mental health professionals for routine evaluations as required by other DA Regulations (i.e. AR 635-200 and AR 135-178, enlisted separations).
- Referrals related to responsibility and competence inquiries conducted pursuant to Rule for Courts-Martial 706 (i.e. sanity board evaluations).
- Referral for mental health evaluations required (pursuant to AR 380-67) for certain duties (e.g. security clearance evaluations or personnel reliability program).

4. NON-EMERGENCY (ROUTINE) REFERRAL

First, prior to making a referral, commanders must contact a Mental Health Care Provider (MHCP) for consultation on the Soldier's "actions and behaviors" and the reasons for the possible referral. Consider the MHCP's "advice and recommendations" before going forward with the referral. If you decide to refer the Soldier, contact an MHCP and make an appointment at least two (2) business days later. Next, provide written notice of referral and rights advice to the Soldier, at least two business days before the referral. For emergency referrals for evaluation or involuntary admissions to a treatment facility, refer to the requirements listed in Paragraph D below. Commanders and their legal advisors should consult DODI 6409.4 or their servicing Behavioral Health assets for sample forms and a list of specific actions commanders must take. The written notice to the Service Member must include the following:

- A description of the behaviors or communications upon which the referral is based;
- The name(s) of the MHCP with whom the Commander consulted before making the referral;
- Notification of the Service Member's Statement of Rights;
- The date and time of the scheduled evaluation;
- The name of the MHCP who will conduct the evaluation;
- The contact information for other authorities who may assist the Service Member, such as attorneys, the IG, and Chaplains; and
- The commander's name and signature.

5. EMERGENCY REFERRALS FOR EVALUATION

When a commander makes a "clear and reasoned judgment" that an "emergency" exists requiring referral for an evaluation, the two-day notice requirements for non-emergency (routine) referrals above do not apply.

A. Emergency Defined

An "emergency" is a situation in which the service member is threatening imminently, by words or actions, to harm himself or others or to destroy property under circumstances likely to lead to serious personal injury or death and to delay a mental health evaluation to complete the administrative requirements for a non-emergency referral could endanger the life or well-being of the service member or a potential victim.

B. Requirements

- After making that "clear and reasoned judgment" that an emergency exists requiring referral, the commander must make every effort to consult with an MHCP prior to referral for an emergency evaluation.
- The commander must safely convey the Soldier to the nearest MHCP.
- As soon as practicable, the commander must provide the Soldier with the notice of referral and rights advice.
- If unable to consult with an MHCP prior to referral, the commander must prepare a written memorandum about the circumstances and observations that led to the emergency referral. That memorandum must be forwarded by fax, overnight mail or courier to the MHCP to whom the Soldier was taken.
- Upon the Soldier's request, a military attorney shall be appointed to advise the Soldier on redress of the referral; if not reasonably available, every effort must be made to provide telephonic consultation.

6. INVOLUNTARY ADMISSION

A. Requirements

When a commander takes a Soldier to an MHCP who involuntarily hospitalizes the Soldier for psychiatric treatment or evaluation, the following requirements apply:

- Commander must coordinate with the MHCP, as soon after admission as the member's condition permits, to inform the member of the reasons for the evaluation, the nature and consequences of the evaluation and any treatment, and the member's rights;
- The member shall have the right to contact, as soon after admission as the member's condition permits, a friend, relative, attorney, or IG;
- The member shall be evaluated by the attending psychiatrist or a physician within two business days after admittance to determine if continued hospitalization and treatment is justified or if the member should be released from the facility;
- If a determination is made that continued hospitalization and treatment is clinically indicated, the member must be notified orally and in writing of the reason for such determination; and,
- A review of the admission of the member and the appropriateness of continued hospitalization and treatment shall be conducted in accordance with required review procedures.

B. Review Procedures

Within 72 hours of an involuntary psychiatric admission initiated under the Directive / Instruction, a review of the admission and of the appropriateness of continued hospitalization shall be conducted. The review shall be conducted by an impartial, disinterested, privileged psychiatrist (or medical officer if a psychiatrist is not available) in the grade of O4 or above (or civilian equivalent) NOT in the member's immediate chain of command, who is appointed by the MTF commander.

C. Special Notes Concerning the U.S. Army National Guard (ARNG) and U.S. Army Reserve (USAR) Soldiers

ARNG/USAR unit commanders will ensure Soldiers identified as at-risk during periods of Active Duty (i.e., Active Duty for Training, Annual Training, or Active Duty Operational Support) or Inactive Duty Training (i.e., IDT or Battle Assemblies) are transported to the nearest military MTF Behavioral Health Clinic to determine the appropriate course of treatment and case disposition. If this resource is not available, the unit commander will ensure that the at-risk Soldier is escorted to the nearest civilian hospital emergency room for evaluation.

If an ARNG/USAR Soldier requires inpatient treatment at a local civilian medical facility, the unit commander and military health care providers will ensure a complete transfer of responsibility to the civilian medical facility. ARNG/USAR commanders will also conduct a Line of Duty Investigation (LDI) in a timely manner to cover the cost of immediate and follow-on care. An ARNG/USAR Soldier is entitled to hospital benefits similar to that for Active Army Soldiers for injury, illness, or disease incurred in the line of duty. Commanders should consult Army Reserve G-1 and AR 600-8-4, *Line of Duty Policy, Procedures, and Investigations*, for additional information on LDI investigations.

If it appears the Soldier will need extended hospitalization beyond the current IDT period or AD order, the command should consider other funding sources, including Active Duty Medical Extension (ADME) or Active Duty Operational Support Reserve Component (ADOS-RC) orders to cover medical expenses for the interim.

Commanders should consult Army Reserve G-1 and the latest update to the *Department of Army Warrior Transition Unit Consolidated Guidance (Administrative)*, for additional information.

An ARNG/USAR Soldier incurring or aggravating any injury, illness, or disease in the line of duty may be entitled to incapacitation pay under AR 135-381. In some cases, incapacitation pay may be an option available and preferred over entering the ADME program. Additionally, a Soldier may not draw incapacitation pay and concurrently be in the ADME Program. Soldiers should contact the chain of command to be considered for incapacitation pay and/or review AR 135-381, *Incapacitation of Reserve Component Soldiers.*

If the at-risk Soldier is judged by the health care provider at the civilian MTF to require extended inpatient treatment beyond 14 days, the senior military MHCP or, in the absence of such at smaller installations, the senior primary care physician at the nearest military MTF, will provide the commander recommendations regarding whether the at-risk Soldier should be transferred to a military MTF for continued treatment once medically stable for transport at the civilian facility.

7. UCMJ VIOLATIONS

Failure to comply with the DoD Directive / Instruction may result in disciplinary action. Become familiar with Directives and Instructions and consult with your servicing Judge Advocate to ensure compliance.

8. RECOMMENDATIONS TO COMMANDING OFFICERS BY HEALTH CARE PROVIDERS

When a MHCP provider returns a Service member to his or her command, either following an outpatient evaluation or upon discharge from inpatient status for which the dangerousness was an issue, the provider shall make written recommendations to the Service member's commanding officer about, at least, the following three issues:

A. Proposed Treatments

Treatments shall be based upon the potential for therapeutic benefit as determined by the MHCP.

B. Precautions

Recommendations shall be based on the doctoral-level MHCP's good faith clinical judgment of the need for, and feasibility of, reducing or eliminating the Service member's ability to cause injury to himself, herself or another; or for avoiding any precipitating events that might lead to such injury. Recommendations for precautions shall be considered especially in cases of those Service members who have demonstrated the potential to become dangerous in the past, as evidenced by violent or destructive behavior. Recommendations for precautions may include, but are not limited to, an order to move into military barracks for a given period; an order to avoid the use of alcohol; an order not to handle firearms or other weapons; or an order to not contact a potential victim or victims. **COMMANDERS SHOULD SEEK OUT THIS INFORMATION IF IT IS NOT PROVIDED. COMMANDERS SHOULD NOT CONFUSE THESE PRECAUTIONS WITH OTHER RESTRICTIONS ON LIBERTY THAT ARE PURSUANT TO THE UCMJ AND MILITARY JUSTICE SYSTEM. IF A MHCP RECOMMENDS CERTAIN PRECAUTIONS BASED ON A GOOD FAITH CLINICAL JUDGMENT, COMMANDERS SHOULD TYPICALLY IMPLEMENT THE PRECAUTIONS. COMMANDERS SHOULD INFORM THE SERVICING JUDGE ADVOCATE OF ALL PRECAUTIONS WHEN IMPLEMENTED ON A SERVICE MEMBER WHO IS FACING OR WILL POTENTIALLY FACE UCMJ PUNISHMENT. SOLDIER AND UNIT SAFETY ALWAYS COMES FIRST.**

C. Fitness and Suitability for Continued Service

The MHCP shall advise the commanding officer about a recommendation for return of the Service member to duty, referral of the Service member to a Medical Evaluation Board for processing through the Disability Evaluation System, or administrative separation of the Service member for personality disorder and unsuitability for continued military service.

D. Other Actions Commanders Must Take

- When a privileged MHCP makes a recommendation to the commander, the commander shall make a written record of the actions taken and reasons therefore. Commanders should involve their servicing Judge Advocate.
- If a MHCP recommends that a Service member be separated from the military service due to a personality disorder and a pattern of potentially dangerous behavior (more than one episode), and the Service member's commander declines to follow the recommendation, the Service member's commanding officer shall forward a memorandum to his or her commanding officer within 2 business days explaining the decision to retain the Service member against medical advice.

THIS PAGE IS INTENTIONALLY BLANK

Chapter 42

COMMAND ACCESS TO SOLDIERS PROTECTED HEALTH INFORMATION (HIPAA)

1. REFERENCES

- DoD 6025.18-R, DoD Health Information Privacy Regulation, (January 24, 2003)
- DoD Instruction 6490.08, Command Notification Requirements to Dispel Stigma in Providing Mental Health Care to Service Members (August 17, 2011)
- DoD Instruction 6490.1, Mental Health Evaluations of Members of the Armed Forces (August 28, 1997)
- DoD Instruction 6490.10, Continuity of Behavioral Health Care for Transferring and Transitioning Service Members (March 26, 2012)
- Army Regulation 40-66, Medical Record Administration and Healthcare Documentation
- Field Manual 6-22.5, Combat and Operational Stress Control Manual for Leaders and Soldiers (March 18, 2009)
- MEDCOM Regulation 40-38, Commander-Directed Mental Health Evaluations (June 1, 1999)
- OTSG/MEDCOM Policy Memorandum 10-042, Release of Protected Health Information (PHI) to Unit Command Officials, 30 June 2010

2. OVERVIEW

The Health Insurance Portability and Accountability Act of 1996 (HIPAA) requires everyone in the Military Health System to safeguard and keep confidential the health information on patients. A patient's health care information is confidential and will not be released to anyone without either an authorization from the patient or an exception to HIPAA. However, HIPAA provides a limited exception for access to Protected Health Information (PHI) for command officials when the patient is a Soldier.

3. COMMAND ACCESS TO PROTECTED HEALTH INFORMATION (PHI) – "THE MILITARY EXCEPTION."

A. Communication is Key

The key to success with HIPAA and medical information-related issues is good communication between the command, the health care provider, the military treatment facility (if applicable), and the servicing judge advocates.

1) Military Health Care Providers and Military Treatment Facilities (MTFs)

Commanders and their designees have a specific exception to receive a Soldier's PHI in certain situations to assure the proper execution of the military mission. Health care providers may provide information to the command pursuant to this exception without the Soldier's consent. **If a commander believes that he or she needs to know about a Soldier's PHI, the commander should immediately contact the health care provider.** Commanders must understand, however, that this exception is limited. Commanders do not have unrestricted access to a Soldier's PHI. MTFs and health care providers will provide timely and accurate information to support a commander's decision-making pertaining to a Soldier's health risk, medical fitness, and readiness. To access a Soldier's PHI, a commander (or the commander's proper designee) must need the Soldier's PHI to carry out an activity under the authority of the commander. This exception does NOT apply to Family members, retirees, or civilians. It applies only to Soldiers.

2) Civilian Medical Facilities

When a Soldier is or was treated at a civilian hospital or by a civilian health care provider, DoD 6025.18-R, paragraph C7.11.1.1 states that a commander may request the Soldier's PHI if the commander needs the PHI for an official purpose. HIPAA, however, leaves it to the civilian hospital or provider's discretion to determine if they will disclose the relevant PHI, as disclosure is generally permissible, but not required. Commanders having difficulty getting PHI from civilian medical facilities or civilian providers should seek the assistance of the MTF's Patient Administration Division (PAD) and their servicing judge advocate.

B. The Minimum Necessary Rule

The HIPAA Privacy Rule requires covered entities, such as MTFs and Unit Surgeons, to take reasonable steps to limit the use or disclosure of, and requests for, PHI **to the minimum necessary to accomplish the intended purpose**. In other words, in most cases, commanders who request PHI pursuant to the military exception will typically not receive all of the Soldier's PHI, as in most cases, not all information is necessary to accomplish the intended purpose. Disclosure may include the diagnosis; a description of the treatment prescribed or planned; impact on duty or mission; recommended duty restrictions; the prognosis; applicable duty limitations; and implications for the safety of self or others.

C. Common Uses of the "The Military Exception" to HIPAA

1) Determine a Soldier's Fitness for Duty.

A commander may obtain PHI to determine a Soldier's fitness for duty, including, but not limited to, the member's compliance with standards and activities carried out under the Army Weight Control Program (AR 600-9), Physical Evaluation for Retention, Retirement, or Separation (AR 635-40), or AR 40-501 (Standards of Medical Fitness).

2) Determine a Soldier's fitness to perform a particular mission

A commander may obtain PHI to determine a Soldier's fitness to perform a particular mission, assignment, order, or duty, including compliance with any actions required as a precondition to performance of such mission, assignment, order, or duty. Common examples are profiles and notice that a Soldier is taking a particular medication that interferes with the performance of duty, such as driving or carrying a weapon.

3) Report on casualties in any military operation.

4) Carry out any other activity necessary to the proper execution of the mission of the Armed Forces. Common examples include:

- to coordinate sick call, routine and emergency care, quarters, hospitalization, and care from civilian providers IAW AR 40-66 and AR 40-400;
- To report Command Directed Mental Health Evaluations IAW MEDCOM Regulation 40-38;

- To initiate Line of Duty (LOD) determinations and to assist investigating officers IAW AR 600-8-4, LOD Procedures and Investigations;
- Most medical appointment reminders concerning Soldiers may be disclosed to Command Authorities (*but see* Section E below);
- To report a Soldier's dental classification IAW AR 40-3;
- To carry out Soldier Readiness Program (SRP) and mobilization processing requirements IAW DA Pam 600-8-101;
- To provide initial and follow-up reports for the Army Family Advocacy Program IAW AR 608-18;
- To complete records for the Exceptional Family Member Program IAW AR 608-75 and MEDCOM Circular 40-4;
- IAW AR 15-6 investigations (but not including Quality Assurance information);
- To review and report Human Immunodeficiency Virus (HIV) IAW AR 600-110;
- To carry out any other activity necessary to the proper execution of the mission of the Army.

D. Command Notification Requirements to Dispel Stigma in Providing Mental Health Care to Service Members (DoDI 6490.08, August 17, 2011).

1) General Information

There is new guidance related to the release of information pertaining to a Service member's involvement in mental health care and substance abuse education (distinguished from substance abuse treatment). Healthcare providers follow a presumption that they are not to notify a Service member's commander when the service member obtains mental health care or substance abuse education services, unless this presumption is overcome by one of the following notification standards.

2) Notification Standards

Command notification by healthcare providers will not be required for Service member self and medical referrals for mental health care or substance misuse education unless one of the reasons listed below apply. Healthcare providers shall notify the commander concerned when a Service member meets the criteria for one of the following mental health and/or substance misuse conditions or related circumstances:

- <u>Harm to Self</u>. The provider believes there is a serious risk of self-harm by the Service member either as a result of the condition itself or medical treatment of the condition.
- <u>Harm to Others</u>. The provider believes there is a serious risk of harm to others either as a result of the condition itself or medical treatment of the condition. This includes any disclosures concerning child abuse or domestic violence consistent with DoDI 6400.06.
- <u>Harm to Mission</u>. The provider believes there is a serious risk of harm to a specific military operational mission. Such serious risk may include disorders that significantly impact impulsivity, insight, reliability, and judgment.
- <u>Special Personnel</u>. Service Members in the Personnel Reliability Program as described in DoDI 5210.42, or is in a position that has been identified by Service regulation or the command as having mission responsibilities of such potential sensitivity or urgency that normal notification standards would significantly risk mission accomplishment.

- Inpatient Care. The Service member is admitted or discharged from any inpatient mental health or substance abuse treatment facility as these are considered critical points in treatment and support nationally recognized patient standards.
- Acute Medical Conditions Interfering With Duty. The Service member is experiencing an acute mental health condition or is engaged in an acute medical treatment regimen that impairs the Service member's ability to perform assigned duties.
- Substance Abuse Treatment Program. The Service member has entered into, or is being discharged from, a formal outpatient or inpatient treatment program consistent with DoDI 1010.6 for the treatment of substance abuse or dependence.
- Command-Directed Mental Health Evaluation. The mental health services are obtained as a result of a command-directed mental health evaluation consistent with DoDD 6490.1.
- Other Special Circumstances. The notification is based on other special circumstances in which proper execution of the military mission outweighs the interests served by avoiding notification, as determined on a case-by-case basis by a health care provider (or other authorized official of the MTF involved) at the O-6 or equivalent level or above or a commanding officer at the O-6 level or above.

4. BEHAVIORAL HEALTH EVALUATIONS

A. Command-Directed

While a commander may inquire into the general nature of a Soldier's status, if a commander has a question about a Soldier's mental ability to perform his or her duty, the commander should immediately initiate a command-directed mental status evaluation. Chapter 38, Behavior Health Evaluations, discusses this situation in depth. Commanders will be provided a copy of a command-directed mental health evaluation.

B. Self-Referral

If a Soldier initiates the mental health evaluation (self-referral), medical conditions that do not affect the Soldier's fitness for duty or fitness to perform a particular mission will not be provided to the unit. Should the Soldier need to be hospitalized or prescribed medications that limit his or her ability to perform his or her duty, such as to carry a weapon, the healthcare provider has an affirmative duty to notify the unit of this change or limitation of duty status. As discussed above, MTFs and military healthcare providers will proactively inform command authorities of conditions that impair a Soldier's performance of duty. Examples include: to avert a serious and imminent threat to health or safety of a person, such as suicide or homicide; if the Soldier's medical condition could impair his or her ability to perform a specific mission; or if the Soldier's injury indicates a safety problem or battlefield trend.

5. MECHANICS OF A REQUEST FOR PHI

A. General Information

It is common for unit commanders to orally ask a health provider about the general status of a Soldier. A commander or his or her proper designee can typically get information on a Soldier's general health status, adherence to scheduled appointments, profile status, and medical readiness requirements over the phone after the commander's identity is authenticated. Commanders may also place requests in writing. These requests should clearly state the purpose for which specific medical information is sought.

B. Medical Records

Requests for medical records should be in writing, using a DA Form 4254, to the MTF's Patient Administrative Division. The servicing Judge Advocate can assist with such requests.

C. Authorized Designees

If anyone other than the commander is to use the PHI, the commander must designate the authorized command official in writing. Commanders must use such delegations judiciously, and instruct each authorized designee about the importance of not further releasing the information without appropriate justification.

D. Disagreements

Contact your servicing Judge Advocate immediately if there is a disagreement regarding the release of PHI. The servicing Staff Judge Advocate serves as an honest broker between commanders and the military treatment providers in such situations.

6. WARRIOR TRANSITION UNITS

Due to the unique nature of a Warrior Transition Unit, WTU commanders typically have access to Soldier PHI without an authorization. WTU Commanders should contact their servicing Judge Advocate about HIPAA-related questions.

7. ADDITIONAL COMMANDER RESPONSIBILITIES

A. Safeguarding PHI

Once medical information is released from the MTF to a commander, it is no longer covered by HIPAA. Commanders, however, have an important responsibility to safeguard the information received and limit any further disclosure in accordance with the Privacy Act and other applicable rules and regulations. Commanders have the same duty as healthcare providers to safeguard PHI. Information provided shall be restricted to personnel with a specific need to know; that is, access to the information must be necessary for the conduct of official duties. Unauthorized release of PHI potentially increases stigma and creates barriers to care. Commanders with questions about the further use of PHI should contact their servicing judge advocate.

B. Reduce the Stigma of Mental Health Treatment

It is DoD policy that the DoD shall foster a culture of support in the provisions of mental health care and voluntarily sought substance abuse and education to military personnel in order to dispel the stigma of seeking mental health care and/or substance misuse education services. Commanders must reduce stigma through positive regard for those who seek mental health assistance to restore and maintain their mission readiness, just as they would view someone seeking treatment for any other medical issue.

C. Transferring and Transitioning Service Members

In conjunction with health care providers, commanders shall notify gaining commanders when adherence to an ongoing treatment plan is deemed necessary to ensure mission readiness and/or safety. In all situations, to include Soldiers transitioning out of the military service, commanders and health care providers should ensure that Service members who require continued behavioral health care or medical addiction treatment or follow-up are properly transferred to prevent a break in care or treatment.

8. OTHER HIPAA EXCEPTIONS

There are numerous other exceptions to HIPAA that are not covered in this section. In addition, laws, regulations, and guidance may frequently change. The Commander should contact their servicing judge advocate with any medical information-related questions or concerns.

Chapter 43

EXTREMIST ORGANIZATIONS AND ACTIVITIES

1. REFERENCES

- DoD Directive 1325.6, Guidelines for Handling Dissident and Protest Activities Among Members of the Armed Forces, dtd 1 October 1996
- AR 600-20, Army Command Policy, dtd RAR 4 August 2011

2. OVERVIEW

Commanders must enforce the Army's policy of providing equal opportunity and treatment for all Soldiers without regard to race, color, religion, gender, or national origin. Participation in extremist organizations and activities by Army personnel is inconsistent with the responsibilities of military service and Army policy. The above-cited references provide guidance on prohibited extremist activities. The following basic principles apply in all cases.

3. EXTREMIST ORGANIZATIONS AND ACTIVITIES DEFINED

Extremist organizations and activities are those that advocate racial, gender, or ethnic hatred or intolerance; advocate, create, or engage in illegal discrimination based on race, color, gender, religion, or national origin; or advocate or use force, violence, or unlawful means to deprive individuals of their rights under the U.S. Constitution, the laws of the United States, or the laws of any State, by unlawful means.

4. PROHIBITED ACTIVITIES

Soldiers are prohibited from engaging in the following activities to support extremist organizations:

- Participating in public demonstrations or rallies;
- Attending meetings or activities knowing that the meeting or activity involves an extremist cause when on duty, in uniform, in a foreign country (whether on or off-duty, or in or out of uniform), in breach of law and order, if likely to result in violence, in violation of off-limits sanctions, or in violation of a commander's order;
- Recruiting or training members;
- Fund-raising.

5. COMMAND RESPONSIBILITIES

In any case of apparent Soldier involvement with extremist organizations or activities, commanders must take positive action to educate Soldiers of the potential adverse effects that participation in violation of Army policy may have upon good order and discipline. These actions include, but are not limited to:

A. Educating Soldiers

Commanders will advise Soldiers that extremist organizations' goals are inconsistent with Army goals, beliefs, and values concerning equal opportunity.

B. Advising Soldiers

Commanders must advise Soldiers that participation in extremist organizations or activities:

- Will be considered in evaluating overall duty performance.
- Will be considered in selections for positions of leadership and responsibility.
- Will result in removal of security clearances, when appropriate.
- Will result in reclassification actions or bars to reenlistment, when appropriate.

C. Command Authority and Options

Commanders have inherent authority to prohibit military personnel from engaging in or participating in any other activities that will adversely affect good order and discipline or morale within the command. This includes, but is not limited to, the authority to order the removal of symbols, flags, posters, or other displays from barracks, to place areas or activities off-limits (when done IAW AR 190-24), or to order Soldiers not to participate in those activities. Commanders' options for addressing a Soldier's violation of prohibited activities include:

1) UCMJ Action

Possible violations include:

- Violation or Failure to Obey a Lawful General Order or Regulation (Article 92, UCMJ).
- Riot or Breach of Peace (Article 116, UCMJ).
- Provoking Speeches or Gestures (Article 117, UCMJ).
- Conduct Prejudicial to Good Order and Discipline or Service Discrediting (Article 134, UCMJ: General Article).

2) Involuntary Separation

The basis for separation may be unsatisfactory performance, misconduct, or conduct deemed prejudicial to good order and discipline or morale.

3) Reclassification Actions or Bars to Reenlistment. (See Chapters 26-33)

4) Other Adverse Administrative or Disciplinary Action. (See Chapters 26-33)

Chapter 44

POLITICAL ACTIVITIES BY MEMBERS OF THE ARMED FORCES

1. REFERENCES

- Manual for Courts-Martial, 2008 Edition
- DoD Regulation 5500.7-R (Joint Ethics Regulation)
- DoD Directive 1344.10, Political Activities by Members of the Armed Forces on Active Duty, dtd 19 February 2008
- AR 600-20, Army Command Policy, dtd RAR 4 August 2011

2. OVERVIEW

Soldiers are expected to fulfill their obligations as citizens but are prohibited, while on active duty, from engaging in certain political activities. The above-cited references provide guidance on participation in non-partisan political activities. Reserve Soldiers not on active duty can participate in political activities in their personal capacity. The following basic principles apply in all cases.

3. PERMISSIBLE ACTIVITIES

The following are examples of permissible activities:

- Registering, voting, and expressing opinions on political candidates and issues – but not as representatives of the Army.
- Providing monetary contributions to political organizations or parties.
- Attending partisan or nonpartisan political meetings or rallies as spectators, when not in uniform.
- Writing letters to the editor of a newspaper in a personal capacity, expressing personal views on public issues or political candidates, as long as this is not part of an organized letter-writing campaign or concerted solicitation of votes for or against a political party, partisan political cause, or candidate.

4. PROHIBITED ACTIVITIES

The following are examples of prohibited activities for Soldiers on active duty:

- Participation in partisan political management, campaigns, conventions, or fundraising.
- Providing monetary contributions to another member of the armed forces serving on active duty or to an employee of the federal government.
- Marching or riding in a partisan political campaign.
- Speaking before a partisan political gathering.
- Wearing a uniform or using government property or facilities while participating in local nonpartisan political activities. This also applies to Reserve Soldiers not on active duty.

- Engaging in conduct that may imply that the Army has taken an official position on, or is otherwise involved in, a local political campaign or issue. This also applies to Reserve Soldiers not on active duty.

Chapter 45

WHISTLEBLOWER PROTECTION

1. REFERENCES

- Whistleblower Protection Act of 1989 (5 USC § 2302)
- Military Whistleblower Protection Act (10 USC §1034)
- DoDD 7050.6, Military Whistleblower Protection, 23 July 2007

2. OVERVIEW

The Whistleblower Protection Acts protect both civilian employees and military members from reprisal for having disclosed certain information evidencing wrongdoing.

3. CIVILIAN EMPLOYEE PROTECTIONS:

The Whistleblower Protection Act of 1989 (WPA) protects civilian employees from reprisal for having disclosed certain information evidencing wrongdoing in Agency operations.

A. What is Whistleblowing?

An employee is "whistleblowing" when he or she lawfully discloses information to a Member of Congress, an Inspector General, agency officials or others that he or she reasonably believes evidences the following:

- a violation of any law, rule, or regulation,
- gross mismanagement,
- gross waste of funds,
- an abuse of authority, or
- a substantial and specific danger to public health or safety.

B. Protections

Under the Civil Service Reform Act, federal agency heads, supervisors, and personnel officials are responsible for preventing prohibited personnel practices, to include reprisal for whistleblowing.

A federal agency violates the WPA if any employee who can take, direct others to take, recommend or approve any personnel action, takes or fails to take (or threatens to take or fail to take) an unfavorable personnel action with respect to any employee or applicant because of any disclosure of information by the employee as described in paragraph B. 1. above or because of the exercise of an appeal right granted by law, rule or regulation, or for assisting another employee in the exercise of an appeal right.

The WPA provides for an individual right of action before the Merit Systems Protection Board for federal employees and applicants who allege that they were subjected to any personnel action because of whistleblowing.

4. MILITARY MEMBERS PROTECTIONS

The "Military Whistleblower Protection Act" (MWPA), protects members of the armed forces from reprisal for certain lawful communication.

The MWPA prohibits taking (or threatening to take) an unfavorable personnel action, or withholding (or threatening to withhold) a favorable personnel action, as a reprisal against a member of the armed forces for making or preparing any lawful communication to a Member of Congress or an Inspector General.

The MWPA also prohibits taking (or threatening to take) an unfavorable personnel action, or withholding (or threatening to withhold) a favorable personnel action, as a reprisal against a member of the armed forces for making or preparing a communication to a Member of Congress, an Inspector General, a member of a Department of Defense audit, inspection, investigation, or law enforcement organization, or any other person or organization (including any person or organization in the chain of command) designated pursuant to regulations or other established administrative procedures for such communications, in which a member of the armed forces complains of, or discloses information that the member reasonably believes constitutes evidence of, any of the following:

- a violation of law or regulation (including a law or regulation prohibiting sexual harassment or unlawful discrimination),
- gross mismanagement,
- gross waste of funds,
- an abuse of authority, or
- a substantial and specific danger to public health or safety.

Where a Soldier alleges that his or her military record has suffered as the result of reprisal for whistleblowing, the member can apply to the Army Board for the Correction of Military Records (ABCMR) for redress. If the ABCMR finds that the Soldier was reprised against for whistleblowing, it may recommend to the Secretary of the Army appropriate disciplinary action be taken against the person who committed the prohibited personnel practice.

Chapter 46

SERVICE MEMBER'S CIVIL RELIEF ACT (SCRA)

1. OVERVIEW

The SCRA is a federal law that provides economic and civil rights protections to service members under specified conditions. The purpose of the law is to assist service members in meeting non-military obligations, so service members can devote their entire energy to the nation's defense.

2. CATEGORIES OF ECONOMIC PROTECTIONS

Primary economic protections include:

A. Six Percent Interest Rate Cap on Pre-Active Service Debts

Service member must request and provide copy of orders. Creditor may not accelerate principle owed to keep payment amount the same.

B. Termination of Residential and Motor Vehicle Leases

Service members may terminate residential, business, and motor vehicle leases after entering active service or after receiving PCS or deployment orders (at least 90 day deployment to terminate residential and business leases, or at least 180 day deployment to terminate motor vehicle leases).

C. Tax Protection

A service member neither loses nor acquires residence for taxation purposes based on absence from or presence in a state based on military orders. Service member spouses sometimes also are protected.

D. Life and Health Insurance Protection

Several service member protections exist for life insurance, including limits on an insurer's ability limit coverage for activities required by military service and federal guarantees of premium payments in some cases. Health insurance protections include reinstatement after service, usually without a waiting period or exclusions.

E. Termination of Telephone Contracts

A service member may terminate cell and land line telephone contracts after receiving military orders to relocate for at least 90 days to an area that does not support the contract. Additional protections apply for cellular family plans.

3. CATEGORIES OF CIVIL RIGHTS PROTECTIONS

Primary civil rights protections include:

A. Sale, Foreclosure, or Seizure of Property Secured by a Pre-Active Duty Service Mortgage During or Within Nine Months after Active Service

The proposed action generally requires a court order; the court may stay the proposed action and adjust the service member's obligation.

B. Eviction of an Active Service Member or Dependents

Eviction requires a court order; the court may stay the eviction and adjust the service member's obligation.

C. Stays of Proceedings in Other Civil Cases

Civil and administrative cases may be stayed for an unavailable service member. The service member must show why duty requirements materially affect his ability to appear, state when the service member is available, and provide the commander's written verification.

D. Stays or vacations of judgments and garnishments.

If a service member is materially affected by military service in complying with a court order or judgment, the court may stay the execution of the judgment, or vacate or stay a garnishment.

4. APPLICABILITY

Some SCRA protections have specific requirements. Particular SCRA protections:

- May apply to all Title 10 service members.
- May apply only to pre-active duty service obligations.
- May apply to service members who receive PCS or deployment orders.
- May require that active service materially affect a service member's ability to meet financial or legal obligations.
- May apply to service member spouses or other dependents.
- May apply to certain types of National Guard, Title 32 active duty service.
- Never apply to criminal matters.

Chapter 47

RELIGIOUS ACCOMODATION

1. REFERENCES

- DoDD 1300.I7, Accommodation of Religious Practices Within the Military Services (3 Feb 88, w/ch.1: 17 Oct 88)
- AR 600-20, para. 5-6
- SECNAVINST 1730.8A, Accommodation of Religious Practices (13 Dec 97).

2. ACCOMMODATION OF RELIGIOUS PRACTICES WITHIN THE MILITARY

It is DoD policy that requests for accommodation of religious practices should be approved by commanders when accommodation will not have an adverse impact on military readiness, unit cohesion, standards, or discipline. Commanders are responsible for the initial determination of appropriate accommodation, but service member can have denial reviewed. Each service establishes procedures for such review. For the Army, appeals are sent through each level of command to the Deputy Chief of Staff, G-1, Washington DC.

A. Four major areas.

1) Worship

Worship services, holy days, and Sabbath observances should be accommodated, except when precluded by military necessity.

2) Diet

Military Departments should include religious belief as one factor for consideration when granting separate rations, and permit commanders to authorize individuals to provide their own supplemental food rations in a field or "at sea" environment to accommodate their religious beliefs.

3) Wear and appearance

Generally, religious jewelry, apparel or articles may be worn while in uniform if they are neat, conservative and discreet. Wear of religious items that are <u>not</u> visible or apparent when in duty uniform is authorized, unless precluded by specific mission related reasons. Wear of religious items that <u>are</u> visible and apparent are governed by AR 670-1. Members may wear visible items of religious apparel while in uniform, except under circumstances in which an item is not neat and conservative or its wearing interferes with the performance of the member's military duties. Hair and grooming practices required or observed by religious groups are not included within the meaning of religious apparel. Jewelry bearing religious inscriptions or indicating religious affiliation is subject to existing Service uniform regulations just as jewelry that is not of a religious nature.

<u>Examples</u>:

- Religious item worn on a chain may not be visible when worn with the utility, service, dress, or mess uniforms. When worn with the PT uniform, the item should be no more visible than ID tags would be.

- During worship service, Soldiers may wear visible religious items that do not meet normal uniform standards. Commanders have discretion to limit this when in field environment.

4) Medical practices

In the Army, there is no accommodation in emergencies or life threatening situations. In other circumstances, a medical board will consider the request.

INTERNATIONAL & OPERATIONAL LAW

Section 6

THIS PAGE IS INTENTIONALLY BLANK

Chapter 48

RULES OF ENGAGEMENT

1. REFERENCE

- Chairman of the Joint Chiefs of Staff Instr. 3121.01B, Standing Rules of Engagement/Standing Rules for the Use of Force for U.S. Forces (13 June 2005).

2. INTRODUCTION

Rules of Engagement (ROE) are the commander's tool for regulating the use of force. The legal factors that provide the foundation for ROE are varied and complex. However, they do not stand alone; non-legal issues, such as political objectives and military mission limitations, also are essential to the construction and application of ROE. ROE ultimately are the commander's rules that must be implemented by the Soldier, Sailor, Airman, or Marine who executes the mission.

This chapter will provide an overview of basic ROE concepts. In addition, it will survey Chairman of the Joint Chiefs of Staff Instruction (CJCSI) 3121.01B, *Standing Rules of Engagement/Standing Rules for the Use of Force for U.S. Forces.*

NOTE: This chapter is NOT intended to be a substitute for the SROE. The SROE are classified SECRET, and important concepts within it may not be reproduced here.

3. OVERVIEW

A. Definition of ROE

Joint Pub 1-02, *Dictionary of Military and Associated Terms*: ROE are directives issued by competent military authority that delineate the circumstances and limitations under which U.S. [naval, ground, and air] forces will initiate and/or continue combat engagement with other forces encountered.

B. Purposes of ROE

As a practical matter, ROE perform three functions: (1) provide guidance from the President and Secretary of Defense (SECDEF), as well as subordinate commanders, to *deployed units* on the use of force; (2) act as a control mechanism for the transition from peacetime to combat operations (war); and (3) provide a mechanism to facilitate planning. ROE provide a framework that encompasses national policy goals, mission requirements, and the Law of Armed Conflict (LOAC).

1) Political Purposes

ROE ensure that national policies and objectives are reflected in the actions of commanders in the field, particularly under circumstances in which communication with higher authority is not possible. For example, in reflecting national political and diplomatic purposes, ROE may restrict the engagement of certain targets, or the use of particular weapons systems, out of a desire to tilt world opinion in a particular direction, place a positive limit on the escalation of hostilities, or not antagonize the enemy. Falling within the array of political concerns are such issues as the influence of international public opinion (particularly how it is affected by media coverage of a specific operation), the effect of host country law, and the content of status of forces agreements (SOFA) with the United States.

2) Military Purposes

ROE provide parameters within which the commander must operate to accomplish his or her assigned mission:

- ROE provide a limit on operations and ensure that U.S. actions do not trigger undesired escalation, *i.e.*, forcing a potential opponent into a "self-defense" response.
- ROE may regulate a commander's capability to influence a military action by granting or withholding the authority to use particular weapons systems or tactics.
- ROE may also reemphasize the scope of a mission. Units deployed overseas for training exercises may be limited to use of force only in self-defense, reinforcing the *training* rather than *combat* nature of the mission.

3) Legal Purposes

ROE provide restraints on a commander's actions, consistent with both domestic and international law, and may, under certain circumstances, impose greater restrictions than those required by the law. Accordingly, commanders must be intimately familiar with the legal basis for their mission. Commanders also may issue ROE to reinforce certain principles of LOAC, such as prohibitions on the destruction of religious or cultural property or minimization of injury to civilians and civilian property.

4. CJCS STANDING RULES OF ENGAGEMENT

A. Overview

The current SROE went into effect on 13 June 2005, the result of a review and revision of the previous 2000 and 1994 editions. They provide implementation guidance on the inherent right of self-defense and the application of force for mission accomplishment. They are designed to provide a common template for development and implementation of ROE for the full range of operations.

B. Applicability

The SROE establish fundamental policies and procedures governing the actions to be taken by U.S. commanders and their forces during all military operations and contingencies outside U.S. territory and ***outside*** U.S. territorial seas. SROE also apply to air and maritime homeland defense mission conducted within U.S. territory and territorial seas. The Standing Rules for the Use of Force (SRUF) apply to actions taken by U.S. commanders and their forces during all DoD civil support and routine Military Department functions occurring ***inside*** U.S. territory or territorial seas. The SRUF also apply to land-based homeland defense missions occurring within U.S. territory and to DoD forces, civilians and contractors performing law enforcement and security duties at all DoD installations.

C. Responsibility

The SECDEF approves the SROE and, through the CJCS, may issue theater, mission, or operation specific ROE. The J3 is responsible for SROE maintenance. Subordinate commanders are free to issue theater, mission, or operation ROE, but must notify the SECDEF if SECDEF-approved ROE are restricted.

D. Purpose

The purpose of the SROE is twofold: (1) provide implementation guidance on the application of force for mission accomplishment, and (2) ensure the proper exercise of the inherent right of self-defense. The SROE outline the parameters of the inherent right of self-defense in Enclosure A. The rest of the document establishes rules and procedures for implementing supplemental ROE. These supplemental ROE apply only to mission accomplishment and do not limit a commander's use of force in self-defense.

E. The SROE are divided as follows:

1) Standing Rules of Engagement

This unclassified enclosure details the general purpose, intent, and scope of the SROE, emphasizing a commander's right and obligation to use force in self-defense. Critical principles, such as unit, individual, national, and collective self-defense, hostile act and intent, and the determination to declare forces hostile are addressed as foundational elements of all ROE.

2) Key Definitions/Issues

The 2005 SROE refined the definitions section, combining the definitions of "unit" and "individual" self-defense into the more general definition of "Inherent right of self-defense" to make clear that individual self-defense is not absolute. Note, however, that if the ROE are made more restrictive, the SECDEF must be notified.

- **Self-Defense.** The SROE do not limit a commander's inherent authority and obligation to use all necessary means available and to take all appropriate action in self-defense of the commander's unit and other U.S. forces in the vicinity.
  - **Inherent Right of Self-Defense.** Unit commanders always retain the inherent right and obligation to exercise unit self-defense in response to a hostile act or demonstrated hostile intent. Unless otherwise directed by a unit commander as detailed below, military members may exercise individual self-defense in response to a hostile act or demonstrated hostile intent. When individuals are assigned and acting as part of a unit, individual self-defense should be considered a subset of unit self-defense. As such, unit commanders may limit individual self-defense by members of their unit. Both unit and individual self-defense includes defense of other U.S. military forces in the vicinity.
  - **National Self-Defense.** The act of defending the United States, U.S. forces, U.S. citizens and their property (in certain circumstances), and U.S. commercial assets from a hostile act, demonstrated hostile intent, or declared hostile force.
  - **Collective Self-Defense.** The act of defending designated non-U.S. citizens, forces, property, and interests from a hostile act or demonstrated hostile intent. Only the President or SECDEF may authorize the exercise of collective self-defense. Collective self-defense is generally implemented during combined operations.
  - **Mission Accomplishment v. Self-Defense.** The SROE distinguish between the right and obligation of self-defense, and the use of force for the accomplishment of an assigned mission. Authority to use force in mission accomplishment may be limited in light of political, military, or legal concerns, but such limitations have NO impact on a commander's right and obligation of self-defense. Further, although commanders may limit individual self-defense, commanders will always retain the inherent right and obligation to exercise unit self-defense. Distinctions between mission, accomplishment, and self-defense, and

between offensive and defensive operations, may vary based on the level of command, array of forces, and circumstances on the ground.

- **Declared Hostile Force** (DHF). Any civilian, paramilitary, or military force, or terrorist that has been declared hostile by appropriate U.S. authority. Once a force is declared to be "hostile," U.S. units may engage it without observing a hostile act or demonstration of hostile intent; *i.e.*, the basis for engagement shifts from conduct to status. Once a force or individual is identified as a DHF, the force or individual may be engaged, unless surrendering or *hors de combat* due to sickness or wounds. The authority to declare a force hostile is limited, and may be found at paragraph 3 of the SROE.
- **Hostile Act**. An attack or other use of force against the United States, U.S. forces, or other designated persons or property. It also includes force used directly to preclude or impede the mission and/or duties of U.S. forces, including the recovery of U.S. personnel or vital U.S. government property.
- **Hostile Intent**. The threat of imminent use of force against the United States, U.S. forces, or other designated persons or property. It also includes the threat of force to preclude or impede the mission and/or duties of U.S. forces, including the recovery of U.S. personnel or vital U.S. government property.
- **Imminent Use of Force**. The determination of whether the use of force against U.S. forces is imminent will be based on an assessment of all facts and circumstances known to U.S. forces at the time and may be made at any level. Imminent does not necessarily mean immediate or instantaneous.

3) Actions in Self-Defense

Upon commission of a hostile act or demonstration of hostile intent, all necessary means available and all appropriate actions may be used in self-defense. If time and circumstances permit, forces should attempt to deescalate the situation. In addition, force used in self-defense should be proportional; that is, sufficient to respond decisively. Force used may exceed that of the hostile act or hostile intent, but the nature, duration, and scope of force should not exceed what is required to respond decisively.

4) Enclosures B-H

These classified enclosures provide general guidance on specific types of operations: Maritime, Air, Land, Space, Information, and Noncombatant Evacuation Operations as well as Counterdrug Support Operations Outside U.S. Territory.

5) Supplemental Measures

Supplemental measures enable a commander to obtain or grant those additional authorities necessary to accomplish an assigned mission. Tables of supplemental measures are divided into those actions requiring President or SECDEF approval; those that require either President or SECDEF approval or Combatant Commander approval; and those that are delegated to subordinate commanders (though the delegation may be withheld by higher authority). The current SROE recognizes a fundamental difference between the two sets of supplemental measures. Measures that are reserved to the President or SECDEF or Combatant Commander are generally **permissive;** that is, the particular operation, tactic, or weapon is generally restricted, and the President, SECDEF, or Combatant Commander implements the supplemental measure to specifically permit the particular operation, tactic, or weapon. Contrast this with the remainder of the supplemental measures, those delegated to subordinate commanders. These measures are all **restrictive** in nature. Absent implementation of supplemental measures, commanders are generally allowed to use any weapon or tactic available and to employ reasonable force to accomplish his or her mission, without having to get permission first. Only when enacted will these supplemental measures restrict a particular operation, tactic, or weapon. Finally, note that supplemental ROE relate to mission accomplishment, not self-defense, and never limit a Commander's inherent right and obligation of self-defense. However, as noted above, supplemental measures may be used to limit individual self-defense.

6) Rules of Engagement Process

The current, unclassified enclosure provides guidelines for incorporating ROE development into military planning processes. It introduces the ROE Planning Cell, which may be utilized during the development process.

7) Combatant Commanders' Theater-Specific ROE

Combatant Commanders may augment the SROE as necessary by implementing supplemental measures or by submitting supplemental measures for approval, as appropriate. Theater-specific ROE documents can be found on the Combatant Command's SIPR website, often within or linked to by the SJA portion of the site. If you anticipate an exercise or deployment into any geographic Combatant Commander's AOR, check with the Combatant Commander's SJA for ROE guidance.

8) SRUF

Much like the SROE, the SRUF sets out the basic self-defense posture under the SRUF. Enclosures M-O provide classified guidance on Maritime Operations Within U.S. Territory, Land Contingency and Security-Related Operations Within U.S. Territory, and Counterdrug Support Operations Within U.S. Territory. Enclosures P and Q provide a message process for RUF, as well as RUF references.

5. MULTINATIONAL ROE

U.S. forces will often conduct operations or exercises in a multinational environment. When that occurs, the multinational ROE will apply **for mission accomplishment** if authorized by SECDEF order. If not so authorized, the CJCS SROE apply. Apparent inconsistencies between the right of self-defense contained in U.S. ROE and multinational force ROE will be submitted through the U.S. chain of command for resolution. While final resolution is pending, U.S. forces will continue to operate under U.S. ROE. In all cases, U.S. forces retain the inherent right and obligation to exercise unit self-defense in response to a hostile act or demonstrated hostile intent as defined in the SROE.

6. ROE TRAINING

Commanders have the primary responsibility for ensuring that their Soldiers are trained on the ROE. The judge advocate can play a significant role in assisting in the training of Soldiers, the staff, and leaders. ROE training is not a one-time event—it is a series of individual and collective training exercises. This training should provide realistic, rigorous scenario or vignette driven exercises. Upon receipt of a mission specific ROE, units should develop a training program and leverage judge advocates to provide individual training for unit leaders. These leaders will incorporate ROE training into the unit's collective training events like situational training exercises and mission readiness exercises. During a deployment to a contingency operation, commanders should continue to conduct refresher training to ensure compliance with the mission specific ROE. Such refresher training can use realistic vignettes generated from the unit's experiences over the duration of the deployment.

THIS PAGE IS INTENTIONALLY BLANK

Chapter 49

LAW OF ARMED CONFLICT

1. REFERENCES

- **Hague IV** – Hague Convention IV Respecting the Laws and Customs of War on Land, Oct. 18, 1907, 36 Stat. 2277.
- **GC I** – [Geneva] Convention for the Amelioration of the Condition of the Wounded and Sick in Armed Forces in the Field, Aug. 12, 1949, 6 U.S.T. 3114, T.I.A.S. 3362, 75 U.N.T.S. 31.
- **GC II** – [Geneva] Geneva Convention for the Amelioration of the Condition of Wounded, Sick, and Shipwrecked Members, Aug. 12, 1949, 6 U.S.T. 3217, T.I.A.S. 3363, 75 U.N.T.S. 85.
- **GC III** – [Geneva] Convention Relative to the Treatment of Prisoners of War, Aug. 12, 1949, 6 U.S.T. 3316, T.I.A.S. 3364, 75 U.N.T.S. 135.
- **GC IV** – [Geneva] Convention Relative to the Protection of Civilian Persons in Time of War, Aug. 12, 1949, 6 U.S.T. 3516, T.I.A.S. 3365, 75 U.N.T.S. 287.
- **AP I** – Protocol Additional to the Geneva Conventions of 12 August 1949, and Relating to the Protection of Victims of International Armed Conflicts, June 8, 1977 (not ratified by the U.S.).
- **AP II** – Protocol Additional to the Geneva Conventions of 12 August 1949, and Relating to the Protection of Victims of Non-International Armed Conflicts, June 8, 1977 (not ratified by the U.S.).
- **CCW** – Convention on Prohibitions or Restrictions of the Use of Certain Conventional Weapons Which May be Deemed to be Excessively Injurious or to Have Indiscriminate Effects, Oct. 10, 1980, 1342 U.N.T.S. 137, 19 I.L.M. 1524
- **DoDD 2311.01E** – Department of Defense (DoD) Directive 2311.01E, DoD Law of War Program
- **FM 27-10** – U.S. Army Field Manual 27-10, The Law of Land Warfare (18 July 1956, Change 1 15 July 1976).
- **OpLaw Handbook** – Operational Law Handbook, International and Operational Law Department, The Judge Advocate General's Legal Center and School (TJAGLCS), U.S. Army, available at http://www.loc.gov/rr/frd/Military_Law/operational-law-handbooks.html (an extensive guide to the law of armed conflict and other operational law topics, published annually by TJAGLCS faculty)

2. INTRODUCTION

This Chapter summarizes key law of armed conflict (LOAC) provisions for commanders and military personnel in the conduct of operations in both international and non-international armed conflicts. It defines LOAC and discusses its purposes, sources, implementation, basic principles, obligations and enforcement. For more information on these and related topics, consult the latest edition of the OpLaw Handbook or an operational law judge advocate.

DoD policy is to comply with LOAC "during all armed conflicts, however such conflicts are characterized, and in all other military operations." (DoDD 2311.01E, para. 4.1). Every Soldier, Sailor, Airman, Marine, and all others accompanying U.S. forces must comply with LOAC.

3. OVERVIEW OF THE LAW OF ARMED CONFLICT

A. Definition

DoDD 2311.01E, para. 3.1, defines the Law of Armed Conflict (LOAC) as "that part of international law that regulates the conduct of armed hostilities." It is also referred to as the "law of war" (LOW) or "international humanitarian law" (IHL). LOAC includes ratified treaties and applicable customary international law (CIL) binding on the United States or individual citizens.

B. Purposes

The purposes of LOAC serve both military needs and humanitarian concerns. These purposes include:

- Protecting both combatants and noncombatants from unnecessary suffering
- Safeguarding persons who fall into the hands of the enemy
- Facilitating the restoration of peace
- Ensuring good order and discipline
- Fighting in a disciplined manner consistent with national values
- Maintaining domestic and international public support

C. Primary Sources

1) Ratified LOAC Treaties

When the United States ratifies a treaty, that treaty becomes the law of the United States, equal to a statute passed by Congress. The U.S. always honors its treaty obligations, including these key LOAC treaties:

- **Hague IV** (1907): Ratified in 1909 by the U.S., this treaty requires belligerents to distinguish themselves from civilians; protect prisoners of war; and limit certain means and methods of attack. The U.S. follows many of Hague IV's basic restrictions in all types of conflicts.
- **GC I-IV** (1949): Ratified in 1955 by the U.S., these treaties govern international armed conflict (between nations). GC I-IV currently bind all United Nations member nations. The four treaties protect (I) the wounded and sick on land; (II) the wounded/sick and shipwrecked at sea; (III) prisoners of war; and (IV) civilians in conflict areas or occupied territory. The treaties define severe violations of terms as "grave breaches," and require nations to train their forces on compliance. Finally, GC I-IV require that in non-international armed conflicts, civilians and the wounded and sick be treated humanely.
- **CCW** (1980): Ratified in 1995 by the U.S., this treaty provides legal framework and dialogue for regulating particular weapons systems through "Protocols," or supplemental treaties. The U.S. is party to the CCW and all its Protocols: (I) banning non-detectable fragments; as well as regulating use of (II/II Amended) mines, booby-traps, and other remote/timed devices (III) incendiaries, (IV) lasers, and (V) explosive remnants of war. The U.S. actively promotes the CCW and its standards.

Many other ratified treaties provide additional protections, or prohibit/regulate use of certain weapons systems. Examples include cultural property protections; recognition of a new "red crystal" symbol for medical personnel, vehicles, and hospitals; prohibitions on asphyxiating or poisonous gases, and biological or chemical weapons; and regulation of nuclear weapons. Consult a judge advocate to determine whether a specialized treaty applies to a particular act or weapon system in question.

2) Customary International Law

Even absent a treaty, the United States always follows certain principles. Beyond policy or doctrine, these customs are established by state practice and followed out of a sense of legal obligation in all operations or types of conflict. LOAC includes two main types of customary international law principles:

- **Basic LOAC Principles:** These include Military Necessity, Distinction, Proportionality, and Unnecessary Suffering, and provide the starting framework for analyzing the legality of military operations. Section IV below defines these principles in greater detail.
- **Fundamental Human Rights:** These include a commitment never to engage in acts violating the life and dignity of human beings. While there is no definitive U.S. list, the following acts are prohibited: genocide, slavery, murder or enforced disappearance, torture or other cruel, inhuman, or degrading treatment or punishment, prolonged arbitrary detention, systematic racial discrimination, rape, or a consistent pattern of gross violations of internationally recognized human rights. These are behaviors beyond the boundaries of honorable combat that all should recognize as illegal.

D. Implementation

1) By U.S. Forces

A variety of statutes, regulations, doctrine, and directives implement LOAC for U.S. forces. Notable examples include the Uniform Code of Military Justice (UCMJ), 10 U.S. Code Section 2441 (the war crimes statute) FM 27-10 (LOAC generally), CJCSI 3121.01B (standing rules of engagement/rules for use of force), JP 3-60 and FM 3-60 (targeting), AR 190-8 (detainee operations), and numerous other references.

Rules of engagement (ROE), tactical directives, and standard operating procedures also implement and must comply with LOAC. These vital sources authorize military action tailored to the overall mission. While ROE change with the mission, LOAC obligations apply in all operations. ROE serve as a Commander's tool to honor those obligations. Chapter 44 discusses ROE in more detail.

2) By Coalition Partners

Other nations may follow additional sources of LOAC. Some are bound by international tribunals, like the International Criminal Court (war crimes) or European Court of Human Rights (regional human rights violations). Some are parties to additional treaties, like the Ottawa Convention (banning antipersonnel land mines) or Convention on Cluster Munitions (banning cluster munitions). Though the U.S. is not bound by these sources, Commanders should be familiar with host and allied nation LOAC commitments and national caveats.

Notably, over 165 nations, including most NATO and other U.S. allies (except Israel and Turkey) follow the 1977 Additional Protocols I and II (**AP I** and **AP II**). These treaties extensively supplement GC I-IV. While the U.S. considers many terms in AP I and AP II to be customary international law, it has not ratified either treaty. Given their wide acceptance, these treaties can impact operations conducted with or within other nations.

3) By Non-Governmental Entities

Non-Governmental Entities frequently take interest in U.S. operations. A few organizations, like the International Committee of the Red Cross (ICRC), or some United Nations (U.N.) bodies, perform essential oversight missions. They should always be assigned an escort (preferably a judge advocate) and permitted to carry out their duties, subject to essential security needs, mission requirements, and legitimate, practical limitations. Treat other interested entities who lack a legal mandate with courtesy and even-handedness.

4. BASIC PRINCIPLES OF THE LAW OF ARMED CONFLICT

A. Military Necessity

This principle justifies those measures **not forbidden** by international law that are **indispensable** for securing the complete submission of the enemy as soon as possible. However, this principle is not applied in a vacuum. It must be applied in conjunction with other law of war principles.

Military necessity generally **prohibits** the intentional targeting of protected **persons** (civilians, hostile personnel who have surrendered or are otherwise "out of combat," etc.) and protected **places** (objects or places used for purely civilian purposes, such as hospitals, schools, and cultural property that have not been converted to or for military/hostile use) because they do not constitute legitimate military objectives in furtherance of the accomplishment of the mission.

B. Distinction

This principle requires parties to a conflict to **distinguish** between combatants and noncombatants (i.e. protected persons), and to distinguish between military objectives and civilian objects (i.e. protected property and places). Parties to a conflict must direct their operations only against military objectives.

Military objectives are combatants and those objects which by their nature, location, purpose, or use make an effective contribution to military action and whose total or partial destruction, capture or neutralization, in the circumstances ruling at the time, offer a definitive military advantage.

C. Proportionality

This principle prohibits attacks that may be expected to cause incidental loss of civilian life, injury to civilians, damage to civilian objects, or a combination thereof, which would be **excessive** in relation to the concrete and direct military advantage expected to be gained.

This principle is only applicable when an attack may possibly affect civilians or civilian objects, and thereby, may cause collateral damage. Proportionality is a way in which a military commander must assess his or her obligations as to the principle of distinction, while avoiding actions that are indiscriminate.

D. Unnecessary Suffering

This principle forbids the employment of means and methods of warfare **calculated to cause** unnecessary suffering. This principle acknowledges that combatants' necessary suffering, which may include severe injury and loss of life, is lawful. This principle largely applies to the legality of weapons and ammunition design, as well as their actual use or any field modifications.

Weapons and ammunition issued by HQDA are reviewed by The Judge Advocate General or his representative for Army-wide use, to ensure compliance with LOAC. However, approved weapons and ammunition also may not be used in a way that will cause unnecessary suffering or injury. A weapon or munition would be deemed to cause unnecessary suffering if, in its normal use, the injury caused by it is disproportionate to the military necessity for it, that is, the military advantage to be gained from its use.

5. OBLIGATIONS AND ENFORCEMENT

A. Always Follow LOAC

As stated above, DoD policy is to comply with LOAC "during all armed conflicts, however such conflicts are characterized, and in all other military operations." (DoDD 2311.01E, para. 4.1). Most rules of LOAC apply across the entire spectrum of conflict.

Commanders are legally responsible for war crimes they personally commit, order committed, or know or should have known about and take no action to prevent, stop, or punish. The U.S. reviews commander and subordinate decisions based on **information reasonably available** at the time an action is planed, authorized, or executed, and not on information that comes to light afterwards.

B. Train Soldiers to Follow LOAC

Commanders have the primary duty to ensure members of their commands do not violate LOAC. Two principal ways include recognizing factors which may lead to commission of war crimes, and training subordinate commanders and troops on LOAC standards, compliance, and proper responses to illegal orders.

1) Factors Leading to War Crimes

Historically, the following factors led to commission of war crimes. They should be monitored and openly addressed at all levels of command and supervision, and simulated in training scenarios or vignettes:

- High friendly losses.
- High turnover rate in the chain of command.
- Dehumanization of the enemy (derogatory names or epithets).
- Poorly trained or inexperienced troops.
- The lack of a clearly defined enemy.
- Unclear orders.
- High frustration level among the troops.

2) Unclear or Illegal Orders

Train soldiers not only to follow the rules of LOAC, but also how to respond to unclear or clearly illegal orders. Troops who receive unclear orders must insist, respectfully and tactfully, on clarification. The superior should clarify the order and ensure all understand there is no intent to order a LOAC violation. If troops are comfortable asking for clarification, this indicates a healthy superior-subordinate relationship.

If the superior insists on the illegal order, the Soldier has a duty to disobey that order and report the incident to the next superior commander, military police, CID, nearest judge advocate, or local inspector general. Obedience to orders is not a defense to war crimes. Never retaliate against Soldiers for such reports. If wrong, it signals communication or training deficiencies. If right, it might stop a war crime.

C. Report and Address LOAC Violations

Violations or perceived violations of LOAC can cripple U.S. operations. From execution of civilian villagers (My Lai, Vietnam) to detainee mistreatment (Abu Ghraib prison, Iraq), to killing and cutting off body parts of random citizens (so-called "thrill kills", Afghanistan), these incidents undermine every purpose for LOAC. Those who violate LOAC, or order or permit others to commit violations, must be held accountable.

1) Reportable Incidents

DoDD 2311.01E, para. 3.2 defines a "reportable incident" as a "possible, suspected, or alleged violation of the law of war [i.e., LOAC], for which there is credible information, or conduct during military operations other than war that would constitute a violation of the law of war if it occurred during an armed conflict."

2) Reporting Requirements

Experience has shown that swift investigation immediately after hearing about an allegation best contributes to good order and discipline. **When in doubt, report and investigate!**

For reporting, DoDD 2311.01E states it DoD policy that:

- All reportable incidents committed by or against U.S. personnel, enemy persons, or any other individual are **reported promptly, investigated thoroughly**, and, where appropriate, **remedied by corrective action.** (Para. 4.4).
- All reportable incidents are **reported through command channels** for ultimate transmission to appropriate U.S. Agencies, allied governments, or other appropriate authorities. (Para. 4.5)
- All military and U.S. civilian employees, contractors, and subcontractors assigned to or accompanying DoD Components **shall report** reportable incidents through their chain of command. Reports may be made to military police, a judge advocate, or an inspector general. If made to anyone else, reports shall be accepted and immediately forwarded through the recipient's chain of command. (Para. 6.3)
- **Commanders shall immediately forward** initial reports through the applicable operational chain of command and Military Department, through the most expeditious means available. (Para. 6.4)
- **Higher authorities** receiving an initial report must require a formal investigation and forward the initial report up the chain to the Combatant Commander and HQDA. Higher authorities must also file supplemental reports on (a) any criminal cases, regardless of the allegation, receiving or expected to receive significant media interest, or (b) any cases suspected to involve "friendly fire." (Para. 6.5).

Additional detail on reporting should be in the OPLAN or OPORD Legal Appendix, and the unit TACSOP or FSOP. Possibly, an OPREP-3 report per CJCSM 3150.03D is also required. The U.S. Army Criminal Investigative Command (CID) normally investigates LOAC violations. Minor violations may alternatively be investigated following AR 15-6 or a commander's inquiry under Rule for Courts-Martial 303.

3) Command Actions

Commanders have wide discretion in responding to the results of reports. If a training deficiency is noted, correct it immediately at the appropriate level. If misconduct is found, consult with a judge advocate, other appropriate advisors, and the chain of command in selecting administrative and/or disciplinary measures, possibly including criminal prosecution. Consider also the overall impact to operations and local national sentiment. Finally, maintain a record of the report so that it can be referenced, if required in the future.

6. CONCLUSION

This chapter reviewed LOAC from a Commander's perspective. It defined LOAC and discussed its purposes, sources, implementation, basic principles, obligations and enforcement. Our nation's experience proves that although the enemy may act otherwise, compliance with LOAC is vital to mission success and discipline, offers the best chance of lasting peace and respect, and is a core command responsibility.

CLAIMS & CLIENT SERVICES

Section 7

THIS PAGE IS INTENTIONALLY BLANK

Chapter 50

ARTICLE 139 CLAIMS

1. REFERENCES

- Manual for Courts-Martial, 2008 Edition
- AR 27-20, Claims, dtd 8 February 2008
- DA PAM 27-162, Claims Procedures, dtd 21 March 2008

2. OVERVIEW

Claims initiated and processed UP Article 139, UCMJ, permit individuals to file claims against Soldiers who *willfully take or destroy personal property*. Soldiers are not the only persons who may file Article 139 claims; any person whose property was taken or destroyed *by a Soldier* may file such a claim, subject to certain limitations.

3. LIMITATIONS ON TYPES OF ARTICLE 139 CLAIMS

Article 139 claims may **not** be processed for the following types of loss or destruction:

- Breach of Contract.
- Property Damaged through Negligence.
- Personal Injury or Death.
- Actions or Omissions of Military Personnel Acting within the Scope of their Employment.

4. LIMITATIONS ON FINANCIAL AMOUNTS OF ARTICLE 139 CLAIMS

Special Courts-Martial Convening Authorities (SPCMCAs) (normally, Brigade or Group Commanders) may approve claims that do not exceed $5,000 on a single claim. General Courts-Martial Convening Authorities (GCMCAs) may approve claims that do not exceed $10,000 on a single claim.

5. PROCESSING ARTICLE 139 CLAIMS

AR 27-20, chap 9 governs the procedures for initiating and processing Article 139 claims. In particular, commanders should be aware of the following provisions.

A. Suspense for Filing

Claimants must file claims within 90 days from the date of the incident causing the loss or destruction of property.

B. Place for Filing

Claimants should file claims with their servicing installation's Claims Office. Installation claims offices traditionally are co-located with respective installation's Office of the Staff Judge Advocate. They may do so either verbally or in writing.

C. Forwarding of Claim

Claims that are properly filed will be forwarded to the suspected Soldier's SPCMCA. If the SPCMCA determines the claim is cognizable, he will assign, within four working days of receiving the claim, an Investigating Officer (IO) to examine the allegations and surrounding facts and circumstances.

D. Investigation

The IO's investigation must comply with AR 27-20, chap 9. In particular, he must take the following steps:

1) Notify the Soldier

The IO must notify the Soldier against whom a claim is filed, and if the Soldier wishes to make voluntary restitution, the IO may (with the SPCMCA's approval) delay the proceedings until the end of the next pay period.

2) Continue the Investigation

If the Soldier refuses to make full restitution or cannot do so, the IO will determine whether the claim is *cognizable* (proper UP AR 27-20) and *meritorious* (supported by the evidence). The IO likely will have to obtain written statements and other supporting paperwork, diagrams, and/or pictures during his investigation.

3) Determination of Meritorious Claim

If the IO determines that a Soldier should be held financially liable, he must submit his written findings and recommendations to the SPCMCA. The assessment must be reviewed for legal sufficiency; normally, the servicing Judge Advocate will perform this legal review.

4) Notification to Liable Soldier

Soldiers against whom financial liability has been assessed must be notified of the determination and of their right to seek reconsideration. A copy of the IO's findings and recommendations must be enclosed with the notice. Unless the approval authority determines that substantial injustice will result, action to recoup money from the liable Soldier must be suspended for 10 working days, in order to afford him an opportunity to respond to the assessment of liability.

E. Disposition of Meritorious Claims

If the investigation into the Article 139 claim ultimately determines that a Soldier is financially liable for the loss or destruction of personal property, an amount equal to the assessed amount of loss or destruction will be taken directly from the Soldier's military pay and awarded to the claimant. Alternatively, the Soldier may choose to make voluntary and full restitution to the claimant at any stage during the claim process. If this occurs, the approval authority may terminate the Article 139 proceedings without findings.

6. RELATED ADMINISTRATIVE AND UCMJ ACTIONS

Commanders may determine, in appropriate circumstances, that a Soldier's actions resulting in the loss or damage of private property warrant adverse administrative or UCMJ action. Commanders are advised, however, that findings of liability under Article 139 are separate and distinct from findings that may result during other adverse actions. Each type of action requires independent findings.

Chapter 51

FOREIGN AND DEPLOYMENT CLAIMS

1. REFERENCES

- U.S. Dep't Of Army, Reg. 27-20, Claims (8 Feb. 2008)
- U.S. Dep't Of Army, Pam. 27-162, Claims (21 Mar. 2008)
- JAGINST 5890.1A, Administrative Processing and Consideration of Claims on Behalf of and Against the United States (18 June 2005)
- Memorandum, Under Secretary of Defense for Secretaries of the Military Departments, et al., subject: Commanders' Emergency Response Program (CERP) Guidance (27 Jul 2009)
- Memorandum, Secretary of Defense for Chairman of the Joint Chiefs of Staff, subject: Response Posture for Noncombatant Civilian Casualty Incidents in Afghanistan
- ALARACT Message, 210236Z Jul 06, Headquarters, U.S. Dep't of Army, subject: Policies and Procedures for the Handling of Personal Effects and Government Property.

2. TYPES OF CLAIMS APPLICABLE DURING A DEPLOYMENT

A. Claims Cognizable Under the Personnel Claims Act (PCA).

The PCA applies worldwide. It is limited to claims for loss, damage, or destruction of personal property of military personnel and DoD civilian employees that occur incident to service. Valid PCA claims commonly arising in deployment situations include: loss of equipment and personal items during transportation; certain losses while in garrison quarters; losses suffered in an emergency evacuation; losses due to terrorism directed against the United States; and the loss of clothing and articles worn while performing military duties. No claim may be approved under the PCA when the claimant's negligence caused the loss. Prompt payment of service members' and civilians' PCA claims is essential to maintenance of positive morale in the unit.

B. Wounded Warrior Personal Effects Processing

(ALARACT Message 139/2006). Over the last several years, CENTCOM has experienced difficulty with processing of the personal effects of Soldiers evacuated from theater. This loss of property results in numerous claims and decreased morale. Once a Soldier is killed in action (KIA), missing in action (MIA), or medically evacuated due to combat injuries from CENTCOM theater of operations, commanders are responsible for processing the Soldier's personal effects in accordance with the following procedures:

Commander appoints summary court-martial officer (SCMO) immediately upon notification. The SCMO will safeguard, inventory, and package all personal effects. Please note that recent implementation guidance allows for NCOs in the rank of E-6 or above to serve as medically evacuated inventory officials, but officers must still serve as SCMO for KIA and MIA Soldiers.

If Soldier is declared KIA, MIA or medically evacuated because of combat-related injuries and will not return to the unit, then SCMO will process personal effects through the mortuary affairs collection point (MACP).

The MACP will send the property to the Joint Personal Effects Depot (JPED), who will then process the property and send it to the Soldier or next of kin.

C. Claims Cognizable Under the Military Claims Act (MCA)

The MCA also applies worldwide, however the claimant must be a U.S. resident in order to recover. Overseas, the MCA will apply only when the claim cannot be paid under the PCA or the Foreign Claims Act (FCA) (discussed below). The MCA may be used to reimburse U.S. contractors and reporters for loss of personal items while serving alongside military members in deployed environments.

D. Claims Cognizable Under the Foreign Claims Act (FCA)

The FCA is the most widely-used claims statute in foreign deployments. Under the FCA, meritorious claims for property losses, injury or death caused by service members or the civilian component of the U.S. forces may be settled "[t]o promote and maintain friendly relations" with the receiving state. Only claims resulting from "noncombat activities" or negligent or wrongful acts or omissions are compensable. Categories of claims that may not be allowed include: losses from combat; contractual matters; domestic obligations; and claims that either are not in the best interest of the U.S. to pay, or are contrary to public policy.

E. Claims Cognizable Under International Agreements (SOFA Claims)

As a general rule, the FCA will not apply in foreign countries where the U.S. has an agreement that "provides for the settlement or adjudication and cost sharing of claims against the United States arising out of the acts or omissions of a member or civilian employee of an armed force of the United States." For example, if a unit deploys to Korea, Japan, or any NATO or Partnership for Peace country, claims matters will be managed by a command claims service under provisions outlined in the applicable status of forces agreement (SOFA).

F. Article 139 Claims

See Chapter 46 of this Handbook.

G. Alternatives to Claims

In addition to the many claims provisions listed above, deployed units must also be aware of alternative sources for payments. Primarily, solatia and Commander's Emergency Response Program (CERP) funds may be used to make payments under certain circumstances in which a claim is not cognizable. Although these payment sources are NOT a part of the claims program, they may be a suitable alternative to claims in certain circumstances.

H. Solatia Payments

If a unit deploys to parts of the world where payments in sympathy or recognition of loss are common, Commander's should explore the possibility of making solatia payments to accident victims. Solatia payments are **not** claims payments. They are payments in money or in-kind to a victim or to a victim's family as an expression of sympathy or condolence. These payments are immediate and, generally, nominal. The individual or unit involved in the damage has no **legal** obligation to pay; compensation is simply offered as an expression of sympathy in accordance with local custom. Solatia payments are **not** paid from claims funds but, rather, from unit operation and maintenance (O&M) budgets. Prompt payment of solatia ensures the goodwill of local national populations, thus allowing the U.S. to maintain positive relations with the host nation. Solatia payments should not be made without prior coordination with the highest levels of command for the deployment area. On 26 November 2004, the DoD General Counsel issued an opinion that solatia payments are a custom in Iraq and Afghanistan.

I. CERP Condolence Payments

The Commanders' Emergency Response Program was originally created to respond to "urgent humanitarian relief and reconstruction requirements," but not for payments to individuals. However, in 2005, the guidance was changed to allow for payment of:

- "Repair of damage that results from U.S., coalition, or supporting military operations and is not compensable under the Foreign Claims Act";
- "Condolence payments to individual civilians for death, injury, or property damage resulting from U.S., coalition, or supporting military operations."

THIS PAGE IS INTENTIONALLY BLANK

Chapter 52

FAMILY SUPPORT OBLIGATIONS

1. APPLICABILITY

- All members of the Active Army, including cadets at the U.S. Military Academy.
- All members of the U.S. Army Reserve on active duty pursuant to orders for thirty days or more. This includes Active Guard/Reserve Soldiers (AGR).
- All members of the Army National Guard of the United States on active duty for thirty days or more.
- Members of the Army National Guard on active duty for thirty days or more pursuant to orders under Title 32, United States Code, except for the punitive provision.
- Soldiers receiving full or partial pay and allowances while confined at the U.S. Disciplinary Barracks or other confinement facilities.

2. COMMAND DRIVEN PROGRAM

- The enforcement authority is the military commander.
- The commander can punish a soldier for failing to comply with certain obligations imposed by the regulation.
- The commander must become involved when the parties are unable to agree on a proper method to provide financial support to the family members. The commander's obligation does not arise until a family member or an authorized representative of the family member complains to the command that the soldier is failing to provide proper support. AR 608-99, para. 2-1b.

3. INTERIM SUPPORT ONLY (AR 608-99, PARA. 2-6.)

Where No Court Order Or Support Agreement Exists, The Army Uses BAH II (RC/T) As A Yardstick For Determining The Amount Of The Interim Support Obligation.

NOTE: A soldier's actual receipt of BAH is **not** a prerequisite to the obligation to pay interim support to family members. AR 608-99, para. 1-7b.

Army Regulation 608-99 creates an interim support requirement that applies **ONLY** when the parties do not have a court order or an agreement concerning support.

This interim amount is not intended to provide adequate support in all cases, and should **not** be used as a guideline for civilian agencies or courts in establishing support requirements.

Purpose. The purpose of interim support is to provide some family support while the parties seek an agreement or settlement by a court. AR 608-99, para. 1-5d.

When the Interim Requirement is not Enough (or Excessive). Soldiers or family members who think the interim amount is not enough, or excessive, must obtain a court order or enter an agreement to change the soldier's support obligation. **Commanders have NO authority to order support less than or in excess of the interim requirement.**

4. FAMILY MEMBERS

Family members, for purposes of AR 608-99, only include:

- A soldier's present spouse.
- A soldier's minor children from the present marriage.
- A soldier's children by any former marriage if the soldier has a current obligation to provide support to that child (includes adopted children, but not children adopted by another person).
- Minor children born out of wedlock to—
  - a female soldier
  - a male soldier, if evidence by a court order, or the functional equivalent of a court order, identifying the soldier as the father: **or** if the soldier is providing support to the child under the terms of the regulation.
- Any other person the soldier is obligated to support by applicable state law (e.g., parent, stepchild).

5. ARREARAGES

- Soldiers cannot fall into arrears without violating AR 608-99
- Collection of arrearages through court procedures is only possible for violations of a court order or a written support agreement.
  - No legal means to collect arrearages based on failure to pay interim support.
  - Army policy is to encourage - but not order - payment of arrearages regarding interim support.
- Punishment for failure to pay interim support is based on failure to pay support when due, not for failure to pay arrearages.

6. DETERMINING THE AMOUNT OF SUPPORT DUE.

The amount of support due comes directly from the BAH RC/T chart provided by DFAS. You may find the chart for the current year at: http://www.dfas.mil. The table is linked to on the front page in PDF form as part of the overall military pay table. The Service member normally owes the "With Dependent" rate based on the Service member's rank regardless of location.

Special circumstances apply for dual military couples or if the family members (dependents) reside in different locations from each other. Consult your legal advisor in these cases.

Chapter 53

DEBT AND CONSUMER PROTECTION

1. DEBT AND DEBT COLLECTORS

A. Basics

- While Soldiers are required to manage their personal affairs satisfactorily and pay their debts promptly, the Army has no legal authority to force Soldiers to pay their debts. In most cases, the Army cannot divert any part of a Soldier's pay even though payment of the debt was decreed by a civil court. Only civil authorities can enforce payment of private debts.
- Commanders must not try to judge or settle disputed debts, or admit or deny whether claims are valid. The Army will not tell claimants whether any adverse action has been taken against a Soldier as a result of a claim.
- It is a Soldier's option on how he or she pays a debt. Soldiers cannot be forced or encouraged to pay a debt with an allotment.
- When a Soldier defaults on a debt, the creditor or debt collector may attempt to contact you to obtain your assistance in collecting the debt.
- Your obligation to assist depends on a number of factors that you may not be able to discern without the assistance of your servicing Judge Advocate. In accordance with Army Regulation (AR) 600-15, creditors must meet numerous conditions prior to getting command assistance in debt processing. Unless a debt collector has a valid court judgment and meets all other prerequisites set forth in AR 600-15, debt collectors are not entitled to command assistance with debt processing. In fact, debt collectors who contact commanders are likely violating the Fair Debt Collection Practices Act (FDCPA).

B. Steps for Commanders Contacted to Assist with Collecting on a Debt

1) Attempt to get contact information

This includes basics such as the caller's name, address, and telephone number. Because of the operation of the FDCPA and other laws and regulations, the caller may not be willing to provide this information. In some cases, the person will just inform you that he or she needs to discuss "an important matter," or something along those lines, with the Soldier. At a minimum, note the date and time of the call, and what was said. This information may later benefit your Soldier. Do not make any promises to the caller, to include a promise to assist with or "check into" the matter.

2) Contact your legal advisor

The level of assistance you must provide to the creditor, if any, as well as the manner in which you may help your Soldier, likely hinges on various complicated federal and state laws and regulations. Provide the information about the phone call to your legal advisor. Ask the legal advisor for advice on how to proceed, particularly if the Soldier is in trouble for other unrelated matters.

3) Counsel the Soldier, as appropriate.

Your legal advisor will give you advice on the nature and specifics of the counseling.

- **Creditors Who Have Satisfied AR 600-15.** If a creditor has satisfied all prerequisites of AR 600-15, you will inform the Soldier of numerous things, to include the debt complaint, the Soldier's responsibility to pay just debts, the possible adverse actions, and the Soldier's legal rights. You will also review all defenses, rights, counterclaims, and will urge the Soldier to seek budget counseling and legal assistance. Your legal advisor can draft the counseling statement to ensure all requirements are met, to include the requirement to read the Soldier his or her Article 31, UCMJ rights.
- **All Other Cases.** In all other cases, you may counsel the Soldier to better understand the Soldier's issue and to help find a solution. If you ever anticipate taking any form of adverse action against the Soldier or are currently doing so, contact your legal advisor prior to the counseling. If you delegate this responsibility, ensure that the counselor understands his or her obligations under Article 31, UCMJ. In these cases, it is also often good practice to provide the Soldier with the information about the call you received, as the Soldier may be able to use that information to obtain relief.

4) Immediately Refer the Soldier to a Legal Assistance Attorney.

The fact that you received a call may indicate that the Soldier is in financial stress. A legal assistance attorney will be able to represent the Soldier individually and assert any legal rights that the Soldier may have, such as under the FDCPA. The FDCPA has numerous penalty provisions for procedural violations that may help the Soldier eliminate an otherwise valid debt. The legal assistance attorney can also assist the Soldier to set up financial counseling. The referral needs to be quick, as the Soldier may only have a short time to assert particular rights. Have your legal advisor assist you if your Soldier has trouble getting an appointment.

5) Contact Your Legal Advisor After Every Subsequent Call.

It may be prudent to share information about subsequent calls with the Soldier's legal assistance attorney or civilian attorney, if applicable.

2. AUTOMOBILES

A. Basics

Most Soldiers do not purchase an automobile the proper way. Soldiers will often inform a car dealer of the maximum monthly payment that he or she can afford. Many car dealers will then seek to maximize the profit by implementing a variety of techniques, none of which are advantageous to the Soldier.

Soldiers are also susceptible to what is commonly known as a "Yo-Yo Car Sale." Dealers who participate in this scam will allow a Soldier to drive a car off of the lot with the understanding that the purchase has been completed. After a few days or weeks, the Soldier is called back into the dealer under some premise, such as "the financing fell through." At this point, the dealer has already sold the Soldier's trade-in vehicle. The dealer will then take possession of the new vehicle, and try to force the Soldier into paying a larger down payment or agreeing to a higher interest rate. Soldiers often agree to a new deal out of a fear of embarrassment, a lack of legal knowledge, or simply because the Soldier feels like he or she has no real choice. While each case is different, this type of practice is typically illegal for a variety of reasons.

B. Preventive Measures

- Contact your servicing Judge Advocate or Army Community Services (ACS) Financial Planning professional to teach a class on how to properly purchase a car.
- Soldiers should shop for 3 things separately when purchasing a car:
  - The price of the car;
  - The financing / credit;
  - The insurance and extras.
- Soldiers should walk into a car dealer with several financing quotes. Soldiers can obtain financing quotes from banks, credit unions, and other reputable lenders. When a Soldier is armed with this knowledge, the most common pricing and yo-yo scams are almost impossible for the dealer to implement.

C. Curative Measures

Commanders who believe that a Soldier was ripped off should immediately refer the Soldier to a Legal Assistance Attorney. Have your legal advisor assist you if your Soldier has trouble getting an appointment. Soldiers who may be the victim of a "Yo-Yo" scam need immediate help.

THIS PAGE IS INTENTIONALLY BLANK

GOVERNMENT INFORMATION PRACTICES

Section 8

THIS PAGE IS INTENTIONALLY BLANK

Chapter 54

FREEDOM OF INFORMATION ACT PROGRAM

1. REFERENCES

- DoD 5400.7-R, DoD Freedom of Information Act Program, 2 January 2008 (Incorporating Change 1, 28 July 2011)
- AR 25-55, Army Freedom of Information Act Program, 1 December 1997

2. OVERVIEW

The basic purpose of the Freedom of Information Act (FOIA) is to provide all persons a statutory right of access to "agency records" that are not specifically exempted from disclosure. If properly requested and not exempt from release, the release authority has twenty working days to respond to a FOIA request. Only an Initial Denial Authority (IDA) can deny a request. The presumption favors release of records.

3. INITIAL DENIAL AUTHORITY

Only an Army IDA or his delegate can deny a FOIA request. The IDAs are specifically designated in AR 25-55, paragraph 5-200(d). The IDAs are authorized to act on records within their area of functional responsibility.

4. PROPER REQUEST

A proper request is a request that is in writing, by any person (U.S. or foreign, organization or business, not a Federal agency), reasonably describes the agency record, asserts a willingness to pay fees, and invokes FOIA (either generally or specifically).

5. EXEMPTIONS

It is the DoD policy to make records publicly available. There are certain types of records that may be withheld if the IDA determines that an exemption applies. Some specific exemptions to FOIA release include Classified information; Purely internal rules and procedures; Privileged Communications including internal advice and recommendations; Records containing personnel and medical files, or similar files (records that contain personal and private information, release of which would constitute a clearly unwarranted invasion of privacy); and Law enforcement records.

6. FEES

Requestors may be charged fees for search, review, and reproduction in accordance with AR 25-55, paragraph 6-104.

THIS PAGE IS INTENTIONALLY BLANK

Chapter 55

PRIVACY ACT PROGRAM

1. REFERENCES

- DoD 5400.11-R, Department of Defense Privacy Program, 14 May 2007
- AR 340-21, The Army Privacy Program, 5 July 1985
- ALARACT 050/2009, PII Incident Reporting and Notification Procedures

2. OVERVIEW

The Privacy Act pertains to three aspects of Government practices regarding individual personal information: collection & maintenance, disclosure, and access & amendment of records. The Privacy Act applies to information that is collected and stored in a "system of records," limits the Government's use, and provides the individual access to their records, unless specifically exempted from disclosure.

3. COLLECTION/MAINTENANCE AND USE

An agency can only collect personal information for a valid purpose in accordance with the applicable "system of records" and cannot disclose the information without the consent of the third party or applicable exception. There are twelve exceptions to the consent rule; the four most relevant to the military are: (1) within agency with an official need to know; (2) required by FOIA; (3) for routine use; and (4) law enforcement purposes.

4. DENIAL AUTHORITIES

Only "Denial Authorities" can deny access to individual files that have been properly requested. Denial Authorities are the same authorities designated as Initial Denial Authorities under the Army Freedom of Information Act Program, AR 25-55, paragraph 5-200(d).

5. PRIVACY ACT STATEMENT (PAS)

When asking an individual for his or her social security number (SSN) or other personal information that will be maintained in a system of records, the individual must be provided with a Privacy Act Statement.

6. UNAUTHORIZED DISCLOSURE OF PERSONALLY IDENTIFIABLE INFORMATION (PII)

In accordance with ALARACT 050/2009, report **suspected OR confirmed** loss of PII: **within One Hour** report to US CERT (Computer Emergency Readiness Team); **within Twenty-Four Hours** report to Army FOIA/PA Office; additional reporting and monitoring IAW ALARACT 050/2009.

A breach is when PII is lost, stolen, or otherwise available to individuals without a duty-related official need to know.

THIS PAGE IS INTENTIONALLY BLANK

FISCAL LAW

Section 9

THIS PAGE IS INTENTIONALLY BLANK

Chapter 56

FISCAL LAW FOR COMMANDERS

1. INTRODUCTION

A. Source of Funding and Fund Limitations

The U.S. Constitution gives Congress the authority to raise revenue, to borrow funds, and to appropriate the proceeds for federal agencies. This Constitutional "power of the purse" includes the power to establish restrictions and conditions on the use of appropriated funds. Congress exerts its "power of the purse" through three primary fiscal limitations: purpose, time and amount.

- An agency may obligate and expend appropriations only for a proper purpose;
- An agency may obligate only within the time limits applicable to the appropriation (e.g., O&M funds are available for obligation for one fiscal year); and
- An agency may not obligate more than the amount appropriated by the Congress.

B. The Fiscal Law Philosophy

The established rule is that the expenditure of public funds is proper only when authorized by Congress, not that public funds may be expended unless prohibited by Congress. The general rule in fiscal law thus requires positive authority – find where it says you can do it, rather than finding where it says you can't do it.

2. AVAILABILITY AS TO PURPOSE

The Purpose Statute provides that agencies shall apply appropriations only to the objects for which the appropriations were made, except as otherwise provided by law. Where a particular expenditure is not specifically provided for in the appropriation act, it is permissible if it is necessary and incident to the proper execution of the general purpose of the appropriation. The Government Accountability Office (GAO) applies a three-part test to determine whether an expenditure is a "necessary expense" of a particular appropriation: 1) The expenditure must bear a logical relationship to the appropriation sought to be charged (i.e. it must make a direct contribution to carryout out either a specific appropriation or an authorized agency function for which more general appropriations are available); 2) the expenditure must not be prohibited by law; and 3) the expenditure must not be otherwise provided for; that is, it must not be an item that falls within the scope of some other appropriation or statutory funding scheme. Agencies have reasonable discretion to determine how to accomplish the purposes of appropriations. An agency's determination that a given item is reasonably necessary to accomplishing an authorized purpose is given considerable deference. In reviewing an expenditure, the GAO looks at "whether the expenditure falls within the agency's legitimate range of discretion, or whether its relationship to an authorized purpose is so attenuated as to take it beyond that range."

3. AVAILABILITY AS TO TIME

An appropriation is available for obligation for a definite period of time. With limited exceptions, an agency must obligate funds within their period of availability. If an agency fails to obligate funds before they expire, those funds are no longer available for new obligations. Expired funds retain their "fiscal year identity" for five years after the end of the period of availability. During this time, the funds are available to adjust existing obligations, or to liquidate prior valid obligations, but not to incur new obligations.

4. LIMITATIONS BASED UPON AMOUNT (THE ANTIDEFICIENCY ACT)

The Antideficiency Act (ADA), prohibits:

- making or authorizing an expenditure or obligation in excess or in advance of the amount available in an appropriation;
- making or authorizing expenditures or incurring obligations in excess of an apportionment or a formal subdivision of funds;
- or accepting voluntary services, unless otherwise authorized by law.

A. Investigating Violations

If an Antideficiency Act violation occurs, the agency must investigate to identify the responsible individual. The agency must report the violation to Congress through the Secretary of the Army. Violations could result in administrative and/or criminal sanctions.

B. Augmentation of Appropriations & Miscellaneous Receipts

Augmentation of appropriations is generally prohibited. Augmentation is action by an agency that increases the effective amount of funds available in an agency's appropriation. This generally results in expenditures by the agency in excess of the amount originally appropriated by Congress. Augmentation often occurs by using one appropriation to pay costs associated with the purposes of another appropriation or by retaining funds received from another source.

5. TYPICAL QUESTIONABLE EXPENSES AND COMMON PROBLEMS

A. Clothing/Apparel

Buying clothing for individual employees generally does not materially contribute to an agency's mission performance. Therefore, clothing is generally considered a personal expense unless a statute provides to the contrary. Exceptions may include purchase of special clothing for personnel that protects them against hazards in the performance of their duties.

B. Food

Buying food for individual employees – at least those who are not away from their official duty station on travel status – generally does not materially contribute to an agency's mission performance. As a result, food is generally considered a personal expense. There are some limited exceptions to this rule that include some training events. Consult a Judge Advocate prior to obligating any appropriated funds for food.

C. Bottled Water

Bottled water generally does not materially contribute to an agency's mission accomplishment. It is generally a personal expense. The major exception to this rule is that appropriated funds may be used to buy bottled water when it has been administratively determined by the agency that a building's water supply is unpotable or unsafe.

D. Workplace Food Storage and Preparation Equipment (i.e. microwave ovens; refrigerators; coffee pots)

Food preparation and storage equipment may be purchased with appropriated funds, so long as the primary benefit of its use accrues to the agency and the equipment is placed in common areas where it is available for use by all personnel. (Note: consult agency regulations and policies prior to applying this decision.)

E. Personal Office Furniture and Equipment

Ordinary office equipment is reasonably necessary to carry out an agency's mission, so appropriated funds may be used to purchase such items so long as they serve the needs of the majority of that agency's employees. With limited exceptions, such as the requirement to make "reasonable accommodations" for qualified handicapped employees, equipment that serves the needs of only a single individual or a specific group of individuals, is considered a personal expense rather than a "necessary expense" of the agency.

F. Entertainment

Entertaining people generally does not materially contribute to an agency's mission performance. As a result, entertainment expenses are generally considered to be a personal expense.

G. Decorations

The use of appropriated funds to purchase decorations so long as they are modestly priced and consistent with work-related objectives rather than for personal convenience is generally permissible.

H. Business Cards

Under a "necessary expense" analysis, the GAO has sanctioned the purchase of business cards for agency employees. However, current policy permits only recruiters and criminal investigators to purchase commercially prepared business cards. All others are permitted to use appropriated funds to purchase card stock and printer ink and then use in-house computing resources to print their own business cards.

I. Telephone Installation and Expenses

Even though telephones might ordinarily be considered a "necessary expense," appropriated funds may not generally be used to install telephones in private residences or to pay the utility or other costs of maintaining a telephone in a private residence. Repair or maintenance of telephone lines in residences owned or leased by the U.S. Government is generally permissible. The prohibition on installing telephones in a personal residence does not prevent an agency from purchasing cell phones for its employees, if they are otherwise determined to be a necessary expense.

J. Awards (Including Unit or Regimental Coins and Similar Devices)

Agencies generally may not use their appropriated funds to purchase "mementos" or personal gifts. Congress has provided specific authority for the SECDEF to "award medals, trophies, badges, and similar devices" to military members for "excellence in accomplishments or competitions" but this authority is limited. Somewhat broader authority exists to provide awards to civilian authority. In both cases, consult the most recent Army Regulation for guidance. See the Commander's Coin chapter for guidance on use of coins as awards.

6. MILITARY CONSTRUCTION

Congressional oversight of the Military Construction Program is extensive and pervasive. There are different categories of construction work with distinct funding requirements. Specified Military Construction (MILCON) Program projects generally cost over $2 million. Unspecified Minor Military Construction (UMMC) Program construction projects generally cost between $750,000 and $2 million. Minor Military Construction projects costing less than $750,000 are typically funded with Operations and Maintenance funds.

Construction includes alteration, conversion, addition, expansion, and replacement of existing facilities, plus site preparation and installed equipment. Splitting a project into multiple projects in order to avoid a statutory threshold is prohibited.

Maintenance and repair projects are not construction, and may therefore be funded entirely with Operations and Maintenance funds. However, the determination of what is maintenance and repair versus construction is a technical decision that should be made by public works, facilities management, or engineering personnel, in close coordination with resource managers and judge advocates.

7. EMERGENCY AND EXTRAORDINARY EXPENSE FUNDS (INCLUDING OFFICIAL REPRESENTATION FUNDS)

A. Definition

Emergency and extraordinary expense (EEE) funds are appropriations that an agency has much broader discretion to use for "emergency and extraordinary expenses." Expenditures made using these funds need not satisfy the normal purpose rules. Not all agencies receive emergency and extraordinary funds, and those that do typically receive a very small amount. Agencies that do receive and expend EEE funds must comply with Congressional notification and reporting requirements.

B. Regulatory Controls

Although extremely broad in purpose by statute, EEE funds have strict regulatory controls. This is largely due to their limited availability and potential for abuse. DOD typically uses these funds in the following ways:

C. Official Representation Funds (ORF) (Protocol)

This subset of emergency and extraordinary expense funds is available to extend official courtesies to authorized guests, including dignitaries and officials of foreign governments, senior U.S. Government officials, senior officials of state and local governments, and certain other distinguished and prominent citizens. In some limited cases, ORF funds may be used to purchase gifts and mementos to specified non-DoD guests. See AR 37-47.

D. Criminal Investigation Activities.

This subset of emergency and extraordinary expense funds are available for unusual expenditures incurred during criminal investigations or crime prevention.

E. Intelligence Activities.

This subset of emergency and extraordinary expense funds are available for unusual expenditures incurred during intelligence investigations.

CONCLUSION

REFERENCES FOR COMMANDERS

The following references may be useful to the commander or new officer who is confronted with a problem in a specific area (*e.g.*, Article 15, Line of Duty Investigation, etc.).

Topic	Reference
Abbreviations	AR 310-50
Absentee and Deserter Apprehension	AR 190-9
Alcohol and Drug Problems	AR 600-85
Apprehension, Restraint, Release, and Release to Civil Authorities	AR 190-9
ARIMS System	AR 25-400-2
Armed Forces Disciplinary Control Boards And Off Installation Military Enforcement	AR 190-24
Army Command Policy and Procedures	AR 600-20
Army Community Service	AR 608-1
Army Emergency Relief	AR 930-4
Army Terms, Dictionary of	AR 310-25
Article 15, UCMJ	AR 27-10
Assignments/Transfers (Enlisted)	AR 614-200
Assignments/Transfers (Officer)	AR 614-100
Awards	AR 600-8-22
AWOL	AR 630-10
Bars to Reenlistment	AR 601-280
Casualty Assistance	AR 600-8-1
Change of Name, SSN	AR 600-8-104
Child Custody	AR 608-99
Claims	AR 27-20
Clothing, Issued, and Sale of Personal Items	AR 700-84
Code of Conduct Training	AR 350-30

Topic	Reference
Commercial Solicitation	AR 210-7
Commissaries	DoD 1330.17-R; DODD 1330.17
Correction of Military Records	AR 15-185
Distribution of Literature	AR 600-20
Dropped From Rolls (DFR)	AR 630-10
Drunk Driving	AR 190-5
Duty Roster	AR 220-45
Eliminations (Enlisted)	AR 635-200
Eliminations (Officers)	AR 600-8-24
Enlisted Personnel Separations	AR 635-200
Equal Opportunity	AR 600-20
Evaluation Report (Enlisted)	AR 623-205
Evaluation Report (Officer)	AR 623-105
Extremist Organizations	AR 600-20
Family Advocacy	AR 608-18
Family Care Plan	AR 600-20
Family Housing	AR 210-50
Family Support	AR 608-99
Family Support Groups	DA PAM 608-47 (rescinded)
Flags (Suspension of Favorable Personnel Actions)	AR 600-8-2
Freedom of Information Act (FOIA)	AR 25-55
Fund Raising	AR 600-29
Gambling	JER
ID Card and Privileges	AR 600-8-14
Indebtedness	AR 600-15; AR 37-104-4
Inspector General	AR 20-1
Law of Land Warfare	FM 27-10
Leave	AR 600-8-10

Topic	Reference
Legal Assistance	AR 27-3
Legal Guide for Commanders	FM 27-1
Legal Guide for Soldiers	FM 27-14
Letter (Memorandum) of Reprimand	AR 600-37
Line of Duty Investigations	AR 600-8-4
Mail, Unit Operations	AR 600-8-3
Military Justice	AR 27-10
Military Police Investigations	AR 190-30
Military Whistle Blower Protection	DoDD 7050.6
Morale, Welfare, & Recreation (MWR)	AR 215-1
Motor Vehicles (Registration)	AR 190-5
Official Military Personnel File	AR 600-8-104
Overseas Service	AR 614-30
Passes	AR 600-8-10
Paternity	AR 608-99
Permissive TDY	AR 600-8-10
Physical Evaluation for Retention,	
Retirement or Separation	AR 635-40
Physical Fitness Program	FM 21-20
Physical Performance Evaluation System	AR 600-60
Physical Security	AR 190-11; AR 190-13
Political Activities	AR 600-20
Post Exchange	AR 60-20
Pregnancy Counseling (Enlisted)	AR 635-200
Privacy Act Program	AR 340-21
Private Organizations	AR 210-22; JER
Promotions (Enlisted)	AR 600-8-19
Promotions (Officers)	AR 600-8-29
Quarters & Commercial Activity	AR 210-50
Qualitative Management Program (QMP)	AR 601-280

Topic	Reference
(Enlisted)	
Reductions (Enlisted)	AR 600-8-19
Reenlistment Program	AR 601-280
Relief for Cause	AR 600-20
Religious Practices (Accommodation)	AR 600-20
Reports of Survey	AR 735-5
Representation Funds of the Secretary of the Army	AR 37-47
Retirement, Voluntary (Enlisted)	AR 635-200; AR 600-8-7
Retirement (Officer)	AR 600-8-24; AR 600-8-7
Salutes	AR 600-25
Security Clearance (Suspension/Revocation)	AR 380-67
Separation, Processing Personnel for	AR 635-10
Separations (Enlisted)	AR 635-200
Separations (Officer)	AR 600-8-24
Serious Incident Report (SIR)	AR 190-40
Traffic Regulation	AR 190-5
Unfavorable Information	AR 600-37
Uniform Wear and Appearance	AR 670-1
Weight Control Program	AR 600-9

CPSIA information can be obtained
at www.ICGtesting.com
Printed in the USA
BVHW012137200220
572955BV00011B/82